County boundaries of England & Wales after April 1974

D1142210

SCOTLAND

CUMBRIA

DURHAM

CLEVELAND

NORTH YORKSHIRE

LANCASHIRE

WEST YORKSHIRE

HUMBERSIDE

MERSEYSIDE

GREATER MANCHESTER

SOUTH YORKSHIRE

CHESHIRE

DERBY

NOTTS.

LINCOLN

CLWYD

GWYNEDD

STAFFS.

SALOP

WEST MIDLANDS

LEICESTER

NORFOLK

POWYS

HEREFORD & WORCESTER

WARWICK

NORTHAMPTON

CAMBRIDGE

SUFFOLK

DYFED

GLOUCESTER

BUCKS.

BEDFORD

HERTFORD

ESSEX

WEST GLAMORGAN

MID GLAMORGAN

GWENT

SOUTH GLAMORGAN

OXFORD

GREATER LONDON

AVON

BERKS.

WILTSHIRE

HAMPSHIRE

SURREY

KENT

SOMERSET

WEST SUSSEX

EAST SUSSEX

DEVON

DORSET

CORNWALL

For the Daughter of the Moon —

George

A guide to the Roman Remains in Britain

IN MEMORIAM

SO·THE·HEART·BE·RIGHT

Joanna Defrates

1945-2000

Roger J A Wilson

A guide to the

Roman Remains in Britain

With a foreword by
Professor J M C Toynbee

Constable London

To my Mother and my Father

who first encouraged my love
of Roman archaeology and
who tolerated countless
detours in search of Roman
Britain

First published in Great Britain 1975
by Constable and Company Ltd
10 Orange Street London WC2H 7EG
Copyright © 1974 Roger Wilson

ISBN 0 09 459870 3

Design Ivor Kamlish MSIA & Associates
Set in Monophoto Times New Roman
Filmset and printed in Great Britain by
BAS Printers Limited, Wallop, Hampshire

Opposite; 1   Dorchester Museum, shale table-leg

Contents

List of illustrations

Photographs, plans and line-drawings

1   Dorchester Museum, table-leg of Kimmeridge shale, 19″ high (Otto Fein, Warburg Institute)

2   Model of Benwell Roman fort, from SE (Museum of Antiquities, Newcastle)

3   Reconstruction-drawing of a typical Romano-Celtic temple

4   Sketch illustrating the working of a hypocaust

5   Plan of the visible remains at Richborough (after Bushe-Fox)

6   Richborough, triple ditches (left), *mansio* (centre), and north wall (background), looking west (the Author)

7   Roman lighthouse at Dover, from south (the Author)

8   North wall of Pevensey fort, looking east (the Author)

9   Glass vessel from Bishopsbourne (Royal Museum, Canterbury)

10   Drawing of Roman inscription in North Street, Chichester; 49″ × 32½″ (after Collingwood and Wright)

11   First-century black-and-white mosaic in room 12 of the Palace at Fishbourne (the Author)

12   First-century polychrome mosaic in room 20 of the Palace at Fishbourne (the Author)

13   The replanted formal garden at Fishbourne, looking NE, as it appeared in 1969 (the Author)

ERRATA

p.30, line 8 :   for 'fig. 4' read 'fig. 5'

pp.238–9 :   numbers 1–19 should be read in
                 the reverse order, i.e. right to left

p.286, line 6 : for 'they have not been indicated'
                 read 'they have also been indicated'

Foreword

by Professor J M C Toynbee

Archaeology, the study of the material, as contrasted with the written, evidence for history, is now firmly entrenched as an important element in a liberal education. It can be studied at school and as part, or even as the whole, of a degree-course in most universities; while the television, the radio, and adult education-classes have placed it within the reach of anyone who has not been confronted with it at the normal student stage. The majority of people would seem to be particularly impressed by the relics of the earliest periods, in this country by the monuments that ante-date the Norman Conquest. And of such series of early monuments none are more rewarding or exciting to investigate than those of Romano–British times, of the 400 years during which this island was a province of a highly-civilized world, at once unified and intensely diversified, that stretched from the Euphrates to the Tyne and Solway, from the Sahara to the Rhine and Danube.

In our present age, with its passion for reality and urge to be ever on the move, no one who is interested in Romano–British archaeology can be content to look at photographs and read descriptions in books. He must be up and out to see the actual monuments, whether in town or country or within museum walls. He must have first-hand knowledge of the things he has heard about; and it is the purpose of the present work to help him (particularly if he is a 'layman') to find how that knowledge may be gained. No Romano–British earthwork or building or collection of objects has escaped the author's net: those most worthy of the reader's attention are given full descriptions in the text, and the rest can be pursued with the help of information given in the appendices. Nearly every site he has personally visited and checked in 1971 or 1972. These journeys he has done by car – a possession now so almost universal that probably most of the users of this guide will follow him on wheels. But his minute and crystal-clear instructions as to how to find a given site will be just as valuable to the humbler, but no less energetic, non–car-owner, travelling by train, bus, and finally on foot. The present book is, in fact, unique for the comprehensiveness of its contents and for the detail contained in its directions. Quite a number of items little-known even to specialists are noted in its pages. If the Introduction covers ground with which some will already be familiar, it will usefully draw the threads of their knowledge together and provide the neophyte with the basic information, succinctly set out, for appreciating what he sees. The numerous illustrations are a very welcome and conspicuous feature.

As the author states, the substance of this guide is primarily factual. But his always lucid and unpedantic and often vivid style of writing brings all the facts to life. He will certainly succeed in kindling his readers' interest and enthusiasm by his personal approach – an approach in which a living scholarship and a controlled imagination are happily blended.

J M C T

Preface

In writing this book I have received help from many people. My first thanks go to Graham Tingay, without whose kindness it would never have been written. He also made useful comments on an early draft of Chapter One. Others whom I must thank for reading parts of the typescript and suggesting improvements are Elizabeth Dwiar, Stephen Johnson (who also checked a few references and generously gave me access to his notes on Saxon Shore forts), and especially Professor Sheppard Frere, who saved me from many errors and who also patiently tolerated the interruption which the writing of this book made in my other studies. Cecilia and Roy Dyckhoff kindly lent me OS maps and checked a site in Appendix One. My brother Donald helped in a number of ways, especially as an intermediary when I was in distant lands. I am grateful, too, for the hospitality I received on my visits to the National Monuments Record from Neil Beacham and especially from Patricia Drummond, who also answered last-minute enquiries from abroad with commendable efficiency. Readers will appreciate the hard work of Kevin Shaughnessy, AIIP, ARPS, who provided prints of all the photographs taken by me which appear in this book. Jessy Kemball-Cook was an invaluable companion on a hectic tour of North Britain, and has also checked references for me. Herta Duncombe and Lynda Blandford helped me out with typing at short notice when I was too pressed to do this myself.

I am equally grateful to the unnamed legion of farmers, custodians, etc., who gave me access to land, answered queries and contributed, usually unwittingly, to the contents of this book. Several museums have given permission to reproduce copyright material: this is acknowledged in the list of illustrations above. An enormous debt is also due to the many scholars whose published works I have plundered: I hope that a mention of their work (though not usually their name) in the bibliography will suffice to appease them.

My greatest debt is to the two people who have read the type-script in full. Firstly, my friend John Crawshaw, who spent countless hours ironing out the inconsistencies and aberrations of my English style, always with alarmingly keen perceptiveness. This book is a great deal more literate than it would have been without his tireless help. Secondly, Professor Jocelyn Toynbee, who made many useful comments on my manuscript and has kindly contributed a generous foreword. But my debt to her is also a much wider one: from the time I went up to Oxford as an undergraduate she has always taken a warm interest in my studies, and encouraged and helped me in numerous ways. To all these, and many others, I am deeply grateful.

A book of this kind is unfortunately doomed to be out of date in some respect even before it appears in print; to the best of my knowledge everything is correct at the time of going to press. In case the book should have a second edition, I shall be very grate-ful to receive any information about omissions and mistakes.

Palermo, March 1973   R J A W

Introduction

Purpose

This book is intended to be a guide to the visible remains of Roman Britain. It does not pretend to give a balanced or complete picture of Britain under the Roman Empire; for that the reader must turn to one of the books listed at the beginning of Appendix Three. It is designed primarily for the ordinary individual who has an interest in his Roman past but no prior specialized knowledge (some background information has therefore been provided in the second half of this introduction); but I also hope that the book may be found useful by those who have been confronted with Roman Britain in the classroom or lecture-hall and who want to know precisely how much of the places they have learnt about remains permanently accessible.

I have also tried to make this guide a comprehensive survey of *all* the antiquities of Roman Britain which are visible *in situ*, with the following exceptions:

(a) Roman linear works, eg roads, frontiers, canals. It has been impossible to describe *every* visible portion of these. Readers interested in Roman roads will find a complete record in I D Margary, *Roman Roads in Britain* (Baker, rev. ed. 1967), and only a few outstanding stretches have been included in this book. Further details about the two Walls can be found in the works listed in the relevant sections of Appendix Three.

(b) The vast majority of native settlements inhabited during the Roman period, as there are many thousands of these. A handful of them, however, has been included (in chs. 2, 6 and 7), in order to give a slightly more balanced picture of the countryside in Roman times.

(c) Sites such as mines and quarries which were used in Roman times but also later, and where it is not certain which, if any, of the workings visible today are Roman.

(d) Antiquities claimed as Roman but of which the Roman date is unlikely or unproven.

Ground-plans of Roman buildings marked out in modern materials, and Roman remains removed from their original position, are not normally included. Some museums are described, others merely mentioned in passing: few have received the space they deserve. Most of the important collections are listed in Appendix Two.

Because of the vast number and diversity of our visible Roman remains, this book sometimes becomes little more than a catalogue. For each site I have tried to give answers to the questions that I think will be asked by the visitor, ie when was it built, why was it built, and what was the purpose of x and y. This means that nearly all my account is purely factual, and I have rarely had the space to provide 'atmospheric colouring'. This I hope the reader will supply for himself at each individual site. For imagination *is* required when visiting Romano–British remains: if you treat knobbly little bits of wall as knobbly little bits of wall you are going to be disappointed. There are no Roman monuments in this country which can compare with the Pont du Gard in Provence, the aqueduct at Segovia in Spain, the temples at Baalbek in the Lebanon or the amphitheatre at El Djem in Tunisia; Roman buildings in Britain are generally reduced to little more than their foundations. The reason is partly that few such colossal structures were ever built here, partly that our country has been intensively inhabited and cultivated since Roman times, and partly that the British climate deals unkindly with ancient structures. I hope, therefore, that with the knowledge of a little background history, and with some idea of their original appearance (aided by Alan Sorrell's excellent drawings), you will be able to picture these places when they were not dead relics but thronging with people and alive with activity.

How to Use this Book
The main text. I have found from experience that to link all the sites in a given area with a single itinerary is impractical. It is infuriating if you happen to be doing the route in the reverse order; and often you will want to see places other than those with Roman remains, and so the itinerary carefully provided by the author becomes useless. In each chapter of this book, therefore, (with the exceptions mentioned below) I have paid little attention

to the geographical proximity of one site to another, but have grouped them according to the nature of the remains, ie forts, towns, villas. When you wish to see some Roman sites, first look at the map on p. 1 which will show you which chapter covers the area you are interested in. Then turn to the beginning of that chapter, where a map is given showing all the sites discussed in the section, and work out your own itinerary from there. If, before doing this, you want to know what there is to see at each place, either use the index or flip through the pages of that chapter, looking at the names in bold type.

In some cases it has proved impossible to treat each site in isolation, especially where several exist very close together. This applies in particular to the Stainmore Pass (ch. 7), Dere Street from Corbridge to the Scottish border (ch. 9, §1), and to Hadrian's Wall (ch. 8) and the Antonine Wall (ch. 9, §2). Here I have had to link sites together to form a coherent itinerary, and I can only apologize to those who have to visit these places in the reverse order. I hope that some, at least, of my directions will still be helpful after they have been 'translated' (ie for 'left' read 'right', etc.).

Particular stress has been laid on giving directions to monuments. The only map I assume you will have is one such as the Bartholomew's $\frac{1}{5}$″ map used by the AA in their Road Books. I do *not* expect readers to have any 1″ Ordnance Survey maps, except in a few instances where I have explicitly said so. You will, of course, find them helpful if you do have them, and a 4-figure National Grid reference is therefore included in brackets after the name of every place. Very occasionally I have provided 6-figure references for greater accuracy (mainly in Appendix One for some remains not marked on current 1″ maps). At each site I have talked about 'left' and 'right' wherever practicable, but this is often not possible and points of the compass are the inevitable alternative.

Outstanding remains which I consider deserve a special effort to see have been given an asterisk (*). The standard, however, is only set in relation to the other sites *in the same chapter*, and not to the book as a whole. Thus, High Rochester (p. 279) would have no chance of an asterisk if it were situated on Hadrian's Wall; it receives one because it preserves stone remains, in contrast to most of the other sites of ch. 9, which are earthworks.

Inevitably, technical expressions keep recurring in a book of

this nature. Rather than waste space explaining these each time
they occur, I have grouped them together in a Glossary at the end
of this Introduction (p. 24). Roman names of forts and towns
are usually given where they are known: note that in Latin V is
used both as a consonant and as the vowel U.

Plans and photographs. I have *only* included a plan of a site
when I think that it is impossible to understand the remains
without one. This means that unimportant sites, usually earthworks, often receive a plan when major monuments do not. It
may be considered perverse that there is no plan of a standard
Roman fort or of a Roman villa in this book; but in all cases I
have felt that these remains are intelligible with the help of a
verbal account alone. For monuments situated in towns, I have
assumed that you will have access to town-plans in a road handbook such as that published by the AA; if you do not, you can at
least ask directions locally.

Photographs of most of the well-known monuments occur
here, but I have also tried to include illustrations of the less
famous sites. The ranging-rod which appears in many photographs to give an idea of the scale is six feet long, divided into
measures of one foot. The caption of each illustration is neces-
sarily brief: further details are given in the list on pp. vi–xii.

Appendix One. All the visible Roman antiquities in Britain which
are not described in the text are listed in Appendix One, usually
referred to as App. I (pp. 333–341). These cannot be found without the help of 1″ OS Maps, and the grid reference and the map
number are therefore given in the first two columns.[1] (*s*) or (*e*) is
added after the type of antiquity has been noted (column 5). In
the case of (*s*), which means that stone remains are visible, it may
be assumed that these are so fragmentary as to be of interest
only to the most avid enthusiast. This is not always so in the case
of earthworks (*e*). In the north of England, Scotland and Wales
many fort-platforms and other military antiquities are still
prominently visible, and it has been impossible to include all of
them in the text. (It must be remembered that 'earthwork' (*e*)
only describes the present state of the site and is no indication of
its original condition: many rampart-mounds cover stone
defensive walls which are not now visible.) What constitutes

---

[1]The number in brackets after the 1″ map no. is that of the new 50,000 scale
maps, which appeared for Southern Britain in March 1974.

'visible' is a difficult problem, and obviously some will think that there is nothing to see at some of the sites that I have listed, whereas other sites that are faintly visible I may have omitted. My guideline has normally been the relevant symbol on the 1″ OS map, though occasionally some places have been included that the OS considers 'site of' (ie nothing visible), and vice versa.

Access

Some of the most important monuments of Roman Britain are in the care of the Ancient Monuments Branch of what is now the Department of the Environment (formerly Ministry of Public Building and Works). These are indicated in the text by 'AM' in square brackets after the name of the site, and by the following letters which correspond to these times of opening:

A: at any reasonable time. S: standard hours:

	Weekdays	Sundays
March–April	9.30–5.30	2.00–5.30
May–September	9.30–7.00	2.00–7.00
October	9.30–5.30	2.00–5.30
November–February	9.30–4.00	2.00–4.00

SM means that, in addition to the above hours, the monuments are open on Sunday mornings from 9.30, April to September.

Opening hours of sites not in the custody of the DOE are also supplied, and as far as possible are correct at the time of going to press. In the case of museums where I give vague closing-times, eg 4.00 or 5.30, it may be assumed that the later hour applies to the summer months only (usually May–September).

The vast majority of the places described in this book, or listed in Appendix I, are on private land. In cases where I know from whom permission to visit can be obtained, I give this information. But in places where I do not, you must NOT assume that you are free to wander. Most landowners are proud of their ancient monuments and are happy to let interested visitors see them, but *only* if the latter make the effort to enquire first, and *only* if they shut gates, keep dogs on a lead, do not trample down standing crops, and do not damage fences or dry-stone walls. A little courtesy will go a long way, and will make things easier for yourself and the other would-be visitors who will come after you.

The Roman army in Britain

Under the Empire, the Roman army consisted of two distinct forces, the legions and the *auxilia*. A **legion**, with a nominal strength of 6,000, was originally recruited only from men with full Roman citizenship (ie Italians and men from Roman colonies during much of the first century AD), but the rule was relaxed in the second century and in the third all provincials were given Roman citizenship. The main body of fighting men was organized into *centuriae*, centuries, of 80 men under the command of a *centurion*. Six centuries formed a *cohort* (about 480 men), and 10 cohorts made up a legion, but the first cohort was bigger (about 800 men). The legionary soldier would normally serve about 25 years before being discharged as a *veteran*. The commander of the legion, the *legatus*, or legate, was a Roman senator, and under him were six *tribunes*, or junior officers. Like the legate, they were not full-time professional soldiers, but held the post as part of their public career.

The **auxilia**, or auxiliary troops, were not Roman citizens, but were recruited from the provinces of the Roman Empire. They usually took their names from the areas in which they were originally levied (eg first cohort of Thracians from Bulgaria), and I have often given these areas when naming auxiliary garrisons. Do not, however, be misled into thinking that British forts were all manned by foreigners from many lands; for each unit, though retaining its original native name, would have received fresh recruits from the area in which it was stationed, ie from the local British population.

The auxiliaries were organized into *cohorts* if they were infantry, or *alae* (wings) if they were cavalry. Both generally had a nominal strength of 500, but units of 1,000 men are also known. A cohort could either be composed entirely of infantry or contain a contingent of 120 (or 240) men on horseback. The *auxilia* were generally commanded by Romans of the equestrian rank (a class below that of senator), who had the title of prefect (*praefectus*) if the cohort was 500 strong, or tribune (*tribunus*) if 1,000 strong; *alae* were commanded by prefects.

Auxilia were placed in forts and were expected to bear the brunt of fighting and frontier-duty. Legions were placed in fortresses behind the main frontier areas, and were the crack troops used only in emergency. In addition to being a soldier, the legionary was also a considerable technician and he was often away from his fortress constructing auxiliary forts or frontier-works.

The original *auxilia* had come from what at the time were the fringes of the Roman-controlled world, but by the third century they were an integral part of the Roman army. In the Later Empire, the tribes on the fringes were also organized into military units, but to distinguish them from the *auxilia* they were called **numeri**. Not attested in Britain before the third century, these forces were composed of light-armed infantry (the cavalry equivalents were called **cunei**). They always served away from their place of drafting. An example of a *numerus* was that stationed at South Shields in the fourth century.

Roman Remains in Britain
Military Remains
Marching Camps. The words 'camp' and 'fort' must be carefully distinguished: the former is used only of temporary earthworks, the latter applies to permanent posts, whether constructed in turf or stone.

An army on the march always defended itself when it stopped for the night by erecting a camp. These are called *marching camps* or *temporary camps*. Their plans are often irregular, to suit the terrain. They consist of an earth rampart, originally perhaps 5–6 feet high and crowned with a timber palisade. Outside was a single ditch, not always dug when the ground was too hard. Poles for the palisade were carried in the soldiers' kit-bags; and the tents which housed the men inside the ramparts were carried by mules. The entrances of temporary camps are of two types: those defended by *titula*, which are short pieces of rampart and ditch set a few yards in front of the gap in the main rampart (in theory they would break the charge of an enemy); and those defended by *claviculae*, which are curved extensions of the rampart (and sometimes its ditch), usually inside the area of the camp, though external and double *claviculae* are also known. Dating evidence from these camps is slight: both types of gateway are found in the first century, but from the second century onwards *claviculae* seem no longer to have been used (Chew Green III, dated to the mid-second century, is the latest known; plan, fig 121). Very occasionally *titula* are found protecting the gates of forts (Hod Hill) and fortlets (Durisdeer). The best examples of marching camps are: Rey Cross (*titula*, fig 86), Y Pigwn (*claviculae*, fig 71).

Practice Camps. Troops also built earthworks as part of their training, but these were never meant to be occupied. The rounded corners and the gateways are the most difficult features of a camp to build, and practice camps are often, therefore, very small, avoiding the need for unnecessary lengths of straight rampart. Today these earthworks are rarely more than 1 foot high; examples near Castell Collen, Gelligaer and Tomen-y-Mur. Others are of normal size and may be built as part of a mock-siege (as Burnswark). At Cawthorn, the troops practised the building of forts, not camps.

Legionary Fortresses. These are larger versions of the fort (see below), and contain similar buildings similarly arranged. They hold a legion and normally cover about 50 acres. There were several short-term legionary fortresses, with turf ramparts and timber buildings, but the three permanent bases, later rebuilt in stone, were at Caerleon, Chester and York.

Forts. These were the permanent bases of the auxiliary units, and except as a temporary measure (Hod Hill is one example) rarely housed even a detachment of legionaries. Their size varies according to the type of garrison, but most forts in the first and second centuries cover between $2\frac{1}{2}$ and 4 acres. Their shape is almost universally like that of a playing-card, with straight sides and rounded corners.

Defences. The earliest forts in Britain had a rampart of turf or clay, on average about 18 feet wide at base, which was crowned with a breastwork and wall-walk of timber. Gateways and towers at intervals round this rampart were also of timber. The best examples of first-century forts in Britain are Hod Hill (fig 16) and the restored Baginton (see figs 49 and 50), but neither represent typical types.

From early in the second century, the front of the rampart was usually cut back and a stone wall inserted in front of it. Henceforth all new forts were usually, but by no means always, built with a stone wall from the beginning, although an earth rampart nearly always accompanied it. This stone wall was originally about 15 feet high, and included a parapet at the top.

Today the facing-stones have usually been robbed away, revealing the irregular core of the wall; and in many places the stone wall is now buried beneath a broad mound which marks the line of the defences. There were normally four gateways, consisting of either one or two arched carriageways, often flanked by guardrooms. Internal towers, perhaps with sloping roofs (fig 62) rather than with open crenellations (fig 2), were placed at the four rounded corners, and at intervals between the latter and the gateways.

Outside the ramparts there were one or more ditches, usually V-shaped. Each had a narrow drainage-channel in the bottom and was never meant to be filled with water like a medieval moat.

Internal Buildings. These conform to a standard pattern. In the earliest forts they were timber-framed with walls of wattle-and-daub, but all visible examples are of stone. In some forts, only the central buildings are made of stone, while the barracks are entirely of timber. Stone foundations need not always imply stone superstructures.

In the centre of each fort is the *principia*, or headquarters building (1 on fig 2). The front part consists of a large courtyard, usually surrounded on three sides by a colonnade. It leads to the covered *cross-hall* which stretches the full width of the building. This was capable of holding the complete contingent standing shoulder to shoulder; here it would have assembled for an address by the commanding officer, who spoke from the raised platform, or *tribunal*, at one end. At the back of the building are some smaller rooms, often five in number. The central one is the *sacellum* or *aedes*, the shrine where the regimental standards and the statue of the emperor stood (see fig 102). Below its floor the pay-chest was kept, sometimes (from the third century onwards) in an underground strong-room. The rooms on either side were used for administrative purposes.

On one side of the *principia* is the *praetorium*, or commandant's house, usually consisting of a range of rooms round a central courtyard (2). Private bath-suites seem to have been a luxury reserved only for the commanders of cavalry regiments. On the other side stand two or more *horrea*, granaries (3). These are always buttressed and have raised floors to keep their contents dry. A *fabrica*, workshop (4), and sometimes a *valetudinarium*, hospital (5), also occupy the central area of a fort.

The rest of the area is taken up by *barrack-blocks* (6), with the provision, too, of *stables* (7) if the regiment was cavalry or part-mounted. A single barrack-block was designed to hold a *centuria* of 80 men. The main part of the building is divided up into approximately 10 portions. Each is further subdivided into two (not always by stone partitions): in one cubicle the men ate and slept, and in the other they kept their weapons and other equipment. There was a verandah running down one side of the building. The centurion and his junior officer(s) lived in the more spacious accommodation provided at one end. The most instructive barrack-block in Britain is the legionary example at Caerleon.

The road running from the front of the HQ to the front gate is called the *via praetoria*; from the back to the back gate, the *via decumana*. The road joining the gates in the long sides and running along the front of the HQ is known as the *via principalis*. There was also a road going all round the fort in the *intervallum*, or the space between the back of the rampart and the internal buildings.

Outside the ramparts lay the garrison bath-house (p. 14) and usually a civilian settlement.

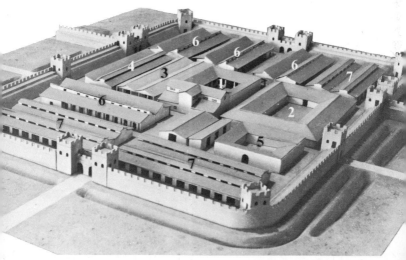

2   *Model of a Roman fort*

The best examples of Roman forts in Britain are Chesters, Housesteads, Hardknott and Caernarvon.

<u>Tactics.</u> Early forts are meant to house garrisons trained to fight in the open : they would sally forth from their gates and meet the enemy outside. Later, there is a trend towards making the fort more of a stronghold impregnable to attack : ditches increase in number, and the ramparts are sometimes furnished with catapult-platforms, *ballistaria*, from which artillery could bombard an attacker. The final move towards the medieval notion of a 'castle' came in the third and fourth centuries with the Saxon Shore Forts.

<u>Saxon Shore Forts.</u> These abandon the conventional (playing-card) shape and layout. They have massive stone walls, probably 30 feet high, usually without an earth bank behind. Most are defended by projecting bastions, to have maximum view of and control over an attacker. Gateways are narrow. These are the forts built along the coastline from the Wash to Southampton to defend SE Britain from Saxon pirate raids (hence their name). The remains of Richborough, Pevensey and Portchester are perhaps the most spectacular monuments of Roman Britain. Similar late forts were built in the west, and the restored example at Cardiff gives an excellent idea of the formidable nature of these strongholds (see fig 75).

Fortlets. These are small guard-posts, often filling gaps between forts. Their size varies : each probably held between 50 and 150 men. Defences usually consist of a rampart broken by a single gate, and surrounded by one or two ditches. Some (eg Maiden Castle) had stone walls, but most were earthworks (eg Castle Greg).

Signal-Stations. Fire, smoke and semaphore were all used by the Romans in transmitting messages, and there are many examples of signal-stations in Britain. Most consist of a timber tower, surrounded by an earth rampart and ditch (eg Bowes Moor), but some first-century towers (eg Gask Ridge) have no rampart. Stone towers are also known (eg one later incorporated into Hadrian's Wall, p. 268). In the late fourth century, a row of strongly-defended stone signal-stations was built along the Yorkshire coast.

Civilian Remains

Towns. The Romans were the first to build towns in Britain, with
streets laid out in a regular chess-board pattern (street-grid).
Most of the sites they chose are still flourishing cities today, but
by modern standards Roman towns were small (the population
of the whole of Britain at the end of the second century is unlikely
to have much exceeded two million people). Very little is
visible of the class of minor settlements called *vici*, except for
those which grew up around the forts of Housesteads and
Chesterholm. More important were the small market-centres
and roadside settlements, but these too have not left many visible
remains (ch. 5, pp. 164–70, for the best examples). Most of the
towns described in this book, therefore, belong to one of the
following two categories:

(i) *coloniae*. These were special foundations for veterans,
retired Roman legionaries, and were composed of Roman citizens. Colchester, Lincoln and Gloucester were founded in this
way. The title later became an honorary one, conferred on a
prosperous town already in existence. We know that York's
civilian settlement received this honour, and it is a fair guess that
at least London (ch. 10) did so too. *Coloniae* were intended to
act as civilizing influences on the surrounding area. They were
self-governing communities, with a city-council (*ordo*) and a
system of magistrates modelled on that of Rome.

(ii) *tribal* or *civitas capitals*. The pre-Roman tribal organization
was not obliterated by the invaders, and towns were founded to
serve as the new market and administrative centre of each
civitas. These, too, were self-governing communities, and their
magistrates would have been elected from among the local
aristocracy. Their size varies from Cirencester, 240 acres, to
Caistor St Edmund, 35 acres. Inhabitants of tribal capitals were
not awarded the privilege of Roman citizenship (though all
provincials became citizens by a decree of Caracalla in 212 or
214).

Public Buildings. The centre of a *colonia* or a tribal capital was
occupied by the administrative unit, the forum and basilica.
The *forum* was the civic centre and market-place, and consisted
of a large courtyard surrounded by a colonnade. The *basilica*
was a long hall, sometimes with apsidal ends, where justice was
dispensed. It lay along one end of the forum. Adjoining it were

administrative offices. The plan of the forum and basilica is
derived from the military *principia*. Unfortunately, no complete
example is exposed in Britain today: the colonnade on one side
of the forum at Wroxeter is the most notable relic.

The *bath-house* was an indispensable part of Roman life, and
examples are found in every town and villa of any note and also
outside every fort. They varied enormously in elaboration. The
system was close to the present-day Turkish baths, and consisted
of a series of rooms heated to different temperatures. The bather
first took his clothes off in the *apodyterium*, undressing room,
proceeded to the *frigidarium* (cold room), started sweating in the
moderately-heated *tepidarium* (warm room), and perspired
profusely in the *caldarium*, the room of intense sticky heat. Here
he would scrape himself down, to remove dirt from the skin, with
an oiled metal instrument called a *strigil*, a sort of blunt 'cut-
throat' razor. He could also take a plunge in the small hot bath
which usually adjoined the *caldarium*. He would then go through
the rooms in the reverse order, taking a dip in the cold plunge-
bath in the *frigidarium*, to close the pores and so avoid catching
cold. This was the most common system, and depended for its
effect on moist heat: steam was created by sprinkling water on
the floor, which was heated by a hypocaust (see Glossary, p. 26).
A more rigorous experience was sweating in dry heat, when the
hot room was known as the *laconicum* (Spartan room) or the
sudatorium (sweating room). A complete bath-house contained
both systems, and the public establishments also had *palaestrae*,
exercise-courts. Swimming-baths as we know them were rare.
The best example of a public bath-suite is at Wroxeter, and of a
military one, Chesters. The thermal establishment at Bath is
exceptionally grand.

Other public buildings within a town included *temples*
(below, p. 17), a *mansio*, or inn (partly for the use of officials
travelling on public business), and (sometimes) *theatres*. The
only completely excavated and visible example of the last, at St
Albans, is described in its proper place (p. 130). The theatre was a
D-shaped building and must be distinguished from the *amphitheatre*. The latter, nearly always outside the built-up area,
consisted of an elliptical arena surrounded by tiers of wooden
seats erected on earth banks. These banks were usually revetted
in stone or timber, but no monumental structures built entirely
of stone, like the amphitheatres of Arles or Nimes or the Colos-

seum, have yet been found in Britain. Gladiatorial combats and animal sports were staged here. Today, civilian amphitheatres survive only as earth banks (eg Cirencester). The amphitheatres outside the legionary fortresses at Chester and Caerleon have been more extensively exposed, but here weapon-training came before gladiatorial entertainment, and the arenas were consequently larger in relation to the seating space than in their civilian counterparts.

Water-supply. *Aqueducts* raised on great arches are unknown in Britain. Where water was brought from a distance it was conducted in an open channel, following natural contours. Dorchester has the best example. Examples of *sewers* have been found at Lincoln, Bath, St Albans and recently at York. *Latrines* are common: the public lavatory at Wroxeter can be seen, but more instructive are the military ones such as that at Housesteads (fig 107). Wooden seats were mounted over a deep sewer, and running water in a gutter in front of the seats washed the sponges which were the Roman equivalent of toilet-paper.

Private houses. The simplest dwelling was a long, narrow building, with one end fronting the street (often a shop, with living-quarters behind). This type was sometimes expanded and had a wing or wings added at the back. The largest house consisted of a series of rooms ranged about a courtyard. The most elaborate were decorated with mosaics and painted wall-plaster. Few town-houses have been preserved in Britain: Canterbury, St Albans and Caerwent have the best examples exposed at present, and one at Cirencester will be on display soon; (but see p. 360).

Defences. All the large towns, and many smaller settlements, were equipped with defences at some time before the end of the Roman occupation. Some, such as St Albans, received an earth bank and ditch soon after AD 43, and Lincoln had a simple stone wall added to its existing earth defences at the beginning of the second century. On the other hand, some very small towns did not receive ramparts until the fourth century. The defences of most Romano–British towns show three distinct phases: an earth bank, a stone wall inserted in front of it, and projecting bastions added to that. Excavation at different sites has produced different dates for each of these phases, as will be noticed by comparing my account of one town-wall with another. It is most unlikely, however, that such diversity in dates is real. Most towns were given earth defences with a wooden stockade or breastwork at the end of the second century. These must have been erected on the command of a central authority, and a likely occasion is AD 193–6, when Albinus was preparing for his attempt to become emperor (see historical outline below, p. 21). In most places the stone wall was inserted in front of the earth bank at a later period, probably in the second quarter of the third century. The third phase, the addition of projecting bastions, is given various dates in the fourth century, but it too may be the product of a single policy. Theodosius' reorganization of the British defences in 369 would have been a suitable occasion. Bastions gave more complete control over an attacker and served as emplacements for *ballistae*, heavy artillery-machines. The best example of the stone defences of a Romano–British town can be seen at Caerwent.

Villas

These are the most popular and familiar monuments of Roman Britain because of the spectacular mosaics which often adorn their floors. Nearly all the mosaics, however, belong only to the last phase of a (usually) complicated development. The simplest houses of just a few rooms have not generally been preserved, though Lullingstone in its final form is a luxurious, expanded example of a very compact house, without projecting wings or spacious courtyards. Most of the villas visible in Britain belong either to the 'corridor-type', in which several rooms open off a long corridor and are often flanked by short wings on either side (eg Newport), or the extensive 'courtyard-type', in which blocks of rooms forming separate wings are grouped around one or more courtyards (eg Chedworth; North Leigh). Most villas were not pleasure-palaces but the centres of agricultural estates, and farm-buildings are usually found on the outskirts of the main living-area (or in the outer courtyard of some courtyard villas). The courtyard-type, usually a development from simpler dwellings, belongs (in the visible examples) to the fourth century. The first-century palace at Fishbourne is quite exceptional.

Even the smallest villas had hypocausts, mosaics or plain tessellated floors, and painted wall-plaster. A bath-house or suite (above, p. 14) was also normal.

Native Settlements

A high proportion of the population of the countryside,

especially in Wales and N and SW England, remained largely uninfluenced by Roman civilization. They used Roman pottery and coins and sometimes even had refinements such as painted wall-plaster, but the settlements they inhabited belonged mainly to the pre-Roman tradition. The dwelling-place was usually a circular hut, though in the Roman period rectangular huts often replaced or co-existed with those of a circular plan. Some of the very few native settlements mentioned in this book are built of stone (Chysauster, Tre'r Ceiri), and are therefore substantial monuments, but most survive only as earth ridges (eg Ewe Close). It is always best to visit the latter on a sunny evening, when long shadows pick out the surviving banks and make the remains more intelligible.

Temples

The true classical-style temple was built on a lofty platform (*podium*) and approached by a flight of steps. The shrine (*cella*) had a front porch of free-standing columns supporting a tri-angular pediment. This type is rare in Britain: Colchester has one.

The most common type is called Romano-Celtic. The ground-plan of the visible examples consists of two squares, one inside the other. The inner wall enclosed the *cella*, the outer wall supported a colonnade and was an ambulatory. The appearance of this type is suggested in fig 3. The best example is at Maiden Castle.

3   *Suggested appearance of a Romano-Celtic temple*

Other temples were of the 'basilican' type, an early forerunner of the Christian church. The outer walls of these are solid, and the interior may be divided into a nave and side-aisles. Lydney and the London temple of Mithras are examples. The Carrawburgh Mithraeum is much smaller and simpler. The rustic shrines of Lullingstone and Scargill Moor (Bowes) were probably thatched.

Roads

Most Roman trunk roads were built in a series of straight stretches, usually changing direction on hill-tops. But straightness was not always possible and in mountainous terrain a Roman road can wind as much as a modern one. The composition of each road varied a great deal: generally there was a foundation of large slabs or stones and the final surface consisted of rammed gravel. The latter has usually been washed away, leaving the foundation-slabs exposed (eg Wheeldale Moor, fig 82). Sometimes iron cinder was used for surfacing (Holtye), but a paving of stone blocks was exceptional (eg Blackstone Edge, fig 83). To ensure good drainage (a vital element when roads lacked the cohesion afforded by modern macadamized surfaces), Roman highways were often built on raised embankments (*aggeres*), and were sometimes accompanied by ditches on either side.

Burials

By Roman law burial was prohibited inside a city, except for infants; in cases which appear to contradict this, eg Canterbury, the burial must have preceded urban expansion. Both cremation and inhumation were practised in Roman Britain: the former was predominant in the first and second centuries, the latter in the fourth. Most burial-places were simple graves perhaps marked by tombstones, and many of such stones are on display in museums. Larger, monumental tombs have remains left *in situ*, and these fall broadly into two categories:

(i) the earth barrow, or *tumulus*, which has a steep, high, conical profile. These are particularly frequent in SE Britain, and are a direct descendant of pre-Roman burial-mounds. Most date from the first and second centuries. The burials, usually cremations and often associated with grave-goods, were placed in a receptacle in the middle of the barrow. *Tumuli* often occur in groups, eg The Bartlow Hills. The most instructive single example is probably Mersea.

(ii) stone-built tombs. The circular structures at Keston and High Rochester were probably merely retaining-walls for a central mound of earth, perhaps with a conical top. Those at Stone-by-Faversham or Harpenden, however, definitely have internal chambers.

Historical outline

55–54 BC	Caesar raids Britain.
AD 43	Invasion of Britain under Aulus Plautius with four legions, II Augusta, IX Hispana, XIV Gemina and XX Valeria, and auxiliaries (about 40,000 men in all). Landing at Richborough. Battle on the Medway. Native chieftain Caratacus flees to Wales. Plautius pauses to await the emperor Claudius before advancing to Colchester.
44–60	Division of the invading army: legion II advances SW, legion IX towards Lincoln, legion XIV and part of XX through the Midlands. Rest of legion XX is kept in a base-fortress at Colchester. Early frontier-line marked by Fosse Way, the Roman road from Exeter to Lincoln.
47–52	Ostorius Scapula governor. Campaigns against the Silures (S Wales) and the Ordovices (mid- and N Wales), who are inspired by Caratacus. Beaten in battle in AD 51 he flees to N Britain, where Queen Cartimandua of the Brigantes hands him over to the Romans.
52–7	Aulus Didius governor. Further campaigns in Wales. Civil war among the Brigantes and Roman intervention there.
60–1	King Prasutagus of the Iceni (East Anglia) dies. Rapacity of Roman administrators causes revolt of Boudicca (Boadicea). Petillius Cerialis with part of legion IX is ambushed by Boudicca – infantry massacred, but he himself escapes. Suetonius Paulinus, governor, rushes back from Anglesey but not soon enough to save Colchester, London and St Albans from going up in flames. 70,000 inhabitants massacred. Poenius Postumus, acting commander of

legion II, refuses Suetonius' call for assistance and
falls on his sword after hearing news of the final
battle, when 80,000 Britons are killed. Julius Alpinus
Classicianus comes to Britain as the new financial
administrator (procurator). Disagreement over
policy leads to the recall of Suetonius.

66   XIV Gemina withdrawn from Britain for service in
the East.

71–74   Petillius Cerialis, now governor, arrives with new
legion, II Adiutrix, and campaigns against the
Brigantes, who make their last stand at Stanwick near
Scotch Corner.

74–8   Julius Frontinus, governor, finally pacifies the Silures.
Legionary fortresses established for II Augusta at
Caerleon near Newport c. 74, and for II Adiutrix
at Chester c. 78.

78   Arrival in Britain of Gn. Julius Agricola, most
famous of the governors of Britain, because of the
surviving biography written by his son-in-law
Tacitus. Final mopping-up in Wales. Base for legion
IX probably established at York c. 78–9, on site of
earlier fort.

79   Advance to the Tyne-Solway isthmus.

80   Advance to the Forth-Clyde isthmus, and reconnaissance as far as the Tay.

81   Consolidation, building of forts and roads.

82   Invasion of SW Scotland.

83–4   Agricola pushes up to the Spey, building forts behind
him, including a legionary fortress for legion XX at
Inchtuthil. Battle of Mons Graupius, in which 30,000
Caledonians under their leader Calgacus are crushed.
Roman fleet circumnavigates Britain.

84–5   Recall of Agricola.

c. 87   Withdrawal from Scotland north of the Forth-Clyde
isthmus. II Adiutrix withdrawn from Britain about
now. Legion XX moves to Chester.

c. 105   Complete withdrawal from southern Scotland,
perhaps after a disaster. Frontier now the Stanegate,
Agricola's road across part of the Tyne-Solway
isthmus.

c. 118   Revolt in Britain, perhaps among the Brigantes.

Suppressed by 119.

122   Emperor Hadrian visits Britain. Hadrian's Wall and its attendant works begun, under the supervision of the new governor, Aulus Platorius Nepos, who brings another legion to Britain, VI Victrix. Disappearance of legion IX, last recorded in 107/8. Probably withdrawn from Britain c. 121–2, eventually to perish in a disaster in the East before 165.

139–42   Antoninus Pius, emperor, orders a new advance in Britain, under Lollius Urbicus. Reoccupation and refortification of S Scotland. Building of the Antonine Wall.

c. 155   Serious revolt of Brigantes in N Britain with heavy Roman casualties. Antonine Wall temporarily evacuated. Gn. Julius Verus arrives as governor with legionary reinforcements, and rebuilding of Pennine forts burnt in the revolt is begun.

c. 159   Antonine Wall recommissioned.

c. 163   Another crisis causes the final abandonment of the Antonine Wall and of S Scotland, probably after enemy destruction. Hadrian's Wall fully recommissioned. More rebuilding of forts in N Britain under Calpurnius Agricola (governor c. 162–166).

c. 169   Possible unrest in Wales.

c. 180   The historian Dio records a war in Britain and the death in battle of a Roman general. Invading tribes cross 'The Wall'. *If* this refers to a barrier in commission, and *if* the Antonine Wall had been evacuated c. 163, this must mean Hadrian's Wall, but there is no archaeological evidence for destruction there at this date. Ulpius Marcellus is sent to Britain, and victory is achieved by 184 (coins).

193–7   Clodius Albinus (governor of Britain from c. 191) claims the imperial throne in 193 and is recognised as assistant (an office with the title of Caesar) by Septimius Severus, who becomes emperor. Growing tension between the two. Probably at this period most of Britain's towns were equipped with earth defences, in preparation for a province without an army; for in 196 Albinus stripped Britain of troops and crossed to France. Defeated and killed by

Severus near Lyon in February 197. Many forts in
N Britain burnt, probably by Brigantes, but it is far
from certain that Hadrian's Wall was destroyed now;
if so, reconstruction was delayed 10 years.

197–201/2   Virius Lupus sent to Britain to restore the situation.
Many Pennine forts rebuilt now. Britain divided into
two provinces (*Superior* and *Inferior*, Upper and
Lower).

205–8   L. Alfenus Senecio, governor, restores Hadrian's
Wall and its forts, possibly after a separate uprising
from that of 196–7. Further rebuilding of Pennine
forts already restored in 197 may also imply this.

208–9   Emperor Severus campaigns in N Scotland to punish
the invaders.

210   Caracalla, his son, conducts campaigning because
Severus is too ill.

211   Severus dies in York, February 4th. Complete withdrawal from Scotland, but probably not before 213.

c. 213–70   Period of peace. Rebuilding and reorganization of
forts in N Britain continues (until c. 230). Towns
given stone walls. From 259 Britain is part of a
Gallic separatist empire.

c. 275–85   Increasing insecurity of SE England because of
Saxon pirate raids. Most of the Saxon Shore forts
built either now or under Carausius.

286–7   Carausius, commander of the British fleet, declares
himself Emperor of Britain and N Gaul. Loses control
of the latter in 293.

294   Carausius is murdered by his finance-minister
Allectus.

296   Constantius (the emperor Maximian's Caesar)
recovers Britain, and Allectus is killed in battle in
S Britain. Destruction of Hadrian's Wall and its forts
at this time. Constantius sets in hand a lot of rebuilding there, in the Pennine forts and at the legionary
fortresses of Chester and York. Perhaps natural
decay partly the reason for the reconstruction.
Britain divided into four provinces. Office established
of *Dux Britanniarum*, commander of all land-forces
in Britain.

306   Constantius returns to Britain, now as emperor, and

campaigns in N Scotland (little archaeological trace). Dies in York, July 25th. His son Constantine proclaimed emperor there.

313   Christianity tolerated by the edict of Milan, and three British bishops attend Council of Arles in 314.

300–42   Peace and prosperity in Roman Britain.

342–3   Trouble north of Hadrian's Wall; several outpost forts destroyed. Emperor Constans comes to Britain, and pacifies the Scottish tribes. Strengthening of the forts of the Saxon Shore (Pevensey added to the series) and a new office established, entitled 'Count of the Saxon Shore'.

360   More trouble with the tribes north of the Wall, the Picts of Scotland and also with the Scots of Ireland. Peace settled by one Lupicinus.

367   Britain is overwhelmed by a great barbarian conspiracy: concerted attacks by Picts, Scots and Saxons. Hadrian's Wall overrun. Nectaridius, Count of the Saxon Shore, is killed, and Fullofaudes, *Dux Britanniarum*, is besieged or captured. Much of the countryside of lowland Britain probably unaffected, though some villas are deserted now.

369   Theodosius comes to Britain to restore the situation. A fifth province, called Valentia, is established (probably in NW Britain). Hadrian's Wall restored and its forts patched up. Some forts in N Britain rebuilt, others abandoned. Signal-stations built on the Yorkshire coast. Bastions added to some town-walls. The Theodosian reconstruction is evidently effective, for towns and villas continue to show signs of prosperity until the end of the fourth century and beyond.

383   Magnus Maximus, probably *Dux Britanniarum*, revolts, removes troops from Wales and N Britain, and crosses to the continent. Irish raids in Wales, but Hadrian's Wall probably remains intact.

395   Stilicho, general of the emperor Honorius, orders some sort of expedition against Scots, Picts and Saxons.

c. 400   Final end of Hadrian's Wall.

401   Troops withdrawn from Britain to defend Italy.

407 Constantine III, a usurper, removes the garrison from Britain, and crosses to the continent.

410 Emperor Honorius tells the British cities to look to their own defence.

c. 446 British cities appeal for military assistance to Aetius, the leading general in Italy at this time ('The Groans of the Britons').

Some Roman Emperors

The dates of some Roman Emperors mentioned in this book:

Claudius	41–54	Caracalla	211–7
Nero	54–68	Geta	211–2
Vespasian	69–79	Gordian III	238–44
Nerva	96–98	(Carausius	287–93)
Trajan	98–117	Constantius	293–306
Hadrian	117–138	Constantine I	
Antoninus Pius	138–161	(the Great)	306–37
Severus	193–211	Constans	333–50

The adjectives *Hadrianic*, *Severan* and *Constantian* refer of course to the years when Hadrian, Severus and Constantius respectively were emperors. *Antonine* refers to the period 138–192, but most of the structures so described in this book belong to the first Antonine phase, ie 138–54. *Agricolan* refers to the years 78–84/5 (Agricola's governorship) and *Theodosian* to 369–70.

Glossary

A page-number in brackets gives a reference to the Introduction, where a fuller explanation of the relevant term may be found.

abutment: masonry platform or earth embankment supporting the central structure of a bridge
agger: cambered embankment-mound carrying a Roman road
ala: unit of cavalry in the Roman auxiliary army (p. 7)
ambulatory: covered portico surrounding the inner shrine of a temple (p. 17)
apodyterium: undressing room in a bath-suite (p. 14)
architrave: the horizontal member above two columns (piers, etc.), spanning the interval between them
bailey: fortified enclosure in a medieval castle
ballista: artillery-weapon discharging arrows and stone balls
basilica: town-hall (p. 13)

berm: in military defences, the level space between two features (eg ditch and rampart)

bonding-course: bands of brickwork (or occasionally stone slabs) which alternate with wider sections of regular stonework; they normally run through the entire thickness of the wall, presumably to give cohesion and stability to the mortared rubble-core; they were also useful as levelling-courses during construction

breastwork: the vertical timber-work built on top of the earth rampart of a fort to provide screening for the sentry; see fig 49

caldarium: hot room (moist heat) in a bath-suite (p. 14)

cella: inner shrine of a temple (p. 17)

centuria: unit of 80 legionary soldiers, commanded by a centurion (p. 7)

chi-rho: Christian symbol composed of the first two letters of the Greek name for Christ (Χρίστος); see fig 140

civitas: tribal unit (p. 13)

clavicula: in a Roman camp, curved extension of rampart (and ditch) protecting a gateway (p. 8)

cohort: unit of infantry soldiers, legionary or auxiliary (p. 7)

colonia: settlement of retired legionaries; for York a title of honour (p. 13)

crop-mark: colour-differentiation in standing crops or vegetation (best seen from the air), indicating the presence of buried ancient features

cross-hall: covered assembly-area in the headquarters building of a fort (p. 10)

culvert: drainage-channel

curtain: wall of fortification

dado: continuous border round the lower part of a wall decorated with painted plaster

field-system: regular pattern of rectangular fields attached to an ancient farming settlement

flue-arch: underfloor arch in a hypocaust (qv) allowing hot air to pass from furnace to room, or from one heated room to another

flue-tiles: open-ended, box-shaped tiles built in the thickness of the walls of a room heated by hypocaust (qv)

frieze: horizontal band above an architrave (qv), sometimes carved with sculpture

frigidarium: cold room in a bath-suite (p. 14)

graffito: writing scratched on tile, pottery, plaster, etc.

guilloche: on mosaics, decorative feature consisting of two or
    more intertwining bands

herringbone: descriptive of a style of construction in which
    stonework or tiles are set in zig-zag pattern

hypocaust: Roman method of central heating: see fig 4. The floor
    was raised, usually on *pilae* (qv), and flue-tiles (qv) acting as
    'chimneys' were built in the thickness of the walls. The draught
    created by these flues enabled hot air to be drawn from the
    stoke-hole (qv; on the right in fig 4), where brushwood or
    other fuel was burnt, to circulate under the floor, and to escape
    up the wall-flues to the air outside. In the channelled type of
    hypocaust, the hot air circulated not around *pilae* but through
    narrow channels built under the floor

imbrex: semi-circular roofing-tile, linking two flat tiles (*tegulae*)

in situ: in its original position

jamb: side-post of a doorway or window

keep: central stronghold of a medieval castle

laconicum: hot room (dry heat) in a bath-suite (p. 14)

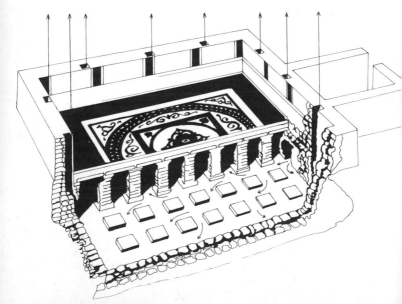

4   *The working of a hypocaust*

latrine: lavatory (p. 15)

leet: aqueduct-channel

lintel: wooden beam or stone slab lying horizontally above a doorway (or window)

mansio: a small town (posting-station, qv); or an inn, especially for government officials

monogram: set of letters combined into one (used of Chi-Rho, qv)

mosaic: floor composed of pieces of coloured *tesserae* (qv) to form geometric or figured designs

motte: earth mound marking site of a small medieval castle

offset: point at which the thickness of a wall is reduced, forming a 'step' in the structure

palaestra: exercise-yard of a public bath-house

parapet: top of a Roman fortification consisting of a wall-walk (qv) and battlements

pediment: triangular gabled end of a roof (usually used of temples)

pilae: pillars of brick (or stone) supporting the floor of a room with a hypocaust (qv)

pilaster: column or pillar incorporated in a wall

piscina: swimming-bath in a public bath-house

plinth: projecting course at the foot of a wall; also used of a base, eg for an altar

podium: raised platform (especially used of temples)

portal: doorway or carriageway, especially of a fort-gateway

post-hole: hole dug to receive a wooden upright

postern: minor gate or door in a late Roman town- or fort-wall

posting-station: small town on a main road, where travelling officials could find an inn (*mansio*, qv)

principia: headquarters building of a Roman fort (p. 10)

procurator: government financial administrator

relieving-arch: arch built as part of a solid wall to take the weight of the construction above, and to divert it from weak points such as doors and windows lower down

revetment: facing of one material given to a structure of a different material (eg stone wall given to an earth bank)

roundel: circular panel containing a design (eg on mosaics)

sacellum: shrine in a fort's headquarters building (p. 10)

samian: high-quality, red-coated pottery, imported from the continent (mainly from France) *sarcophagus:* coffin of stone or lead

Saxon Shore: coast of SE England exposed to Saxon pirate raids (p. 12)

sleeper wall: low wall supporting a raised floor, especially in a granary

springer: the voussoir (qv) which rests on the cap above a jamb (qv) and marks the beginning of an arch

stoke-hole: furnace-area for a hypocaust (qv)

street-grid: regular pattern of streets crossing at right-angles

sudatorium: hot room (dry heat) in a bath-suite (p. 14)

tepidarium: warm room (moist heat) in a bath-suite (p. 14)

tesserae: small cubes of coloured stone, glass or tile, of which a mosaic (qv) or tessellated (qv) floor is composed

tessellated: composed of *tesserae* (qv), usually used of a floor without decoration

titulum: short detached stretch of rampart (and ditch) protecting the gateway of a marching camp (p. 8)

tribunal: platform for commanding officer in *principia* (qv) (p. 10), or on a parade-ground

triclinium: dining-room

tumulus: burial-mound (p. 18)

vexillatio: detachment of a legion (normally 1,000 men)

via decumana: road in a fort running from back of *principia* (qv) to back gate

via principalis: road in a fort linking the gates in the long sides and passing in front of the *principia* (qv)

vicus: small civilian settlement, especially one outside a fort

voussoir: wedge-shaped stone forming one of the units of an arch

wall-walk: level platform for the sentry on top of a fortification (see parapet)

wattle-and-daub: wall-construction consisting of wickerwork plastered with mud

Chapter I

South-East England

Kent and Sussex

(Appendix I only – Surrey)

In 55 and 54 BC, Gaius Julius Caesar made his famous invasions into Britain. On the second expedition he crossed the Thames and penetrated into what is now Hertfordshire; the great ditch known as Devil's Dyke at Wheathampstead is probably part of the fortress of the native king Cassivellaunus, which Caesar successfully assaulted. But there was no permanent Roman occupation, and the marching camps which Caesar must have built have never been found.

We have, therefore, to turn to **Richborough*** (TR 3260) [AM; SSM] for the earliest visible traces of Roman Britain. The site lies $1\frac{1}{2}$ m NW of Sandwich in Kent and is reached by taking a minor road to the right just before the level-crossing on the Canterbury road (A257) out of Sandwich. It is difficult to imagine the place as it was in AD 43, the year of the Roman invasion under Aulus Plautius, as the coastline is much changed: the whole of the NE corner of Kent, the isle of Thanet, was indeed an island,

and Richborough itself lay on a small peninsula attached to the mainland. In particular, the steep escarpment on the east, where the railway-line and river Stour now lie, has carried away the east wall of the later stone fort, and in AD 43 the ground must have extended flat for some way beyond this.

On arriving at the fort, ignore for the moment the massive walls and go straight into the interior; leaving the triple ditches on the right, head northwards and you will see (1 on plan, fig 4) a line of double ditches interrupted by a causeway, just inside the west gate of the later stone fort. These ditches (and a now-vanished rampart) have been traced in both directions for a total length of 2,100 feet, but only this short portion has been dug out

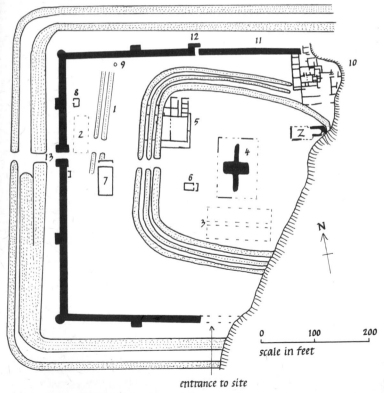

entrance to site

5   Plan of Richborough

and left visible. Everything that is described in this book – all the villas, towns and forts of the Roman occupation – are later than these ditches, dug by the invading army in AD 43 to defend their beach-head.

These ditches were soon filled up once the progress of the invasion had ensured that a defended base was no longer necessary at RVTVPIAE (as the Romans called Richborough). The area then became a supply-base; several buildings, all of timber, are known, and the plans of three of them have been marked out in concrete on the site. One (2 on plan) had a row of posts (now concrete circles) forming a verandah; the outline only of two other buildings, granaries, are marked 3 on fig 5.

By about AD 85, the area of the storebase had been cleared for the erection of a great marble-faced monument, of which all that remains is the enormous cruciform mass of concrete rubble that dominates the centre of the site (4). Its full mass can be appreciated by going down into the tunnel burrowed underneath the monument in the nineteenth century. Above this you have to imagine a magnificent four-way arch, towering nearly 90 feet high, sumptuously adorned with bronze statuary and marble imported from Italy, fragments of which are visible in the museum. The building was rectangular, the present cross-shape merely being the platform for the marble-paved passageway between the arches; massive piers of masonry (now gone) must have filled the spaces between the arms of the cross, and the level of the cross itself was reached by four flights of steps. Richborough was the chief port of Roman Britain, at least during the first century, and the monument was evidently a piece of propaganda, probably celebrating the completion of the conquest of the province and designed to impress the many visitors passing through. About the middle of the third century, the monument was stripped of all its ornament and served as a signal-tower, surrounded by an earth rampart (not visible) and the triple ditches which surround it on three sides. Shortly afterwards the monument was totally levelled and the triple ditches filled in when the walls of the Saxon Shore fort were built in the late third century.

The rest of the visible remains inside the fort can be dealt with briefly. Building 5 (fig 5) is that of a block of shops rebuilt in stone in the second century. It consists of three large rooms with a courtyard in front and a corridor with rooms for living-quarters

or storage behind. Only half the building remains, as the rest
was removed when the triple ditches were dug. No. 6, close to the
monument, belongs to the fourth century (note the difference in
surface-level – this and the top of the monument-platform
represent the ground-level of the Saxon Shore fort); the function
of this and a similar but larger building (7) is unknown, but they
may have been meeting-rooms for military guilds. No. 8 is an
early second-century cellar, the only surviving part of an otherwise timber building. No. 9, a hexagonal structure in the NW
corner, is of fourth-century date and was interpreted by the
excavator as a water-tank. A recent suggestion, however, is that
it is the baptismal font of a Christian church, the main construction of which is visible in some of the excavation photographs but
was entirely removed without proper record. A *Saxon* church
has in fact been found at Richborough, in the NE corner where
its plan has been marked out (Z on fig 5). Finally, a substantial
stone building in the NE corner (10) had a long history. The
earliest building of c. AD 85 (plan marked by brown concrete-
dressing) was rebuilt on a larger scale in the second century
(white concrete). It was clearly an official building of some sort,
perhaps a *mansio* or inn, as it was respected by the ditches of the
third-century earth fort which stopped short of it (fig 6). It
remained in use until the construction of the Saxon Shore fort,
when a small military bath-building (the remains on a higher
level, including a hypocaust and semi-circular plunge-bath) was
built on the site.

6   *Richborough, the north wall (inside face)*

From here you can easily reach the outside of the walls of the
Saxon Shore fort. This was one of a series of forts, running from
the Wash to Portsmouth, which was designed to protect SE
England from Saxon pirates. It is usually believed that Richborough was put up by Carausius (287–293), who revolted from
Rome and made himself master of an independent empire of
Gaul and Britain; but it has recently been suggested that it
belongs to the decade before him. At some time towards the end
of the third century, at any rate, these massive walls were built,
probably 30 feet high and faced, as can be seen, with rows of
squared stones separated at intervals by bonding-courses of tiles.
This facing is best preserved on the north side, which presents
other interesting features; you can study here, for example, the
various sections in which the wall was built: the join is very clear
(11) to the east of the north postern – note the row of patterning
in chalk and ironstone blocks, which are not on the same level in
each section. Next you reach the first bastion (12), which has an
opening for a postern gate; its outer face contains a large re-used
stone, now much worn, once representing the head and mane of a
lion. Just beyond the bastion a sharp eye will spot that the
bottom tiling-course changes its level at one point, indicating
another section-break in the building of the wall. Rounding the
circular corner bastion, you reach the west gate (13), a single
passageway defended by a guard-chamber on either side, one of
which is visible. Here began the Roman road later called Watling
Street, which ran through London and the Midlands to Chester.
Rounding the SW corner bastion, you arrive back at the entrance
to the site, where a small museum displays a selection of finds.
The area beyond the fort-walls was also intensively occupied in
Roman times, but no surface features are visible except for the
amphitheatre, now an unimpressive hollow; it is difficult to find,
lying in a field to the west of the minor road where the track to
Richborough Castle joins it.

Richborough is only one of four Saxon Shore forts in Kent;
others were at Reculver, Dover and Lympne. **Reculver**, the
Roman REGVLBIVM, (TR 2269) [AM; A], lies 3m east of Herne
Bay. Here too the coastline has changed dramatically, but
whereas Richborough is now some way inland, the fort at
Reculver has been eroded by the sea and only the south half of the
original eight-acre enclosure remains. A fortlet connected with
the Roman invasion in AD 43 was built here, but the surviving

walls belong to the first half of the third century. This was confirmed by the finding in 1960 of a fragmentary but important inscription referring to the building of the *principia* and cross-hall under a certain Rufinus, probably Q. Aradius Rufinus, who was governor of Upper Britain c. 230. The fort is therefore considerably earlier than that at Richborough, and the absence of bastions and tile bonding-courses at Reculver confirms this. Excavations since 1952 have shown that it was supplied with the customary buildings of a Roman fort, but these were much robbed and are not now visible. Coin evidence shows that occupation ceased about 350–60. The garrison was the first cohort of Baetasians from Brabant, on the Belgium–Holland border.

To see what remains of the defences (and if you have just come from Richborough be prepared for disappointment), take the path from the sea-shore car-park which leads up to the twin towers of the Saxon and medieval church. Passing this, you reach the east gate, excavated in 1967. The guardroom which defended its north side can be seen, and another on the south may lie under the path. Turning right, the path follows the most impressive stretch of wall. It is about 8 feet high, but only rubble-core remains, as all the facing-stones have been robbed. About 130 feet from the SE angle a rough bit of projecting masonry indicates a repair to the wall in late Roman times. Along the south side the wall is more overgrown, but its line can be followed (except at the SW corner) right round to the inn opposite the car-park. One or two blocks half way along the south wall are all that remain of the south gate, excavated in 1964.

The village of **Lympne** (TR 1134) lies on B2067, 3m west of Hythe. To find the remains of the Saxon Shore fort, known today as Stutfall Castle but as PORTVS LEMANIS under the Romans, take the turning in the village to Lympne Castle; where the road turns 90° to the left, by a building called 'The Cottage', walk down the path which leads straight on. After climbing a stile, continue down a narrow muddy path between two barbed-wire fences, and after ten minutes you will see the forlorn Roman walls in a field on your right. They have been much tossed around by landslides, and the sea has now retreated far away, but the overgrown ruins have an air of impressive, almost romantic, solitude. Some fragments are still about 25 feet high and 14 feet thick, even though fallen from their original position. The walls originally formed a pentagon enclosing about ten acres, and tile-courses and bastions (one good example survives on the NW) make it likely that they are contemporary with those of Richborough (second half of the third century), although pottery indicates the presence of a naval base here in the second century.

The fourth of the Kentish Saxon Shore forts was at **Dover***(TR 3141), DVBRIS, but until rescue excavations in 1970–1 along the path of the inner relief-road, its exact position was uncertain. Now, however, the south and west walls of the fort are known, together with three bastions – a later addition and not, as at Richborough, of one bond with the wall. A totally unexpected find was that of another fort on a slightly different site. This was built in the second century and, on the evidence of tile-stamps (CL BR), it is almost certainly the headquarters of the British fleet, the *Classis Britannica*. Unfortunately, nothing of either fort is now visible, as the new road covers the remains. One discovery of 1971 has, however, been salvaged: several rooms of a house belonging to the civil settlement which grew up outside the *Classis Britannica* fort. The walls, still standing nine feet high in places, are covered with brightly-painted plaster. This consists of a dado below a series of panels separated by columns. Ritual objects, including two reversed flaming torches, can be seen in the panels. Its preservation is due to the fact that it lay under the earth bank piled behind the wall of the Saxon Shore fort, the building of which removed the rest of the house. Because of our climate, substantial finds of painted wall-plaster are rare; Dover can boast, in fact, of by far the largest area of Roman wall-plaster visible *in situ* in this country – over 400 square feet. It is to be found near Market Street, close to the new relief-road. Dover Corporation plan to build a museum and cover-building over the house, which at present (1973) is not yet open to the public.

As well as this spectacular new find, Dover possesses another monument unique in Britain. This is the Roman *pharos*, or lighthouse, [AM; A], which adjoins the church of St Mary close to the car-park in the grounds of Dover Castle (reached from the Dover–Deal road, A258, on the east side of the town). The top 19 feet are entirely medieval, but the lower 43 feet are good Roman work, built of flint-rubble, originally faced in ashlar blocks, with external tile bonding-courses (fig 7). The outer face, octagonal in plan, is now much battered by decay and by medieval refacing (especially on the NW); in Roman times it rose in a series of

eight vertical stages, with a set-back of about one foot at each
stage. It was probably about 80 feet high, or 20 feet higher than the
whole monument is today; and from the top a column of smoke
would have risen by day, and a beacon of fire by night, to guide
ships using the Channel. The Roman entrance survives on the
south, and some of the upper windows retain their stone voussoirs
interlaced with brick. The square interior, now a roosting-place
for pigeons, is equally impressive. The lighthouse was probably
built in the second century. The church, which incorporates
Roman material in its walls, also has a small collection of finds
to the right of the entrance.

A second lighthouse was built at Dover, on the Western
Heights. Paintings show that it was still standing at the end of the
seventeenth century, but a drawing of 1760 depicts a mere

7   Dover, *the lighthouse*

shapeless chunk of masonry, known as the Bredenstone. What was left was mutilated when the Western Heights fortification was built in 1805–6. All that survives today is a long stretch of flints and tile-course encased in stonework of 1861 and, on the surface above, three chunks of concrete propped up against one another. At present these pathetic remnants are not accessible, the staircase to them being dangerous; but the fortifications are in the care of the Department of the Environment who may, one day, tidy up the area and allow visitors to see where the western *pharos* stood. Re-used material, including stamped tiles, indicates that this lighthouse belongs to the later Roman period.

One more Saxon Shore fort belongs to this chapter, and it is even more impressive than the examples in Kent. It is at **Pevensey*** (TQ 6404) [AM; A], which lies between Eastbourne and Hastings on the A259. This, too, now lies inland; in Roman times the walls were built on a peninsula, with the sea coming right up to the south wall and the harbour situated to the east in the area of the present car-park. The Roman walls enclose an oval area of about nine acres. That on the south has entirely gone except for two bastions, incorporated into the keep and the outer wall of the medieval castle which lies at the SE angle. Going through the east postern, which is on the site of a Roman gate (the existing masonry is medieval or modern), you reach the interior of the fort, where excavations in the early years of the century found only a few timber buildings and hearths. On the right, just before the gap where the wall has fallen away, the internal face has been cleared down to Roman ground-level. Here you can see that the thickness of the wall is reduced by offsets; note, too, how the lowest eight feet retain their facing-stones, as this part of the wall was covered by earth in the post-Roman period and so escaped the later stone-robbing and weathering which have battered the top part. On the far side is the west gate. This consisted of a central arched entrance nine feet wide, with two guardrooms on either side, of which only the lowest courses of one survive; the whole was then flanked by the two gigantic bastions (the existing gate-jamb is medieval). In front of this entrance a ditch was dug across the isthmus joining the peninsula on which the fort stood to the mainland, and part of it is visible. From here you can follow the walls right round to the east gate again: they are about 12 feet thick and stand virtually to their original height except for the parapet. Facing-stones and bonding-courses are well preserved, and the few patches of flintwork used in the facing (where the parapet survives, for example) show how little repair the Roman walls needed during medieval times. From the west gate you first reach three bastions; here, as elsewhere, they are bonded into the wall and therefore were built at the same time. Then comes a magnificent stretch of wall (fig 8) where section-joints between building-parties can easily be spotted (note how the rows of green sandstone or brick bonding-courses do not tally with those of adjacent sections). Next, immediately before the fallen sector, was a small postern-gate, a simple curved passage in the wall. Between here and the east gate are three more bastions; the herringbone patchwork especially clear on the middle one is due to Norman repair-work.

ANDERIDA, as the Romans called it, was not built until the fourth century (as a coin of c. AD 330 found *under* a bastion shows), although earlier occupation of the site cannot be ruled out. Most of the coins date from the late third and early fourth centuries. The Anglo-Saxon Chronicle relates how a vain defence of the fort was made in 491, ending in a terrible massacre. The site then lay derelict until the Normans used the walls as an outer bailey for their castle.

So far, I have dealt almost exclusively with military antiquities, and this may have given the impression that SE England was predominantly a garrisoned area. This was not the case; the forts I have described belong to the later phase in the Roman occupation of Britain when the peace and security of SE England was threatened by Saxon pirates. Both before and after the erection of the forts, civilian life continued in the towns and villas, and to these I must now turn.

Two trunk-roads, both built in the early years of the occupa-tion, served SE England. One was Watling Street, which started at Richborough and reached London by way of Canterbury and Rochester; the A2 follows the Roman road for much of its course. The other was Stane Street, which linked London and Chichester (for the posting-stations en route at Alfoldean and Hardham, see App. I). From Canterbury there were roads to Reculver, Dover and Lympne, the last one surviving as the B2068 (Stone Street); and another road branched off Watling Street near London and headed for the south coast near Lewes, enabling swift transport to the Thames of corn from the Downs and iron from the Wealden mines. The road is unusual in being

metalled for many miles with iron slag, and a portion of this has
been preserved by the Sussex Archaeological Trust. It is reached
by a footpath just south of the B2110 East Grinstead to Tunbridge
Wells road, 1m west of the crossroads with the B2026, and about
100 yards east of the White Horse Inn at **Holtye** (TQ 4638). The
road was exposed in 1939, since when frost has loosened the
smoothness of the cinder surface. The shallow hollow running
diagonally across the road marks the site of a ford.

Of the settlements linked by these roads, only three, Chichester,
Rochester and Canterbury, have any Roman remains, and most
of these are meagre. **Canterbury** (TR 1457) was DVROVERNVM
CANTIACORVM, the tribal capital of the Cantiaci. Excavation
since the war has revealed many new features of the Roman town,
but little is now visible. The medieval walls follow the line of their
Roman predecessors, but no Roman masonry is now exposed
except for one tiny fragment of a gateway (the 'Quenin Gate'),
consisting of two large ragstone blocks and a few courses of
bricks marking the turn of an arch. This can be seen, embedded
in the medieval wall about 4 feet from the ground, at the most
northerly (right-hand) end of the car-park in Broad Street, very

8   *Pevensey, the north wall*

close to the last square tower in this NE sector of city-wall. Excavation has shown that the Roman walls and a contemporary earth bank behind them were built c. 270–90, later than their counterparts in most other Romano–British towns.

Of public buildings, we know most about the theatre which lay at the junction of St Margaret's Street and Watling Street. This was of two main periods: about AD 80–90, when the first building was erected with timber seats on banks of gravel; and about 210–20, when the whole theatre was rebuilt in stone on a larger scale. To the later period belong the two fragments of the theatre which are the most easily accessible: a portion of the back wall is visible in the dining-room of the restaurant at 37, St Margaret's Street; and an imposing fragment, 4 feet high, of the curving outer wall of the auditorium can be seen in the 'Cella Romana' of Slatter's Restaurant on the opposite side of the street. For the fanatic, other fragments are visible on private property in the cellars of 23, Watling Street and 5 and 6, St Margaret's Street.

Much less disappointing are the remains of part of a town-dwelling preserved in a basement in Butchery Lane (Apr.–Sept. 10–1 and 2–6, Sunday 2–6; Nov.–Mar. weekdays 2–4). The most impressive feature here is a corridor paved by a tessellated floor, with two mosaic panels with leaf- and flower-motifs and fragments of a third. Excavation in 1946 showed that the corridor itself was a second-century addition to a late-first-century stone house, but that the mosaic was added later, probably in the third century. A block of limestone visible on the left of this corridor represents a Roman repair. The other main feature of the site is a room with a hypocaust, of which only the *pilae* supporting the vanished floor remain. The skeleton of a baby and a small hoard of bronze coins (c. AD 270) were found in the area of the hypocaust. The central part of the basement, now covered with concrete but originally a courtyard open to the sky, has showcases of small finds; note in particular a lamp showing a slave with a wine jar. Around the walls are tiles, pots and a small mosaic from Burgate Street.

The main collection of finds, however, is housed in the Royal Museum, High Street (weekdays 9.30–5.30). This is small but excellently arranged; only from here (and not from looking at isolated masonry lumps in private cellars) can one get some idea of life in Roman Canterbury. Note especially the collection of pre-

9   Canterbury, a glass vessel from Bishopsbourne

Roman coins; the reconstruction-drawing; some superb glass, especially a beautiful flagon from Bishopsbourne with ornate handles (fig 9); and above all, the hoard of silver-ware in the case in the centre of the room. This was deposited in the late fourth century and found in 1962. It includes 11 silver spoons, one with the Chi-Rho monogram and another inscribed VIRIBONISM (= ? 'by the hand of Viribo'); also a curious silver implement with a prong and another Chi-Rho.

Two other Roman relics in Canterbury deserve a brief mention. One is the Dane John, a Roman burial-mound of the first or second century, much obscured and altered by landscape-gardening (in Dane John Gardens, on the south side of Canterbury). The other is St Martin's church, which lies on a hill to the east of the city on the Sandwich road (A257). Inside, a wall of Roman brickwork is clearly visible on the right-hand side of the chancel, pierced by a Saxon doorway. More impressive is the rear wall of the nave which, though much repaired, contains unmistakable Roman tile bonding-courses. Bede, writing in 731, mentions 'a church built in honour of St Martin while the Romans still lived in Britain'. The presence of Christianity in Roman Canterbury is confirmed by the silver hoard mentioned above; it is uncertain whether these walls are part of a Roman church, or of another Roman building only later converted to Christian worship, or are of Saxon date and merely incorporate Roman material brought from elsewhere.

The remains of DVROBRIVAE (TQ 7468), Roman **Rochester**, need not detain us long. The town, 23 acres in size, defended the important crossing of the Medway by Watling Street. An earth rampart and ditch of c. 150–175 was replaced, probably at the end of the second century, by a stone wall. The SW corner of this wall, faced with ragstone but without tile-courses, stands to an impressive 10 feet in a public garden called Eagle Court, which is reached by an alleyway between the Eagle Tavern (public house) and a butcher's shop (Kemsley's), on the south side of High Street. All the facing-stones are present. Note that just after the Roman wall begins to turn the corner, the medieval wall carrying straight on abuts onto it. Then cross High Street and go down Free School Lane opposite. The medieval wall turns the corner and you will see, under a hideous stretch of modern brickwork, the core of the Roman wall. Other bits of core, unimpressive and difficult to reach, are visible in the Deanery Garden and elsewhere in the Cathedral precinct; and another forms part of the bailey-wall of the Norman Castle fronting the Medway.

Of Roman **Chichester** (SU 8604), the NOVIOMAGVS REGNENSIVM ('Newmarket of the Regnenses'), even less is visible. It had a military origin, perhaps as a base for the Second Legion during its thrust to the west (ch. 2). By the end of the first century it had already developed into a flourishing town. Today, there is virtu-ally nothing. The museum in Little London contains the best of the small finds (Tues.–Sat. 10–6; closes at 5 in winter). The site of the amphitheatre is visible as a hollow surrounded by a low elliptical bank in a recreation-area on the east side of the city, reached by a passage called Whyke Lane from A259 (The Hornet); it was built about AD 80 and abandoned at the end of the second century. The walls follow the Roman line but no Roman masonry is visible. There is a portion of second-century mosaic on show *in situ* in the south aisle of the Cathedral's retrochoir. And, for the record, Messrs. Morants' shop in West Street has a fragment of black-and-white mosaic from a bath-house; and part of a massive flint foundation is visible in the cellars of the Dolphin and Anchor Hotel (perhaps belonging to a colonnade on the south side of the forum). Much more important is an inscription found in 1723 and now placed in the wall under the portico of the Assembly Rooms in North Street (fig 10). This records a temple to Neptune and Minerva erected by a guild of artisans (*collegium fabrorum*) on the authority of Tiberius Claudius Cogidubnus, who is described as *rex et legatus Augusti in Britannia*, 'king and legate of the emperor in Britain'. This Cogidubnus established his kingdom (*Regnenses* = people of the kingdom) at Chichester and did his best to foster romaniza-tion in the early years of the conquest. In return the Romans respected his authority as a native client-king and only after his death was the area formally assimilated into the Roman province. He is recorded by Tacitus as one 'who maintained his unswerving loyalty down to our own times'. It was as a reward for this loyalty that the next site, Fishbourne, was erected.

Fishbourne* (SU 8404) is the success story of post-war British archaeology. It has, rightly, attracted enormous publicity and brought renown to its excavator Barry Cunliffe, who began digging here as an undergraduate in 1961 and was a professor before it was opened to the public in 1968. Visitors should be equally grateful to Ivan Margary, whose generosity saved the area from housing-development and allowed the modern cover-building to be erected. The site lies 1¼m west of Chichester on the A27 to Portsmouth, and can be visited every day from 10 a.m. (March to October), closing at 4 p.m. in March, April and October, and at 7 p.m. in other months; during November it is open only at weekends, and it is closed from December to February.

The first occupation at Fishbourne was military: the remains of two timber store-buildings excavated under the east wing of the later palace belong to what is probably a supply-depot for the fort underlying Chichester in the early years of the conquest. The depot was soon cleared away, and sometime in the late 40's or early 50's a timber house with a separate building (perhaps a servants' range) was constructed. It had clay or mortar floors, and there were traces of painted plaster, so a man of some status must have lived here. Then, in the 60's, the first masonry building was erected at Fishbourne. Its site lies astride the main road and so could not be completely excavated, but trenching was able to show that it comprised a large colonnaded garden, a bath-suite, a set of living-rooms and servants' quarters. The whole was elaborately decorated with stucco and painted plaster; its floors were paved in mosaic or marble. It was no ordinary building; yet its magnificence was to be far outstripped by what was to come.

Sometime after 75, a start was made on the building of the great palace which has made Fishbourne famous. It is important

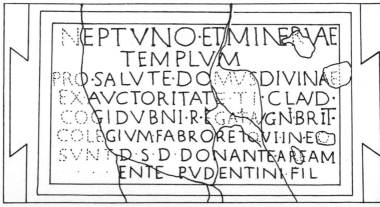

10   Chichester, the Cogidubnus inscription

to realize that only a small portion of the whole complex is visible today: it originally consisted of four wings arranged around a formal garden. The main living-rooms of the owner lay on the south, and are now largely under the A27; this wing had a colonnade on both sides, overlooking the formal garden on one side and a natural garden stretching down to the sea on the other. The official wing was on the west; its chief room, in the centre, was an apsed audience-chamber where the owner would have received official visitors. The east wing contained an entrance-hall designed to impress (as, indeed, was the whole palace), and suites of rooms arranged around courtyards, probably for visitors of lower rank as the standard of comfort was less than that of the north wing. The latter, protected in its entirety by the modern cover-building, had a sumptuous series of guest-rooms ranged about two private courtyards. Servants' quarters must lie elsewhere, still to be uncovered.

We have here, then, a palace of some ten acres – a staggering complex of colonnades, halls and rooms magnificently adorned with painted plaster, stucco, and mosaic, built by an army of skilled craftsmen from the continent, at an estimated cost in modern-day terms of about one and a half million pounds. It is true that some British villas approached the size of Fishbourne, but that was not until the fourth century: for the first century AD the Fishbourne Palace is entirely without parallel not only in Britain but in the whole of Europe outside Italy: it is a piece of Italy transplanted into a distant, newly-conquered province. Who, then, could be the owner of such a palace – a high-ranking Roman official, or a local landowner of great distinction? This is where Cogidubnus (above, p. 43) fits into the picture. For a Roman official residence to be built so close to the capital of a loyal ally would have been an intolerable snub; and it is therefore more likely (though we shall never know for certain) that the palace was the home of king Cogidubnus in his old age, and that the earlier structures at Fishbourne (the timber house and the first masonry building) represent the earlier stages of his rise to luxury.

Drastic changes occurred at the beginning of the second century, no doubt after Cogidubnus' death. A bath-suite was inserted into the north wing, and another into the east, suggesting the splitting up of the palace into separate units (the palace baths lay at the SE corner – convenient for the owner, but a long way for

his guests in the north wing!). Various other modifications to the
north wing, including the laying of more mosaics, will be noted
in turn below; the villa, though lacking its former grandeur, still
maintained a level of affluence markedly higher than elsewhere
in the contemporary Romano–British countryside. Finally, at the
end of the third century, a disastrous fire brought the life of
Fishbourne to a close until its resurrection in 1960, the year of the
laying of a water-main which caused its discovery.

On arriving at the site, first pay a visit to the museum where all
the phases described above are imaginatively set out and
illustrated with photographs, models and plans; here too are the
principal small finds. In the main concourse is a model of the
palace as it may have appeared in about AD 80. From here you
can begin your tour of the north wing.

The first room (labelled 1) which you see on the left of the
viewing-platform was also the last addition: this hypocaust was
still being constructed when fire destroyed the whole building at
the end of the third century. No trace of the floor above was
found, and it had probably never been laid. The floor-level here
was in the process of being raised: a fragment of the mosaic laid
when the palace was first built can be seen on the right. Of the
floor in 2, of second-century date, little remains, but the adjoining
room (5) has preserved its polychrome floor (also second-century)
which can be viewed either as a pair of scallop-shells or as the
splayed tail of a peacock, the main body of the bird destroyed
but the feet (?) surviving. On the other side of the catwalk (rooms
3 and 4) are two simple geometric mosaics and a solid dividing
wall which *do* belong to the original palace; these floors seem to
have survived later use without the need for replacement. (The
masonry in the corner of room 4 represents the flue of a second-
century oven.) Moving on, you reach a courtyard of the palace-
phase, originally open to the sky. Its stone gutter has been largely
replaced in modern materials. The tiles seen here are part of the
collapsed superstructure. Opposite (behind you) is (7) the best-
preserved mosaic at Fishbourne, of mid-second-century date and
again, therefore, laid when the palace had ceased to operate as a
single unit: remember that only half of the visible mosaics belong
to the original palace. The central roundel depicts a winged cupid
riding a dolphin, with sea-panthers and sea-horses in the
surrounding semi-circles. Compare the two sea-horses: that
nearer the catwalk is much more skilfully executed. Note, too,

how the guilloche border which surrounds the mosaic changes its colour-composition. Clearly several craftsmen were at work on the same mosaic. At the same time as the laying of this floor, the little rooms on either side (6 and unnumbered) were given hypocausts; only the *pilae* bases remain, the heating proving so ineffective that they were destroyed in the third century, when the mosaic in an adjoining room (8) was laid. This is a simple knot-motif and a guilloche circle surrounded by dolphins.

Now come down the steps and examine room 12, which contains the best preserved of the first-century palace mosaics – a pleasing geometric design – as it was never refloored even when a timber partition chopped it in two (fig 11). The success of the design is shown by the poor imitation of it which was laid in the mid-second century in the room beyond (14). Return to the cat-walk now, which skirts rooms 9–11. The skeleton in 9 was buried in the ruins of the building some time after its final destruction. 10–11 have plain or simple mosaic floors laid in the second or third century. After this, on the right, is the mosaic already mentioned (14). The primary interest of the room beyond (13) is that it displays two superimposed mosaics, the original floor

11   *Fishbourne, first-century mosaic (black-and-white)*

being replaced about AD 100, when the palace first changed hands.
The centre of the new mosaic depicted a head of Medusa, of
which part of her right eye and eyebrow and some of her snaky
hair can be made out (upside-down from this angle). The floor
has been much damaged by medieval ploughing, but enough
remains to show its rather poor technical standard, and it is
perhaps the work of a local, not a foreign, mosaicist. Behind you
is the site of another of the open courtyards of the original
palace.

Of the north wing beyond this point very little remains, as
before the mid-second century the whole of it, including a newly-
inserted bath-suite, was demolished because of serious
subsidence. Parts of three mosaics, however, which belonged to

12 Fishbourne, first-century mosaic (polychrome)

the original palace, survive. Little is left of one (19), largely
destroyed by the water-main trench of 1960. The next room (20)
has a fine, if fragmentary, polychrome mosaic (fig 12). The central
portion is destroyed, but enough remains of the surrounding
rosettes and vine-leaves, the band of guilloche, and the corner
vases, to show the skill of the mosaicist both in his mastery of
composition and in his use of colour. The adjoining mosaic (21)
is much simpler but quite effective. The small white diamond on
its border is clearly not part of the design and may be the craftsman's signature. A few fragments of the early-second-century
bath-suite survive at the far end of the cover-building.

Now you should go out into the garden, flanked by parts of
the east and west wings. The plan of the former is marked out in
modern materials, but the latter is at present grassed over. What
you see here is not guesswork : excavation revealed the pattern of
the bedding-trenches, and these have been followed in the
reconstruction. Although pollen analysis could not determine
what shrub was used, box is the most likely and that is what has
been planted (fig 13). At the west end of the central path
(remember that only half the formal garden is visible today), just
in front of the steps leading up to the site of the audience-
chamber, is a square construction made of tiles, probably the
base for a statue. Finally, going back towards the modern
entrance along the outside wall of the west wing, you reach the
NW corner, where the gutter, column-bases, and the projecting
corner of the stone foundation for a water-tank (to feed the
fountains which adorned the garden), can be seen. Here your
visit to this extraordinary site ends. Nowhere else in Britain will
you see a Roman garden, nowhere else will you see mosaics laid
as early as some of those in the north wing : such is the uniqueness
of Fishbourne.

Another villa-site can easily be reached from Chichester : it is at
Bignor* (SU 9814), a village situated about 14 miles away,
midway between the A285 and the A29, but more conveniently
approached from the latter (minor road via West Burton,
leaving the A29 near the inn at the foot of Bury Hill). It is open
from 1st March to 31st October, every day except Monday,
10–6.30 ; also on Bank Holidays and every Monday in August.
In contrast to Fishbourne, Bignor has long been known. It was
found in 1811 and the entire plan of the villa was uncovered in the
following years. But it was not until partial re-excavation in the

late 1950's and early 60's that anything of its historical sequence
was revealed. We now know that the first stone building, a simple
rectangular construction, was not erected before about AD 225,
though a timber house or houses preceded it. It was given a
corridor and small wings later in the third century, but only in
the fourth was the villa expanded to enclose a courtyard. To get
some idea of its size in this last phase, stand with your back to the
modern huts and face the driveway up to the villa. On your right
the west wing has been marked out: in front of you, part of the
corridor serving the south wing is exposed. The south wing ended
at the point where a modern hut covers the Medusa mosaic (far
left, by the trees), and another corridor then turned to join up
with the north wing, half of which is represented by the huts
behind you. The present car-park covers about two-thirds of the
area of the Roman courtyard. Farm-buildings lay further still to
the left, and the whole complex was enclosed by a boundary-wall.
The general plan of the villa, together with some of the finds, can
be seen in a room, still floored with its Roman mosaic, to the right

13   *Fishbourne, the garden (1969)*

of the present entrance. Here too is a reconstruction-drawing
showing the villa on fire and the inhabitants escaping to safety:
but there is no evidence of destruction by a looting party, and it is
more likely that the great house declined gradually until its final
abandonment in the early fifth century.

The glory of Bignor is its splendid series of mosaic pavements
laid in the mid-fourth century. The mosaic in the first room (left
of entrance) is divided into two parts: one represents a large
well-drawn eagle carrying off the shepherd Ganymede to serve
as Jupiter's cup-bearer on Mount Olympus; Ganymede, naked
except for boots, a red cap and a red cloak, carries his shepherd's
crook. The rest of the room contains six hexagonal panels of
dancing girls, now much destroyed, with an ornamental stone
water-basin in the centre. If symbolism is to be looked for in
these mosaics, perhaps the soul's ascent to heaven (Ganymede)
and the joy that awaits it (the dancers) is the meaning here.

The next room, entered from the far end in antiquity (there
being no access then from the Ganymede room), has a pleasing

geometric mosaic in good condition. From here you go outside and reach, on the right, the hut containing the best-preserved pavement, restored in 1929 partly with modern materials. The main portion of the floor is destroyed, exposing the hypocaust *pilae* and flue-tiles in the walls. Of the mosaic here only parts of five dancing cupids survive, but in the apse is a superb, delicate rendering of the goddess Venus, with head-dress and halo, flanked by birds and festoons. Below it is a charming panel of winged cupids engaged in gladiatorial combat. The mosaic in the next hut, viewed from the outside through a wooden hatch, depicts a powerful head of Winter, heavily muffled in cloak and hood, with a bare twig over her left shoulder (fig 14). Of the mosaic in the next hut, probably heads of Medusa and the Seasons, virtually nothing remains, but you can see the two steps which inadequately fill the gap between the corridor of the north wing and the beginning of the west wing. From another wooden hatch, on the other side of the hut, a fragment of mosaic with a dolphin and the letters TƎR can be made out. Perhaps this stands for Terentius and is the mosaicist's signature. The site of the west wing, marked out in different colours to distinguish separate building-periods, lies nearby.

Finally, do not forget to cross the car-park to the trees at the far side to see the cold plunge-bath and, beyond it, the floor of the undressing room. This has a central panel depicting the snaky head of Medusa, which is often used on floors as a charm to ward off evil (according to the myth, a single gaze on it would turn you into stone).

The third outstanding villa-site in SE England is at **Lullingstone*** in Kent (TQ 5365) [AM; SSM], reached by a road (signposted) off the A225 in Eynsford. That a Roman building stood here had been known from the eighteenth century, but systematic excavation began only in 1949 and continued for 12 years. The first stone house, with a simple range of rooms served by a back corridor, was built towards the close of the first century. A major change occurred about 100 years later when a new owner added a bath-suite to one end of the villa and a series of cult-rooms to the other. He was a man of some distinction and wealth, his rooms being adorned with two portrait-busts of his ancestors, finely executed in Greek marble. About AD 200 the villa was suddenly deserted: the owner had to leave in a hurry, for even the busts were left behind. After lying derelict for over 50

years, it was reoccupied by a new family in the last quarter of the
third century. The cult-rooms were demolished and a long heated
room built over them; the baths were refurbished; and a large
granary (no longer visible) was built between the house and the
river. From now until the early fifth century the villa was
continuously occupied. Mosaic floors were laid in the mid-fourth
century in the new apsidal dining-room and in the main living-
room. Then, about 360–70, the owner became a Christian, and
part of the villa was converted to Christian use. At the same time
the baths were filled in, and a little later the granary was pulled
down. Finally, in the early fifth century, a fire destroyed the villa,
whether deliberate or accidental is unknown.

Passing the ticket-office and moving clockwise, turn the corner
and pause in front of the Deep Room, labelled no. 6. It was
probably first used for storing grain, but in the late second
century a pit containing ritual water was sunk into the centre of
the room and a niche built in the left-hand wall. This was decorated with a fine painting of three, now two, water-nymphs; the
head of one is still in good condition, with green leaves in her
hair and water falling from her breasts. The room was presumably

14   *Bignor, mosaic of Winter*

dedicated to the worship of these water-goddesses, and was
connected on the right to another cult-room, surrounded by a
corridor on all four sides (partly under the modern concrete
concourse). All this was swept away in later alteration and only
the tiled stairway which served the cult-rooms is clearly visible
now (to the right of and behind the Deep Room). In the late third
century the Deep Room was blocked off and the niche containing
the water-nymphs covered up: one of them was totally destroyed
and the central portion of what remained was marred by the
erection of a shelf. The busts belonging to the previous owner
were also placed here; the originals are now in the British
Museum, but casts may be seen in a showcase at Lullingstone.
Meanwhile, a new long heated room was constructed to the
right of the Deep Room, concealing the second-century staircase
and cult-rooms. Its floor was of timber supported on wooden
rafters and therefore, of course, no longer visible: all we can see
now is the area below the floor where the hot air circulated,
passing from one compartment to another through the flue-arch
prominently visible here.

  In the second half of the fourth century, as we know from a

15   Lullingstone in the fourth century, reconstruction-drawing

reconstruction of the painted plaster which was found in tiny
fragments among fallen debris in the Deep Room, the room
above the latter was converted into what was probably a
Christian house-chapel, although no specific object was found to
prove its use in Christian worship. Along the end-wall facing us
were painted six human figures in beaded robes, with arms outstretched (the way early Christians prayed), separated by ornate
columns resting on a dado. Next to the figures, on the left-hand
wall, was a large painted representation of the Christian Chi-Rho
monogram within a wreath. Perhaps there was also an altar on
the wooden floor, but no sign of it was found in the collapsed
debris. The chapel was approached by an anteroom (labelled 10),
which had another Chi-Rho, and a vestibule (11). This house-
chapel, and the probable churches at Silchester and Richborough,
constitute the earliest known Christian shrines in Britain. The
original wall-plaster is now in the British Museum (fig. 140), but
copies can be seen at Lullingstone on the wall by the exit.

Moving on, and passing the reconstruction-drawing (fig 15)
and the coloured plan of the villa where all the building-phases
can be studied, you reach the bath-house at the far end, built at
the close of the second century and demolished 200 years later.
The various rooms – hot, cold, and tepid – are labelled, and there
are two plunge-baths at one end (underneath the walk-way), the
smaller being a fourth-century addition. Turning the corner, and
passing the well which supplied the house with water, you can go
up to the balcony and look down on the whole building from
above. In one room a large fourth-century pot, made at Farnham
in Surrey, marks the site of the kitchen, but the main feature
which strikes us is, of course, the splendid mosaic floors laid in
the mid-fourth century. That nearer us is the dining-room: the
couches would have been arranged on the semi-circular border to
look down on the main panel of Europa being abducted by
Jupiter in the guise of a bull, accompanied by winged cupids on
either side (fig 16). The smiling bull, evidently delighted with his
prize, leaps over the sea (the dark blue portion of mosaic) with
lively charm. Above is a Latin verse-couplet referring to a passage
in the Aeneid of Virgil – a reflection of the owner's literary
tastes – and can be translated: 'if jealous Juno had seen the
swimming of the bull, she might have more justly gone to the
halls of Aeolus'. Juno was the wife of Jupiter; Aeolus was ruler of
the winds and therefore capable of producing a tempest to upset

Jupiter's amorous adventure. Part of the mosaic has been disfigured here by burning rafters in the final conflagration.

The mosaic in the principal room (13) has a skilfully-executed
central panel. It depicts the hero Bellerophon, seated on the
winged horse Pegasus, killing the Chimaera, which is a monster
with a lion's head and a serpent's tail. Surrounding this and much
less realistically drawn are four dolphins and two opened-out
mussel-shells, representing the sea-journey which Bellerophon
had to make in order to carry out his task. Heads of the Seasons
fill out the four corners – Winter, an old woman with a hooded
cloak (top left); Spring, a girl with a bird on her shoulder (top
right); and Autumn, a middle-aged woman with corn in her hair
(upside down). Summer was destroyed when a fence was being
put up in the eighteenth century. The rest of the mosaic is composed of a medley of geometrical patterns, poorly designed and
laid, and clearly the work of the craftsman's assistants. The
finding of these pagan mosaics so close to the almost
contemporary Christian rooms suggests a symbolical meaning for
them, and it is significant that Bellerophon also appears on a
Christian mosaic in the British Museum. His killing of the

16   *Lullingstone, mosaic of Europa and the bull*

Chimaera represents the triumph of life over death and good over evil – the Roman equivalent of St George and the dragon; and the rape of Europa probably symbolizes the freeing of the soul from the body at death.

Showcases at Lullingstone give a selection of the many finds from the site. One of the most interesting is a complete set of gaming-pieces which came from the burial-goods of a young man and woman in a mausoleum constructed in the early fourth century on the terrace behind the villa. The remains of this, now largely overgrown, and of a small circular temple erected about AD 80–90 can be seen; they are not strictly open to the public, but a word with the custodian will probably be sufficient if you are interested in seeing them.

Apart from the Lullingstone mausoleum, two other Roman burial-sites in Kent are worth visiting. One is about 10 miles away at **Keston** (TQ 4163). It lies in the grounds of Keston Foreign Bird Farm, and although the site is owned by Bromley Council access to it is private; permission to visit, therefore, should be sought at the farm on arrival. The farm is signposted on the west side of the A233, the Bromley Common to Westerham road, on a sharp bend just south of its junction with the B-road from Hayes Common. The site has been known for over 150 years and sporadically dug on a number of occasions, but proper excavation and consolidation was not carried out until 1967–8. The main feature is a large circular tomb strengthened by six buttresses, originally rendered externally with red plaster and perhaps 20 feet high. It was clearly a monumental tomb, probably for the family who owned a large villa on the lower part of the hill. Adjoining it is a rectangular tomb with a large buttress on one side, and from it came the stone coffin set up nearby on the perimeter of the site. This coffin has quite a history of its own: it was found about 1800 and performed a variety of tasks in the district, including that of a garden-box and a horse-trough; in 1941 it was smashed by a German bomb and only in 1968 was it restored and brought back to the site. A third tomb had eluded all the earlier excavators as it lay between two buttresses of the large circular tomb. It consists of a small chamber covered by a vault made of tiles set in mortar; a lead casket with the remains of an adult cremation was found inside. This tomb is now protected by an easily-liftable wooden door. A number of simple graves were also found in the area but are not now visible. Pottery from them suggests a mid-second- to mid-third-century date for the cemetery, but the monumental tombs may be later.

The other site is at **Stone-by-Faversham** (TQ 9961), which lies by a group of trees in a field 100 yards north of the A2 opposite a minor road leading to Newnham; this is at the foot of Judd's Hill, ½m west of Ospringe and 1¼m west of Faversham. Most of the masonry here belongs to a medieval church, but it incorporates a square Roman building into the west part of its chancel. The Roman work is unmistakable, consisting of regularly-tooled stones separated after each layer by tile bonding-courses. This is especially clear on the exterior south face (that nearest the road), where the break between the neat Roman work and the medieval masonry without the tile-courses is obvious. The Roman building is entered on the west by a massive stone sill, and the pivot-hole for the door is clearly visible. It was built in the fourth century and is most probably a mausoleum. No trace of a burial was found in the excavations of 1967–8, but it may have been robbed in medieval times or in later probes at the site. Many other burials have been found in and around Ospringe, and the finds are displayed in the Maison Dieu Museum [AM; S], ¾m east, at the junction of the A2 with Water Lane. The Roman settlement of DVROLEVVM was here-abouts, but the earthworks on Judd's Hill, sometimes claimed to be the site, are probably due to landscape-gardening and the real site lies in or near Ospringe village.

Chapter 2

Wessex and the South-West

Hampshire, Wiltshire, Dorset, South Somerset, Devon and Cornwall

(Appendix I only – Berkshire)

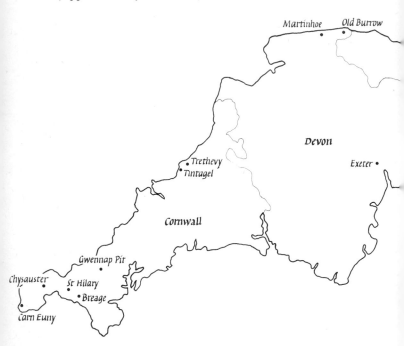

In AD 44, with SE England reasonably secure, the invading army split up into separate units to attempt the subjugation of the rest of Britain. The division chosen to advance south-westwards was the Second Augustan Legion, then commanded by the man who was later to become the Emperor Vespasian. His biographer Suetonius has left us the bare information that he fought thirty battles, overcame two powerful tribes and more than twenty hill-forts, and reduced the Isle of Wight to surrender. Archaeology, however, has been able to shed light on the nature of the opposition offered by the two tribes mentioned, the

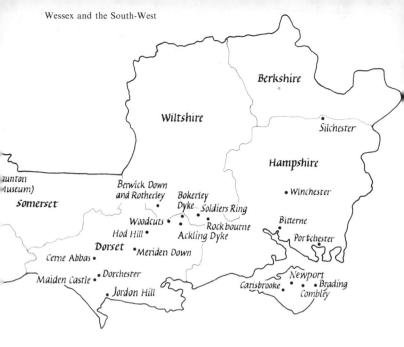

Durotriges of Dorset and south Somerset, and the Dumnonii of
Devon and Cornwall; and this opposition resulted in the building
of a series of forts which held the area in check during the early
years of the Roman occupation. Few of these have left any
features traceable on the ground today. Even the earliest base of
the Second Legion is still not known, but a 42-acre fort near
Wimborne Minster in Dorset (not visible) is one possibility.
By about AD 55, however, the Legion was in Exeter, where recent
excavations have revealed its fortress.

Ramparts of the smaller forts, designed for auxiliary forces
with perhaps a sprinkling of legionaries, are visible at Hod Hill
(see below) and, less impressively, at Waddon Hill in Dorset,
Wiveliscombe in Somerset, North Tawton in Devon and
Nanstallon near Bodmin in Cornwall (App. I). Excavation at the
last indicated an occupation of c. AD 55–80. Better preserved are
two fortlets on the north Devon coast, at **Old Burrow** (SS 7849)
and **Martinhoe** (SS 6649). Excavation in the early 1960's showed
them to be successive, not contemporary, constructions. The

former was the earlier, with occupation beginning perhaps about AD 48 and lasting only a short time. It was abandoned in favour of the slightly less exposed site at Martinhoe, where a fortlet was built about AD 60 and evacuated on the final subjugation of the Silures of South Wales in 78: for these posts were designed to patrol the Bristol Channel as well as to keep an eye on possible trouble in Devon. Accommodation at Martinhoe was provided by a couple of timber barracks for about 80 soldiers, but at Old Burrow the men lived in tents. All that can be seen at either site today are the earth defences, which in both cases consist of an outer, circular rampart and ditch with an entrance on the south, and an inner square rampart and ditch or ditches with an entrance on the north. The position of the entrances ensured that an attacker who had stormed the outer gate would have to traverse half the circuit of the outer compound before attempting the gate to the fortlet proper. The earthworks at Old Burrow are better preserved than those of Martinhoe, where part of the outer rampart has slipped over the cliff. The former is reached from the A39 (Minehead–Lynmouth), by the first path on the right (north) of the road ½m after crossing the Somerset–Devon border at County Gate (if you are coming from Minehead). The village of Martinhoe is reached by a minor road leaving the A39 at Martinhoe Cross, 4m west of Lynton; then follow the track leading north out of the village, take the right fork, and when this finally ends walk across two fields to the fortlet.

The most interesting of the early Roman military works in the area covered by this chapter is the fort built, exceptionally, inside the ramparts of the prehistoric hill-fort of **Hod Hill** in Dorset (ST 8510). Take the Shaftesbury road (A350) for three miles out of Blandford Forum, turn left at 'The White Horse' in Stourpaine and right again at the crossroads. When the road peters out at a stream, go through the barbed-wire 'gate' on the left and so up the cattle-track to the SE corner of the hill-fort, which is here entered by a breach of medieval or modern origin. The main pre-Roman entrances were at the NE and SW, while the gap in the middle of the eastern side was made by the Romans. Once inside the ramparts, the visitor will notice in front of him a mass of circular platforms and depressions. These mark the sites of the huts occupied by Iron Age peoples immediately prior to the Roman invasion; and excavation has shown that one of them, surrounded by a hexagonal enclosure, was the target for Roman artillery-fire during the assault on Hod Hill in AD 44. It is assumed, therefore, that this was the chieftain's hut and, as no evidence was found of fighting at the gates or of massacre within, this bombardment alone was apparently sufficient to secure the surrender of the hill-fort's inhabitants. The Romans then proceeded to build a garrison-fort inside the NW corner of the hill-fort (diagonally opposite the corner at which you entered), using the prehistoric rampart to form its north and west sides, but building their own defences on the south and east. The latter have been damaged by ploughing over the centuries, but are still impressively preserved. The Roman rampart consisted of packed chalk, faced with turf back and front, and was originally 10 feet high to rampart-walk; it still stands to about five feet near the NE angle. Outside the rampart were three ditches, all only about five feet deep but skilfully designed. The innermost two each had a nasty ankle-breaking channel at the bottom. Then came a flat platform 55 feet wide before the outer ditch, which was so shaped as to be easy to cross in attack but deceptively difficult in retreat. These ditches are interrupted by causeways leading to the south and east gates, both defended by *titula* (visible in fig 17).

17   Hod Hill from the air, looking south

The entrance in the NW corner of the hill-fort is also Roman, as is the causeway crossing the ditch here. It was made to provide the garrison with convenient access to water from the river Stour below.

The entire plan of the interior of the fort was recovered in excavations between 1951 and 1958. These revealed the foundation-slots cut in the chalk to receive the timber-framed buildings of which the fort was composed. The layout of these indicates that the garrison consisted of about 600 legionaries supplemented by an auxiliary cavalry-unit 250 strong. It was evacuated after a fire had destroyed some of the buildings, probably by accident, and coins and pottery show that this cannot have happened more than about eight years after the original building of the fort in AD 44 or 45.

Hod Hill, as we have seen, can be included among the twenty hill-forts which Suetonius records as being captured under Vespasian's command. Much more dramatic evidence, however, was found in excavations in 1934–7 by Sir Mortimer Wheeler at the most famous and impressive of all British hill-forts, **Maiden Castle*** (SY 6688) [AM ; A]. It is reached by the signposted lane off the Weymouth road (A354) in the southern outskirts of Dorchester. The massive triple ramparts which surround the site were erected in the early first century BC, and the defences are even more intricate at the two entrances. The west gate (that nearer the car-park) is the more strongly defended and has not been excavated. It is not, therefore, known if the Romans attacked it, but it seems more likely that Vespasian concentrated his assault at the less complex east gate. Here, in contrast to Hod Hill, the Romans met with tough resistance. First their artillery fired some rounds of arrows, one of which landed in a defender's spine ; the vertebra and arrow-head are now in a case in the Dorchester Museum. Then an advance party gained access to the interior and set some huts on fire, and the resulting smokescreen enabled the gate to be stormed by the rest of the troops. It cannot have been easy : try running up and down the slopes at the east gate today, then imagine determined natives raining sling-stones down on you, and you will appreciate that even for tough, well-disciplined Roman soldiers the battle cannot have been a walk-over. This is confirmed by the fury they showed on gaining entrance : the inhabitants, regardless of age or sex, were brutally hacked down before a halt to the slaughter was called. The

natives were left to give a hasty burial to their dead. The evidence
for all this can be read in Wheeler's report and some of it is
displayed in Dorchester Museum. No trace of the battle can be
seen at the site today.

There are, however, Roman remains visible at Maiden Castle,
though they date from nearly 350 years later than the battle of
AD 44. In the closing years of the fourth century, at a time when
Christianity was the official religion but paganism still apparently
flourished, a new temple was built in the eastern half of the
hill-fort. It is one of the best examples of the typical Romano–
Celtic temple to be seen in Britain, and consists of the normal
central shrine and surrounding ambulatory (fig 18). Next to it is
a tiny two-roomed construction interpreted as the priest's
dwelling. The name of the deity worshipped is not known, but as
representations of several were found in the excavation there may
have been a plurality of deities. The very slight remains of another
Roman temple can be seen a short distance away, on **Jordon Hill**
(SY 6982) [AM; A], dug in 1843 and 1931–2. Here, however, the
outer wall is not visible and has not in fact been found: the stonework had probably been completely robbed and its position

18   *Maiden Castle, the Roman temple*

escaped the notice of the excavators. Coins indicate that it flourished, like the one at Maiden Castle, in the second half of the fourth century. To reach it, follow the A353 out of Weymouth, and keep straight on where the A-road swings inland by a filling-station (DOE signpost). The temple lies on the brow of the hill, to the left of the track, after ¼m.

The native occupation of Maiden Castle did not cease immediately after the battle of 44, but it does not appear to have continued beyond AD 70. We must assume that by that date its inhabitants had been shifted elsewhere, probably to the new town which the Romans founded in the valley below, at **Dorchester*** (SY 6990). Finds and topography make a military origin certain, but no structural remains of a fort have yet been identified. The town which took its place was known as DVRNOVARIA and served as a tribal capital for the Durotriges, though in the fourth century it may have shared this role with Ilchester in Somerset (App. I). At any rate it was then that both towns reached the height of their prosperity, and the many mosaics found in and around Dorchester indicate the existence of a flourishing school of mosaicists in the town at that date. To the fourth century, too, belongs the town-house in Colliton Park, situated behind

19   *Dorchester, a channelled hypocaust*

County Hall in the extreme NW corner of the Roman walled
area. It is reached by a path from the Hardy Statue, and can be
visited at any time. The building consists of two separate ranges,
both built in the early fourth century but enlarged c. 340. The
south range (that nearer the entrance-gate) first consisted of the
three central rooms only, but in the enlargement the big room
(nearest the gate), the corridor and the heated room at the end
were built. A dwarf column, found amongst rubbish in the
adjacent well, has been re-erected on the corridor wall. The
heated room is an excellent example of a channelled hypocaust.
Some of the paving-flags of the floor are in position and the
hollows once containing flue-tiles for the escaping hot air can be
seen in the walls (fig 19). Opposite this room is the shed covering
a geometric mosaic. Next to this is a rare survival from Roman
Britain – the splayed opening for a window, originally closed by a
wooden frame and glass. Fragments of this had collapsed,
together with the stone framework, into the room below.
Mosaics were laid in all the rooms of this western range, but
except for the one on show only fragments survived. Another
hypocaust is visible in one of these rooms. Coins cease c. 375,
when the cobbled path by the well was built, but slum occupation
went on, perhaps into the fifth century.

The course of the defences of Roman Dorchester is not
precisely known over their entire circuit, but they enclosed an
area of between 70 and 80 acres. An earth bank and ditch came
first, towards the end of the second century, and this was fronted
with a stone wall at some later date, probably just before AD 300.
A rather wretched fragment of this, penned behind railings and
capped by a modern brick wall, is visible in West Walk, a short
distance south of the Hardy Statue. Only the core of the wall is
left, at most eight feet high, and displaying a double course of
limestone bonding-slabs near the top. Nearby, in High West
Street, is the Dorset County Museum's important archaeological
collection (Mon.–Sat. 10–5, closed Mon 1–2 and Sat. 1–2). The
most interesting items to note are the finds from Maiden Castle,
the coin-hoard from South Street, the table legs (fig 1, Contents
page) and other products from the Kimmeridge shale industry,
and the mosaic floors which reflect the opulence of fourth-
century Dorchester (see also p. 360).

The rest of the Roman remains in the Dorchester neighbourhood lie outside the walled area of DVRNOVARIA. The most

impressive is the amphitheatre, known as Maumbury Rings,
which lies on the left (east) side of Weymouth Avenue just before
the railway bridge in the southern outskirts of the town. The
earthwork started life as a Neolithic monument c. 2,000 BC, when
the banks were about 11 feet high. The Romans converted it into
an amphitheatre by lowering the ground level to create an arena
floor and raising the banks to their present 30 or so feet. There
was a timbered gangway round the arena, which had a single
entrance less wide than the present gap. There is no reason to
suppose that it was built before the second century, and it was
certainly still in use in the fourth. Later ages employed it in other
ways. In the seventeenth century it was used as a gun-emplace-
ment and the internal terraces on the banks belong to this period.
In the eighteenth century it was used as a place of public
execution, and as recently as 1952 the people of Dorset assembled
here to greet HM the Queen.

   The second Roman feature outside the walls is interesting
rather than spectacular. It is the aqueduct, built in the late first
century, which carried water to the town over a winding course
some twelve miles long. It is a puzzle to understand why it was
ever necessary when water could easily be obtained by sinking
wells; perhaps civic pride was responsible. It consisted of an
open leet about six feet wide and four feet deep, now visible (in
part) as an embanked shelf following the contours of the hillside.
Take the Bridport road at the roundabout by the Hardy Statue
and then turn immediately right along Poundbury Road. On the
right, after you cross the railway bridge, are the ramparts of the
prehistoric Poundbury Camp. Walk to the NW corner of the
latter, and just outside, near the entrance to the railway-tunnel,
you will see the shelf of the aqueduct. It is particularly prominent
curving round the hillside away to the left, by the river. After
$\frac{1}{4}$m the road descends steeply and the aqueduct can be faintly
seen on the left on Fordington Down before returning close to
the road: it is particularly clear as the road climbs again, for the
aqueduct has become a field-boundary and a cattle-track. The
rest of its course is less well preserved.

   Finally mention may be made of two other relics in the
neighbourhood of Dorchester, this time to the east. One is a
finely-carved marble tombstone which was erected to a certain
Carinus, in the mid-second century, by his wife and three children.
It is now inside St George's church at Fordington, a suburb of

Dorchester. The other is what is almost certainly a Roman milestone, nearly six feet high, which can be seen on the south side of the A35 one mile NE of Dorchester. It is situated on the verge immediately before the A-road makes a left bend, at the point where a minor road turns off for Stinsford village. The *agger* of the Roman road, at first in a coppice, but then in the open, can be seen on the north side of this lane before the latter also changes direction. The milestone, no longer inscribed, was moved a short distance from its original spot in the nineteenth century. It stands beside the Roman road heading for the hill-fort of Badbury Rings near Wimborne, where there was a small road-side settlement.

Three other tribal capitals were founded by the Romans in Wessex and the south-west, at Exeter, Winchester and Silchester. The military origin of **Exeter** (SX 9192), long suspected, was confirmed first by the discovery of a fort-ditch near the south gate in 1964, and then of military buildings in the centre of the city in 1971–3. These included barracks, a workshop and a granary of timber and a fine stone bath-house, and it is now clear that a legionary fortress was built at Exeter during the 50's, presumably by and for the Second Legion. At some stage, still uncertain, the soldiery moved on, and before the end of the first century the place was laid out as a town-centre for the Dumnonii, ISCA DVMNONIORVM, with a street-grid and the usual public buildings. At this time the legionary baths were converted into the basilica : the hypocausts were filled in, the floor-levels raised, and a range of steps provided to enter the basilica from the forum. At the time of writing, the future of this site, which lies opposite the west front of the Cathedral, is uncertain, but a plan has been drawn up for displaying the remains in an underground museum. If this is implemented, visitors will be able to see the *caldarium* and part of the *tepidarium* of the military baths, together with some later alterations, including the basilica steps (but see p. 360). Otherwise the only visible remains of ISCA are the defences, which enclosed about 100 acres, an average size for a Romano–British tribal capital. As usual, a clay bank and ditch came first, in the late second century, and in the early third the bank was faced in stone. The walls have been much repaired and altered in medieval and later times, and consequently the Roman masonry is not everywhere apparent. Look out, therefore, for regularly-coursed blocks of purple-grey volcanic stone, with a projecting plinth at the base, and you will know that you are looking at Roman work. The plinth is often a few feet above ground and was underpinned by medieval masonry when the ground-level was lowered.

The best place to start is in Northernhay Gardens, entered from Queen Street opposite Northernhay Street. The walls have been mostly refaced here, but the Roman plinth and a few blocks above it are visible near the war-memorial 20 yards south of the modern arched opening. The plinth is again visible north of the opening, but is here four feet above the present ground-level. In the east corner of these gardens is the archaeological museum (10–5.30, Mon.–Sat. only), one room of which has a display of Roman finds. Come out of the museum, go down to the end of Castle Street, then turn left and first right by Eastgate House. Here the wall again becomes visible, with plinth and about five feet of Roman masonry above it. Continue on, past a much-botched portion, until you reach a modern brick structure projecting into the car-park. Immediately beyond this is a superb stretch of wall 15 feet high, with plinth and 20 courses of Roman masonry above it. Continue walking straight down Southernhay West, past the Devon and Exeter Hospital (there is another piece of plinth visible at the south end of the car-park opposite the hospital). Then turn right (on foot only, since it is a one-way street) and right again at the traffic-lights. The stretch of wall here has been largely repatched, but part of the Roman plinth survives. A green plaque on the modern wall behind points out the foundations of a guard-tower of the Roman south gate, adjoining the pavement. The rear face of the Roman wall is well preserved here. Finally, on the other side of the inner by-pass, there is a fine stretch of wall (fig 20), with Roman facing-stones impressively visible at first and medieval patching beyond. The ranging pole in the photograph (on the right) stands on the plinth marking Roman ground-level.

Of Roman **Winchester** (SU 4829) virtually nothing is visible. It was VENTA BELGARVM, the capital of the Belgae, the tribe which occupied much of what is now Hampshire and part of Wiltshire. There was a pre-Roman settlement here, and the earthwork called Oram's Arbour in the western outskirts of the town is now dated to this period (first century BC). A Roman fort in the conquest period is a probability, for the town was not properly laid out until about AD 90. The forum, situated immediately north

of the Cathedral, was built about AD 100 and enlarged 50 years
later. There was a defensive bank at the end of the first century,
but about AD 150 new earth defences were erected to enclose an
area of 138 acres, making it the fifth largest town in Roman
Britain. Timber houses were rebuilt in stone from the mid-
second to the third century, and about AD 200 VENTA received
stone walls. There was apparently decline in the fourth century,
when part of the forum fell into disuse and houses were
demolished without being rebuilt. The only readily accessible
relic of Roman Winchester *in situ* is a fragment of the city-wall
visible behind a grating from a footpath called the Weirs, which
runs south from the river-bridge on the east side of the city.
(There is also some core of the Roman wall in the private grounds
of St Bartholemew's Maternity Home, Hyde Street.) A portion
of mosaic has been relaid on the floor beneath the entrance to the
Deanery, south of the Cathedral. Otherwise, the remains of
VENTA must be examined in the museum, at the NW corner of the
Cathedral Green, where finds from the city and nearby are on
display (weekdays from 10 a.m. closing at 4, 5 or 6 according to
the time of year; Sundays 2–4.30). A near-perfect geometric
mosaic from a villa at Sparsholt is the outstanding exhibit.

To attempt to give coherent directions to the most famous of
all Romano–British towns, **Silchester*** (SU 6462), is virtually
impossible, for it lies in the middle of a maze of minor roads in

20   *Exeter, Roman town-wall*

the extreme north of Hampshire, inside a triangle formed by
Newbury, Reading and Basingstoke. The site is marked on most
maps, and I will leave readers to make their own way there. It is a
charming place, peacefully set in deep countryside far from the
bustle of the twentieth century. It is truly a 'dead' city, for,
whereas most Roman towns in Britain continue in occupation to
this day, Silchester did not find favour with later town-planners
and it remains deserted, with only a medieval church and a farm
within its walls. Yet, paradoxically, the fact that it is dead makes
CALLEVA ATREBATVM, as the Romans called it, very much alive
with the spirit of the past, and most people find a visit to the spot,
whatever the season and whatever the weather, a moving and
uncanny experience.

The reason for Silchester's fame is the fact that the area within
the walls was totally excavated between 1864 and 1878 and, more
especially, between 1890 and 1909. Techniques were not scientific
in those days and so a chronological sequence for the history of
the town was not revealed. But the excavations did provide not
only a wealth of objects but the complete plan of a Romano–
British town – the forum and basilica in the centre, the baths to
the SE where the ground slopes down to a stream, several temples
and, of course, many houses. A tiny building, 42 feet by 33 feet,
found near the forum 1892 and re-excavated in 1961, was
almost certainly a church, though no specific objects conclusively
proved its use for Christian worship. All these buildings, however,
unfortunately now lie under a blanket of soil; and apart from the
forum, which was visible from 1875 to 1909, no attempt has been
made to leave the remains open in an accessible form. Today the
cost of conserving anything but a tiny area would be
prohibitive.

Despite the lack of visible remains within the walls there is
still plenty to see at Silchester today. Apart from the town-walls a
series of earthworks once encircled the site; the dating of these
is still disputed. The earliest seems to have been the inner earthwork, not marked on the plan (fig 21). It was erected about AD
43–4 over the pre-Roman settlement of the Atrebates, and
enclosed a slightly smaller area than that of the later town-walls.
The earthwork soon fell into disuse and was levelled, and the
outer earthwork (5 and 12 on fig 21) was thrown up shortly
afterwards, probably c. AD 61–5. But the Roman town was not
formally laid out until the end of the first century. The planning,

however, was a little too ambitious, for the earth defences of the late second century enclose a smaller area than that envisaged by the original street-grid. Finally, in the early third century, the existing stone wall was built along the same line as the earth bank.

The church provides a car-park and a good starting-point for a tour of the visible remains (1 on fig 21). By the path behind the church is a sun-dial, supported on part of a Roman column which comes from a temple-precinct underlying the churchyard. Walking south from here you will soon see the wall, preserved to a good height but much overgrown at present. It provides a vivid contrast with the next stretch (2), newly freed from its shrubbery and conserved by the Department of the Environment, which has recently taken over responsibility for the walls. As can be seen from this magnificent stretch (fig 22), almost all the facing-stones have been robbed, leaving visible the concreted flint-rubble core, separated at intervals by bonding-courses of large flat slabs. It is a spectacular sight, still standing 15 feet high, probably close to its original height apart from the patrol-walk. Then the wall changes direction and runs along to the south gate

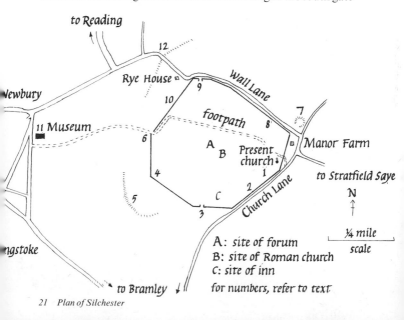

21   *Plan of Silchester*

(3), still cluttered up at the time of writing with barbed-wire and corrugated sheeting. Its single arch was set at the back of the passage formed by in-turning the curtain-walls, and only these side walls remain now. From here you have a fine view of the interior of CALLEVA. Close to the walls on your right you have to imagine a large inn with rooms ranged round a courtyard; in the middle distance a polygonal temple; and beyond, in the centre of the town, close to the footpath, the forum with, along its western side, a basilica rising 70 feet above the ground.

Visitors pressed for time should now return to their cars, and resume the itinerary from the beginning of the next paragraph. Others may like to continue following the walls right round to the west gate. This stretch is much less impressive, but the ditch accompanying the wall is visible here. At the SW corner (4) a detour can be made to Rampier Copse, where the outer earthwork survives to an astonishing height of 20 feet (5). At the west gate (6), now a simple breach, but originally a twin-portalled gate with guard-chambers, you should go inside the wall and follow the footpath back across the buried city to the churchyard.

From here the amphitheatre (7) is only a short distance away.

22 Silchester, the Roman town-wall

It has not been excavated, but the tree-grown elliptical banks are still 18 feet above the level of the arena, which is now a stagnant pond. The adjacent stretch of city-wall (8), which near the amphitheatre stands to an impressive height and displays the base-plinth marking the original front face of the wall, can be viewed over the hedge from Wall Lane. Next, pause at the barbed-wire farm-gate (where a notice informs would-be visitors that the property is private) to view the north gate (9) which, like the south gate, consisted of a single carriageway; it is now a total ruin. Should you also wish to see the remaining sector of city-wall (on the NW (10)), you must ask permission at Rye House. The most interesting feature is the long sag which the wall displays here; this is because the inner earthwork and ditch, now invisible, passed obliquely under the line of the later wall and the foundations of the latter have settled into the earlier ditch. Otherwise go on to the museum (11), passing through a well-preserved section of the outer earthwork (12) on your way. This museum, which is very tiny, contains some models and casts of the more important objects found in the excavations, but the main collection is excellently displayed at Reading Museum

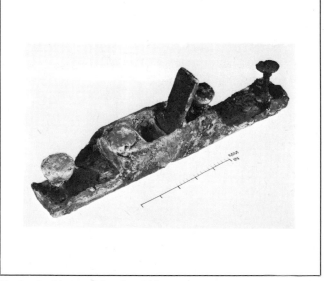

23   Reading Museum, a plane from Silchester

(weekdays 10–5.30). The objects in the showcases there speak for themselves; many of them, especially the iron tools (fig 23), look remarkably similar to their modern counterparts. The inscriptions, too, are interesting: one has the word CALLEVA inscribed on a stone slab, a confirmation of the Roman name for the town (there is a cast of this in the Silchester site-museum); others scrawled on tile, such as 'Clementinus made this box-tile', show a high standard of literacy among the ordinary inhabitants of the town. Another *graffito*, reading *conticuere omnes* (the opening words of Aeneid II), suggests that Virgil was read in Romano–British schools.

Turning now from the towns to the countryside, we find a complex pattern of settlement. Romanized villas are absent west of Exeter and on the downs of Wiltshire and Dorset. Instead, they stick to the more cultivable and better-watered valleys, especially around Ilchester in south Somerset (App. I), Winchester, and, to a lesser extent, Dorchester. Apart, however, from the examples in the Isle of Wight, described below (p. 85–8), only the villa at Rockbourne in Hampshire is permanently visible, though an outstanding mosaic from another site deserves a mention here. It was uncovered in 1946 at a villa at Low Ham near Langport (Somerset) and is now in **Taunton** Castle Museum (weekdays 9.30–5.30). Unfortunately it has been displayed on the wall, and only one of the five scenes can be viewed in comfort. The mosaic tells the story of Dido and Aeneas as recounted in the Aeneid and presumably reflects the literary tastes of its owner. A detailed explanation of the panels is given in the museum and further comment here is unnecessary, except to say that the figure on the right in the bottom panel is not Anna but Dido herself, as her obvious interest in Aeneas on the left amply demonstrates (fig 24).

The **Rockbourne** villa (SU 1217), privately owned and open only from Good Friday to October 1st (Mon.–Fri., 2–6; Sat. and Sun. 10.30–6), is signposted from the A354 5m SW of Salisbury and can also be reached by turning right off the B3078 at Sandleheath, 2m west of Fordingbridge. We ought to be grateful that its excavator, a retired architect, has thrown his villa open to the public instead of back-filling after excavation, which has continued every year since 1956. Unfortunately, however, much of the villa is badly overgrown and little attempt has been made to tidy up or consolidate the excavated remains.

It is also unfortunate that little accurate knowledge has been
gained from the excavations about the history and development
of the villa. There was occupation here in the first century, and
the first stone villa belongs to the second, but it cannot have
reached its final form, of at least three wings enclosing a courtyard, until the fourth century. A visit to the site itself may, therefore, prove disappointing, but the new museum, crammed full
of the copious finds, some of them rare, is richly rewarding.
From the museum you first reach the NW corner of the villa,
and the bath-house belonging to the west wing. The hypocaust is
especially interesting here, for the floor, partly in position at one
point, is supported on pillars made from semi-circular roofing-
tiles (*imbrices*) placed together (fig 25). Now turn left, past the
projecting room 26, which was the kitchen; there is an oven in
one corner. Nearby (room 8) is a well-preserved geometric
mosaic. Then the path descends two steps and passes between a
large overgrown room on the right (massive walls and a
hypocaust containing 66 *pilae* bases), and another bath-suite on
the left. Mosaics are visible here in rooms 1 and 4, and the
octagonal room 2 is a cold plunge-bath. The path leads into the

24   Taunton Museum, the Low Ham mosaic (detail)

courtyard and passes the rest of the west wing. Then, after a gap, are the rooms put to agricultural uses. A corn-drying kiln is visible here (room 66).

In addition, however, to romanized villas there are hundreds of native settlements which could be mentioned, ranging in size from single homesteads to large villages and displaying varying degrees of romanization. Their economy was based on small-scale mixed farming, consisting of both corn-growing and sheep- or cattle-raising. In Cranborne Chase, immediately west of Rockbourne, however, a change seems to have been introduced in the late third century, if not before, when the area may have been appropriated as an imperial estate. At this time several of the settlements were deserted, field-systems fell into disuse, and new cattle-enclosures were erected. It looks, therefore, as if government-controlled sheep- and cattle-farming replaced arable farming – a theory supported by the record that there was an imperial weaving-mill in the fourth century at VENTA, probably Winchester rather than Caistor in Norfolk. One such cattle-enclosure, known as **Soldier's Ring** (SU 0817), is close to the Rockbourne villa. To reach it from the latter, take the road towards the village of Rockbourne, and turn first left and then first right (signposted Martin). Continue along this road for 1¼m, and take the first track on the left after South Allenford Farm (double wooden gates). The polygonal enclosure's slight earth-works, now crowned by wire fences, lie in the field at the end of this track.

25 *Rockbourne villa, a hypocaust*

Several other Roman sites can be visited in close proximity
on Cranborne Chase, and so I will describe them in geographical,
not chronological, order. Continue along the minor road at
Soldier's Ring through the village of Martin to the A354. Turn
left at this junction and keep going for 1¼m until you cross the
Hampshire–Dorset border, where there is a lay-by on the right.
Running alongside the left of the road here for 100 yards, before
it changes direction, is a bush-covered stretch of the impressive
barrier known as the **Bokerley Dyke** (SU 0319). It was designed
to protect the downland of NE Dorset against marauders from
the north by running across a neck of land four miles wide,
flanked on either side by forest, of which some remnants exist.
In its first phase, the bank and ditch stopped some 500 yards
east of the A354, having started from Martin Wood, 3m SE, and
run over Blagdon Hill and Martin Down. This sector, still visible
over its entire length though difficult to reach, is dated to c. AD
325–30. Later, in phase II, the barrier was extended up to and
across the modern road, though west of the latter the dyke is not
now visible. It was even built over the Roman road at this point,
and the road's *agger*, heading northwards towards Old Sarum,
is clearly visible on the right (west) of the modern road. The fact
that the new extension was built across the Roman road, thus
blocking the major trunk route to the south-west, suggests a
period of crisis; and the archaeological evidence makes the
barbarian invasion of 367 the most likely occasion. A year or two
later, however, the road was re-opened through it: the crisis had
clearly passed. Finally, sometime after 395, in the closing days of
Roman rule, the dyke west of the road was replaced by another on
a different and more commanding line. To sum up, then, the
Bokerley Dyke belongs to three periods: west of the road it dates
to the end of the fourth century; east of the road for just over ¼m
it dates to c. 367; and the long sector beyond was thrown up
about 330.

I have already mentioned the *agger* of the Roman road visible
here near the Bokerley Dyke. Its alignment touches the A354 at
this point and joins it at the village of Woodyates for one mile,
before the modern highway swings away towards Blandford and
leaves the Roman line altogether. The best place to examine the
Roman road is a little further south. Continue along the A354
for another mile and turn left for Ringwood along the B3081.
The *agger* of the Roman road, known here as the **Ackling Dyke**

(SU 0116), crosses the B-road after ¼m (first field-boundary on the left) and forms a striking sight. From here it strides magnificently over the downland, dead straight and visible for miles, aiming for the hill-fort of Badbury Rings, over eight miles away. The whole of this stretch is a right-of-way and it provides a wonderful walk. Here the *agger* is at its best, 40 feet wide and 5 or 6 feet high. Such an embankment is unnecessary on this dry ground, and it has been suggested that the road was deliberately built in this fashion to impress the natives.

Return now along the B3081 and cross the A354 to Sixpenny Handley. Two miles beyond this village is a turning to the left, signposted Cashmoor and Dean, and immediately after this, on the right by a telephone-booth, is a grass track. In the field at the end of this lies the classic native settlement of **Woodcuts** (ST 9618). Excavated in 1884 by General Pitt-Rivers, the pioneer of scientific archaeology, and later re-interpreted by Professor Christopher Hawkes, the site is now known to have had three separate phases. The first lasted from the early first century, before the Roman invasion, to the third quarter of the second century, and was entirely non-Roman in character. The homestead was surrounded by a circular bank and ditch within which were 80 storage pits for grain, though only a few were dug at a time. From the late second century Roman influence was certainly present in the form of wall-plaster, two wells (now marked by modern stone slabs), and corn-dryers, the latter in one of the two separate enclosures tacked on to the original perimeter-bank. There was further remodelling of the enclosure-banks at the end of the third century, and in the later fourth the place was deserted. The visible earthworks, restored by Pitt-Rivers, belong to all periods, but still give some idea of the level of native occupation under Roman rule.

Of the many hundreds of similar settlements in which Wessex is so rich, I will mention just three more – sites which I have visited and which are generally reckoned to be among the best-preserved of their kind. Giving directions to these is not easy and readers will find it better to locate them with the help of the 1″ OS maps. At none of them is there anything to see beyond some confusing ridges, mounds and building-platforms, but they ought to be visited for the sake of reminding ourselves that it was only a minority of the inhabitants of Roman Britain who enjoyed the plush luxury of the stone-built villas, with their hypocausts and mosaics, that are popularly associated with the countryside. Very close to Woodcuts, and reached from the bridleway leading due north from Tollard Royal on the B3081 (turn right at the pillar-box and telephone-booth) is the native settlement on **Berwick Down** (ST 941197). It adjoins the right-hand side of the track one mile from Tollard, at the point where the pylons cross over it from left to right. There are three separate areas here: behind the beech trees is a U-shaped bank enclosing an oblong hut-enclosure which has yielded finds of the first century AD; 100 yards to the north, where the trees end, is a circular enclosure over two acres in extent, with a mass of rectangular building-platforms, certainly of Romano–British date; and north again is a concentration of pits and a large circular hut which belong to pre-Roman times. ½m due east, across the other side of the valley and on the edge of another wood, is **Rotherley** (ST 948196), which is very remote and best reached by another path from Tollard (see OS map). It was excavated by Pitt-Rivers in 1885–6 and, like Woodcuts, restored by him. The main layout of the earthworks must be dated to the immediate pre-Roman period, but occupation continued with few changes, except for the introduction of Roman coins and pottery, until about AD 300. The main feature is a large circular enclosure where the principal house was situated, a smaller enclosure to the NE, where there was a granary, and other hollows, working-areas and gulleys to the east. The settlement never seems to have been more than a single community with at most two or three dwelling-huts.

Finally in Wessex I will mention the settlement on **Meriden Down** (ST 862049), as visitors are welcome even though the land is private, and there is a plan of the earthworks displayed on the site. There is very little of interest to see, but it is set in some of the most peaceful and delightful countryside in Dorset, and the walk alone should make the visit worthwhile. Take the minor road signposted Milton Abbas in Winterbourne Whitchurch on the A354, 5m SW of Blandford Forum. Keep straight on without going into Milton, and then turn left at the fork (sign-posted Bulbarrow). After nearly two miles you will see a gate on the left marked 'Delcombe Woodlands; private property'. Opposite is a short track leading into a field. Walk across this field, following the edge of the wood on your right until you come to a wooden gate. Cross this and you will come to an exercise-ground for horses. The site lies at the far end of this field and the plan is displayed near the trees on the right. Part of the settlement lies behind these trees, and three embanked loops, probably the compounds for three large buildings, are clearly visible here. The main part of the settlement is honeycombed with banks and level platforms indicating the site of working-areas and building-structures. Four roads (a–d on the site-plan) lead to open spaces outside the nucleus; one of the western roads (f) is accompanied by four small mounds of unknown purpose. To the south is a large area of perfectly-preserved contemporary fields, tilled by the inhabitants of the settlement.

An interesting sidelight on Romano–British Wessex is shed by the **Cerne Giant** (ST 6601), a chalk figure cut into the hillside above the village of Cerne Abbas on the A352, a few miles north of Dorchester. He is a powerful muscular figure, 180 feet high, emphatically displaying his potency and wielding a knotted club above his head. Nipples and six ribs are also rather crudely shown. The club makes it almost certain that the figure is a native representation of the god Hercules, carved by the local population to promote the fertility of their crops. Its precise date is unknown, but its Romano–British origin seems certain.

In the Cornish peninsula, Roman influence was virtually non-existent, and only a single example of a romanized house is known in Cornwall, at Magor, Camborne (not now visible). For the vast majority life must have been little changed by the Roman conquest. The classic native settlement in this part of Britain is **Chysauster** (SW 4735) [AM; SSM] on the Land's End peninsula. It is signposted from the B3311 Penzance to St Ives road at Badger's Cross and from the Penzance to Zennor road at New-mill. The well-preserved remains consist of eight oval stone-built houses arranged in pairs, with another to the right of the path near the entrance-stile. Pass this and go to the next two houses, no. 3 on the left and no. 5 on the right. It is best to study house 5 first, since its plan is simple and characteristic of the 'courtyard-house' of which this and other similar villages are composed. The entrance-passage leads into a courtyard, open to the sky, in the centre of the enclosure. On the left is a recessed portion. perhaps covered by a lean-to for cattle, and on the right is a long narrow room, perhaps used as a workshop or for storage. The living-room was the round or oval hut at the far side of the courtyard opposite the entrance, and its roof was supported by a central beam in a stone socket (here *in situ*). There are sometimes other small rooms or recesses opening off the central courtyard, but the other houses all display these same basic features. No. 3, however, is more complicated as it is 'semi-detached': there are two entrances, two round rooms and two recesses on the left, all enclosed in the single unit. Many of the houses have terraced areas (?gardens) adjacent. Pottery indicates that the Chysauster village goes back to the first century BC, but the main occupation occurred in the first and second centuries AD until peaceful abandonment c. AD 300. The inhabitants existed on small-scale mixed farming, and the custodian, if asked, will point out the remains of the nearby field-system.

Another peculiar feature of some Cornish settlements is a subterranean chamber known as a *fogou*, apparently used as a cellar for keeping food cool and dry. There is a very ruinous example at Chysauster, reached from the main area by a separate footpath, but the best *fogou* is at a nearby village, **Carn Euny** (SW 4028) [AM ; S], 4m west of Penzance and signposted from the A30 at Drift. It is approached from one of the houses by a roofless stone-lined passage, which leads to the main curving gallery, five feet wide and six feet deep, still roofed with massive stone slabs. Opening off it at one end is a tiny tunnel leading to the surface and also to a circular chamber, which had a domed roof now fallen. It is believed that the *fogous*, like the villages themselves, are of pre-Roman origin, but continued in use during the Roman period. Carn Euny also has several stone 'courtyard-houses'. Excavations in the 1960's showed that these replaced earlier timber huts from the first century BC onwards.

Apart from the early invasion-period, official Roman interest in the far west was confined to the exploitation of the tin-streams of central Cornwall in the third and fourth centuries AD, after the Spanish tin-mines, Rome's previous major source, had dried up. The workings themselves have been largely destroyed by later activity, but five crudely-cut Roman milestones, all of them just a few yards from their original find-spots, bear witness to road-building or repair in Cornwall, though actual traces of these roads have not been found. Two milestones imply a short stretch of road on the north coast: one, dated to 251–3, is at St Piran's, **Trethevy** (SX 0588), a hamlet midway between Tintagel and Boscastle on the B3263; and the other, which is dedicated to Licinius, emperor between 308 and 324, is in the south transept of **Tintagel** Church (SX 0789). Further west is a better example,

found in 1942 and now erected in the garden of Mynheer Farm at
Gwennap Pit (SW 7241), a hamlet 1m due east of Redruth, south
of the minor road to St Day (ask for directions locally). It is
dedicated to the Emperor Caesar Antonius Gordianus Pius
Felix (AD 238–44) and belongs either to a road running down the
spine of Cornwall or to a cross-road linking the north and south
coasts, to assist in the transport of tin from the mines to the ports.
In south Cornwall two more milestones are known: one erected
to Postumus, emperor 258–68, is now in the church at **Breage**
(SW 6128), a village north of the A394, 4m west of Helston; and
the best-preserved of all the Cornish milestones is now cemented
into the floor of the south aisle of the church at **St Hilary** (SW
5531), which lies north of the B3280, 1¾m east of its junction with
the A394 near Mazarion. It was set up in AD 306–7 'To the
Emperor Caesar Flavius Valerius Constantinus Pius, most
noble Caesar, son of the deified Constantius Pius Felix Augustus'
(fig 26).

I have stayed long enough on the fringes of Roman Britain and
it is time to return and deal with a more familiar monument of the
Romano–British countryside, the villa. The Rockbourne villa

26   St Hilary, Roman milestone

has been noted above, but three more are clearly visible in Wessex, all of them on the Isle of Wight, or vects as the Romans called it.
Brading* Roman Villa (SZ 6086), open only from May to September (9.30–6, Sun. 3–6) except by prior arrangement with the custodian, lies to the west of the A3055, 1½m SW of the town. It is signposted from the main road during the summer. The excavations, conducted during the 1880's, paid little attention to chronology, but pottery finds indicate that the site was occupied from the first century AD onwards. In its final form, in the fourth century, it consisted of a main residential block of 13 rooms and two subsidiary wings arranged around a courtyard. Nothing is now visible of the south wing (left of the car-park when facing the shed), and only two separate elements of the north wing, a hypocaust and a well, are under cover. These wings seem, partly at least, to have been put to agricultural uses, for the villa was the centre of a large estate and the ancient fields visible on the hillside 600 yards NW of the villa are probably contemporary. The main block of the villa is completely visible and is chiefly notable for the remarkable fourth-century figured mosaics in four of its rooms. The first mosaic seen on entering lies in the middle of a long corridor and represents Orpheus charming the animals with his lyre: on the left is a monkey, on the right a bird and a fox. Eight other British examples of this scene are known, but only the Brading mosaic puts charmer and charmed within the same circle. To the right, a corn-drier has been inserted into the floor, presumably at a time when this part of the villa no longer mattered as a residence while the site continued in use as an agricultural centre. Moving now to the left, you come to the second mosaic, which is unfortunately badly damaged. The central roundel has a bust of Bacchus, but of the side-panels only one is substantially complete. On the left is a cock-headed man dressed in a tunic, in the centre is a small hut approached by a ladder, and on the right are two griffins (fig 27). This extraordinary scene has no parallel anywhere and is perhaps symbolic of some mystic rite of initiation connected with the after-life, in which the ladder represents the soul's ascent to heaven and the griffins are guardians of the dead. The adjacent panel depicted a gladiatorial combat, of which a man with a trident and net survives: it too must surely have an allegorical meaning, perhaps of the ordeals which the soul has to suffer in life on earth.

Other rooms nearby have little of interest except for a poorly-displayed selection of finds. In the room projecting at the back of the block, possibly a kitchen, a section of stone roofing-tiles has been re-assembled. Mount the wooden catwalk again, and pass on the right a simple geometric mosaic and, on the left, a couple of small rooms. The first of these, paved with red tiles, has a masonry bench or shelf round two walls. But it is the magnificent mosaics of the remaining two rooms which will claim your attention. The floor of the larger has mostly disappeared, but one side-panel is nearly complete. It represents Andromeda (on the left) being rescued by the hero Perseus, who holds aloft the head of the newly-slain Medusa. To the right of this panel is the bust of Summer, and of the other seasons Winter (diagonally opposite) and Spring also survive.

Go now to the far end of the shed to admire the superbly-preserved mosaics of the remaining room. In the foreground is a lively strip showing tritons and mermaids. The central roundel of the main section contains a sad-looking, snaky head of Medusa and the four oblong panels which surround it depict the following mythological scenes (clockwise, starting with left-foreground):

27   Brading villa, cock-headed-man mosaic

(i) Lycurgus, carrying his two-headed axe, pursues the nymph Ambrosia, who in response to her cry for help is being swallowed up by the earth, while Lycurgus is entwined by a vine-tendril and throttled; (ii) a young shepherd with crook and pipes is lost in admiration for a girl with a tambourine; (iii) Ceres, goddess of the crops, gives seed to Triptolemus, the inventor of the plough; (iv) nymph pursued by a man. In the triangles between these scenes are busts of the Four Winds, each blowing a conch. Finally, in the panel separating the two parts of the room, is the enigmatic figure of an astronomer pointing to a globe, above which is a pillar surmounted by a sundial. Once again, symbolism must be intended here: the astronomer perhaps signifies that by wisdom man could become immortal, and other symbols of immortality can be read into the Perseus-Andromeda and the Lycurgus-Ambrosia scenes (victory over death and evil), Ceres' gift to Triptolemus (bread and wine sustains us both on earth and in after-life), the Winds (carrying the soul to heaven), etc. Such a significance cannot be proved but seems highly probable. At any rate, though the standard of figure-drawing is far from masterly, the peculiarity of the subject-matter puts these Brading mosaics in a class of their own.

The second villa on the Isle of Wight, at **Newport** (SZ 5088), deserves to be better known. It is open only on some weekday afternoons during the summer, not on Saturdays or Sundays, but arrangements can be made to see it at other times (check opening hours at the IOW Information Office, Newport). The entrance is in Avondale Road, a turning to the west off the A3056 on the Sandown road. It is an excellent example of the corridor-type of villa, the corridor itself and four of the rooms which led from it lying outside the modern shed. Inside can be seen three rooms with tessellated floors, and the largest of these also has the unusual feature of a fireplace, built of tiles, projecting from the far wall. Beyond is a well-preserved bath-suite: there is a semi-circular hot plunge-bath, a cold plunge with lead pipe *in situ*, and the hypocaust *pilae* of three rooms of varying heat still preserved to a good height, though the floors they once supported are missing. A masonry base near the cold bath, outside the villa but inside the present shed, is believed to have supported a water-tank. Showcases contain a plan and finds from the villa, which was probably built in the third century. The site was discovered in 1926.

The third villa, at present under excavation (1972), is designed
to be part of a recreation-park called Robin Hill at **Combley**,
Arreton Down (SZ 5387). The park, which is only open in
summer, is entered by a gate on the minor road between Wooton
on the A3054 and Arreton on the A3056, near 'The Hare and
Hounds' Inn. (If the gate is closed, the site can also be approached
from Combley Farm, with the permission of the owner; this is
reached by the straight track which leaves another minor road
immediately west of the railway bridge at Havenstreet.) A small
set of baths, with a mosaic portraying aquatic beasts, and a good
third-century geometric mosaic in another room, are the main
features. Dating is uncertain, but the site was abandoned,
probably because of flooding, towards the end of the fourth
century.

A fourth villa-site on the island, partly excavated in 1859 and
1970, is situated at Carisbrooke, but it is not worth visiting now
(see App. I). There are, however, Roman remains to see at
Carisbrooke Castle (SZ 4887) [AM, S, but closes on Sundays at
5.30 p.m., May–Sept.]. Go out into the castle-bailey by the small
gate below the keep on the east side and you will see, embedded
in the lower banks of the later castle-ramparts, a stretch of walling
five feet high, and a small round turret. In this east side there is
also a gateway, 22 feet wide, visible to the right where the wall
curves inwards. These walls are also exposed along the whole of
the west side of the castle, both in the grounds of the tea-rooms
and on the other side of the Gatehouse. A late-Roman date for
this enclosure is almost certain, although positive dating material
is absent and excavation virtually impossible. If so, it is presumably one of the forts erected during the third or fourth centuries
to protect south and south-east England from the growing
menace of Saxon pirates. Unlike the rest, Carisbrooke is not on
the sea, and so its precise purpose must remain uncertain.

There is no uncertainty, however, about another of the forts
in this series, **Portchester*** (SU 6204) [AM; A], which is one of the
best-preserved and most impressive Roman structures anywhere
in Britain. It is signposted on the A27 between Fareham and
Portsmouth. The entire defensive wall of this fort, 10 feet thick
and over 20 feet high, together with 14 of the original 20 bastions,
still survives, except at the NW corner where the Normans built
their keep. In many places medieval refacing has covered up the
Roman work, but it can be spotted by the neat rows of coursed

flints separated at intervals by stone and tile bonding-courses. The bastions are hollow and were originally floored with timber to mount artillery. In addition, each was provided with a tiled drain at the bottom to allow water to escape, and this drain can be seen in places, for instance in the east side of the second bastion from the keep along the north wall (fig 28). The inner face

28   Portchester, a bastion

of the walls has been largely cut back in medieval times, but the original Roman width can be seen in the places where the walls have been excavated down to Roman ground-level, eg south of the Landgate and in the middle of the south wall. The battlements are mainly Norman work.

The fort was defended by four gates, of which only part of one is visible. In the north and south walls there were simple posterns, now blocked up, but the main gates in the middle of the west and east sides were formed by in-turning the curtain-walls to form a forecourt 45 feet wide and 36 feet deep, and closing the inner end of this passage with a gate 10 feet wide flanked by two square guard-chambers. The idea of this arrangement is that an enemy attacking the gate would be surrounded on three sides by defenders on the battlements above. The east gate is entirely buried beneath the medieval Watergate, but part of the lower courses of the west gate are traceable immediately south of the Landgate, inside the walls. Part of the Roman ditch-system is also visible and on the east the water still laps up to the walls as it did in Roman times. This magnificent site hardly qualifies for the description 'ruin', such is its state of preservation, and, unlike the majority of Roman sites in this country, it needs little imagination to visualize the fort in its heyday (fig 29).

Inside the walls excavation has revealed some traces of timber barracks and pits, but the Roman levels have been much disturbed by later occupation. First-century finds have been made, but the walls belong to the end of the third century. It was

29   Portchester, the south wall

disused for a time in the early fourth century but reoccupied on a
large scale again c. AD 340. It was finally abandoned c. 370, in
favour of a different site with a better harbour, a few miles away.

This was **Bitterne** (SU 4313), CLAVSENTVM to the Romans,
situated on a promontory jutting out into the river Itchen and
now a suburb of Southampton. A port was founded here c. AD
70, and the export of Mendip lead is attested by two (lost)
ingots. It continued to flourish in the second century, when the
promontory may have been defended by an outer bank and ditch.
There was decline in the third century, but towards the end of the
fourth a triangular area at the end of the promontory was
surrounded by a stone wall which, on the landward (east) side,
was built on wooden piles and defended by a ditch. The dating of
this new defence to c. 370 ties in with the abandonment of Portchester at this time, and the turning of port into fort was probably
due to Theodosius' reorganization of the British defences.

To see the fragmentary remains of CLAVSENTVM, take the
Portsmouth road (A3024) from the centre of Southampton.
Immediately after crossing the river bridge, by an 'Accident
Black Spot' sign, is a driveway leading to Bitterne Manor House,
now a block of flats. At the western end of this are the foundations
of a small square building. This was first built about AD 175 as a
private bath-house with four rooms: in front, a changing-room
and an apsed *tepidarium*, and behind, a *caldarium* and a *frigidarium* with cold plunge-bath. The internal partitions were then
demolished at some later stage and another wall built to divide
the building into two rooms of uncertain purpose. Finally, c. 370,
the whole was razed to the ground and new walls built to enclose a
slightly larger area. This too was intended to be a bath-house
(there is a stoke-hole opening in the north wall), but it was never
finished. Beyond this building is a small section of the fort-wall
erected c. 370, made of flint rubble and about five courses high;
it is now totally overgrown but the change in ground-level can be
appreciated. The site of the ditch which protected this wall on
its eastern side lies on the other side of the hedge to the right of the
entrance-driveway. The outer, earlier, bank and ditch are also
virtually obliterated. Their line lies parallel to and slightly east
of, Rampart Road, but only a marshy bank behind the sewage-
works survives today.

Chapter 3

Mendips and Cotswolds

Gloucestershire, Oxfordshire, North Somerset

(Appendix I only – Herefordshire)

The tribe that inhabited the area of the Cotswolds and the Upper
Thames in the pre-Roman period was known as the Dobunni.
They appear to have caused little or no trouble to Roman armies
in the early years of the invasion, but forts were established in
their territory to protect them and the province behind from the
aggressive Silures of South Wales. There was one at Cirencester
and probably another at Bath, both places on the great trunk-
road, the Fosse Way, which formed the earliest boundary of the
new Roman province. Much of its course in the area covered by
this chapter is followed by modern A-roads, but, for a three-mile

stretch going north from Shepton Mallet over Beacon Hill, the Roman highway has become no more than a track, and plenty of traces of the original metalling survive. Other forts were established beyond the frontier road, notably at Gloucester and Sea Mills, but hardly anything from this military phase is visible anywhere now.

The Roman invaders did not waste much time before exploiting the Mendip lead-mines around **Charterhouse** (ST 5056), which were already in operation only six years after the conquest. Lead was important not only in itself (eg to make water-pipes and coffins) but especially for the extraction of silver by a process known as cupellation. The lead remaining after the silver had been removed was cast in the form of ingots, often inscribed with the emperor's name, the date, and the authority in control of the mines. These ingots, therefore, furnish valuable historical information: one in the British Museum is dated to AD 49, so that we know when mining was started; one was found near Southampton and another in north France, and so we know they were exported to the continent. Indeed metallic tests have shown that a cistern at Pompeii, buried by the eruption of Vesuvius in 79, was made of British lead, probably from Charterhouse. The French ingot also tells us that the Second Augustan Legion was in control of the mines in Nero's reign (AD 54–68), but another in the British Museum dated to AD 60 is marked 'from the lead-silver works of Gaius Nipius Ascanius', making it clear that early military control soon gave way to private lessees. Finally, several Mendip ingots read BRIT.EX.ARG.VEB., 'British lead from the Veb . . . lead-silver mines'. VEB may be the abbreviation of the Roman name for Charterhouse, but the full name we do not know. The last datable ingot (in Taunton Museum) was made between 164 and 169, but coin finds at Charterhouse indicate that occupation continued into the fourth century.

Very little of the Roman mines or the associated settlement can be seen today; the former have been worked for a long time, especially in the nineteenth century, and the latter has never been adequately explored. A few earthworks, mostly of uncertain date and purpose, are the main features. The site is most conveniently approached from Cheddar. Take the road through the famous gorge (B3135), and then fork left along the B3371. One mile after the fork, turn left at the crossroads, signposted Charterhouse. After another mile, on the right of the road as it bends to ascend

the hill to Charterhouse church, near the notice announcing
Mendip Farm to be private property, deep trenching and pitting
are visible and these probably belong to the Roman exploitation.
Just beyond the church is a crossroads where you should turn
right. After 200 yards, on the left-hand side of the road just
beyond a group of trees, are the faint traces of a small earthwork
(504558) about 70 yards square; the south and east sides are
largely destroyed. It may be a small Roman fort created to guard
the lead-mines. Now return to the crossroads and turn right;
after $\frac{1}{4}$ mile take the track which goes off to the left. Just before
this, on the left of the minor road, is another small earthwork
(503561), which could be Roman or medieval. The site of the
Roman town lay on the right of the track at its junction with the
road; it lies in 'Town Field', but nothing is traceable now,
although aerial photography has revealed something of the street-
plan. A small earthwork enclosure, which may be Roman, can
just be traced on the ground immediately next to an iron stile on
the right of the track, where the stone wall stops. Finally, and
most conspicuous of all, is the small amphitheatre (498565),
which can easily be spotted away to the left a little further on.
The banks are still about 15 feet above the arena floor, and the
entrances at either end are clear. The field in which it lies is
entered by a gate $\frac{1}{4}$m further on, where the track swings away to
the right. The amphitheatre was inconclusively excavated in
1908. Finds from here and other sites in Charterhouse can be
found in Bristol and Taunton Museums.

Charterhouse was not a normal Roman settlement in so far as
its position was dictated by the nearby lead-mines. Another
Roman town which owes its existence to natural phenomena –
this time hot springs emerging from the ground at 120°F. – is
Bath* (ST 7564), where the thermal establishment is perhaps the
most famous Roman antiquity in Britain after Hadrian's Wall.
And rightly so, for it was no ordinary bathing-station: it was a
spa designed on the most elegant and ambitious scale.

The deity of the natural springs had probably been worshipped
before the Roman period, and, although no pre-Roman occupation has ever been found, the name of the place, AQVAE SVLIS,
indicates that the waters were sacred to the native goddess Sulis,
whom the Romans identified with Minerva. There was probably
a fort here in the period of the Roman conquest, as the spacing of
forts along the Fosse Way demands it, but of this, too, not a trace

has been found. Towards the end of the first century, the centre
was laid out with an outstanding series of monumental buildings.

The focus of the whole complex was clearly the sacred spring
itself, surrounded by its reservoir; into this, now under the later
King's Bath, all kinds of votive offerings were thrown. The
spring was viewed from a hall in the baths (where the Circular
Bath now is), and beyond it, on the same axis, the bather would
catch a glimpse of a great altar, its corners richly carved with
figures of deities. One of these was found in 1790, another in 1965
(both in the Museum), and a third, now much weathered, is built
into a buttress of the church at Compton Dando, seven miles to
the west. While the altar lay on a north-south axis from a bather's
viewpoint, it also lay on an east-west axis in front of a splendid
temple dedicated to Sulis Minerva. Part of the plan of this temple
was plotted in 1867–8 on the west side of Stall Street, but the
precise dimensions, including the position of the bottom step
leading to the temple-platform (*podium*), were only established
in 1964–5 during judicious trenching in cellars under the Pump
Room. This was not the usual Romano–Celtic temple with
central *cella* and lean-to ambulatory: it was a full-scale classical-
style temple on a lofty *podium*, approached by a flight of steps,
and fronted by a porch four columns wide and two deep supporting a frieze, architrave and pediment. The centre of the pediment
was formed by the striking head of Medusa, found in 1790, and
now in the Museum. The temple and altar were set in a large
paved courtyard enclosed by a colonnade. But of this
magnificent temple-complex nothing, alas, remains for the visitor
beyond the sculptured stones in the Museum.

The baths themselves were at first quite simple, though on a
monumental scale. From the entrance-hall, with its vista of the
spring and the altar, the bather could either turn right to the
Great Bath and to the two smaller swimming-baths at its east end,
or he could turn left and indulge in the artificial heat of the
conventional Roman baths, which at this stage were very simple
in layout. This set of baths with damp heat ('turkish' baths) was
found insufficient, for in the second phase (probably early
second-century) a set of dry-heat (sauna) baths was added,
including a *laconicum*, a large circular plunge-bath, and a small
courtyard for exercise. At the same time, the last swimming-pool
at the far end was replaced by a second set of turkish baths. The
third period, also second-century, saw the entire re-roofing of the

Great Bath with a grandiose barrel-vault, but only minor alterations elsewhere. Some years later (period IV) extensive reorganization occurred: the eastern baths were rebuilt on a much larger scale; the alcove north of the tepid plunge-bath at this end was converted into an immersion-bath; and at the west end further additions and alterations meant that both sets of baths here were probably now of damp heat. Finally, before the end of the Roman period, there was trouble with the drainage, and in the late fourth or early fifth century the flooding became serious: the baths were abandoned, the area became a marsh, the vault of the Great Bath collapsed. Not until the eighteenth century was something of Bath's former grandeur and popularity to be regained.

Of this elaborate and complicated sequence of baths just over half is at present visible, but excavations now in progress (1972) are clearing the area at the western end, and the intention is for the whole of the Roman establishment as so far known to be laid open on permanent show. For the moment, however, a temporary staircase leads to the Circular Bath which served as a cold plunge for the sauna baths (dry-heat) added in the early second century; before this the room was an entrance-hall. In the re-roofing phase of the later second century, it was provided with a vault springing from new piers fitted between the bath and the side-walls. The double arcade built for vaulting the corridor on the south side of the Circular Bath (right-hand side when facing the Great Bath) is very well preserved; the inner one is now filled up with modern concrete, but beyond it an entire pier and two voussoirs of an arch survive.

From the Circular Bath a few steps lead up to the viewing point over the King's Bath. As you duck your head to look at this, you are passing under one of the most substantial pieces of Roman architecture in Britain: the rounded arch above and the square-headed arch to the right, both now partially blocked with modern stonework, still display superb masonry in the same position as it was when built in the first century AD. They form two of originally three vast windows to the entrance-hall, designed to give an impressive view over the sacred spring and the altar of the temple-complex beyond. Of the Roman reservoir enclosing the sacred spring nothing can now be seen as the King's Bath covers it; it was an irregular octagon about six feet deep and lined with lead, which was ripped up and sold in 1880 to provide money for

excavations! The outflow-arch and an impressive vaulted drain
taking excess water from this reservoir can be seen inside the
Museum, to the left and right of the entrance.

The most impressive feature of the Roman remains at Bath is
of course the Great Bath, which until 1880–1 was still covered by
houses of the Georgian city. It belonged to the original scheme
and remained the chief feature of the establishment throughout
its life. It is one of the rare Romano–British structures which need
no description, for its appeal is immediate and obvious: a great
rectangular swimming-bath still lined with its Roman lead and
still fed by the constant flow of water from the sacred spring. But
although the bath is still intact, the hall that enclosed it is not,
and the present open-air effect is misleading. From the beginning
it was roofed over, at first with a simple timbered ceiling
supported by twelve simple piers lining the bath and the exterior
walls. In the third period, sometime in the second century, the
whole area was re-roofed with an enormous barrel-vault, over 50
feet high – much higher than the modern colonnade. It was made
of hollow box-tiles, to lessen the weight, and was left open at
either end to allow the steam to escape. One of the ends, neatly

30   Bath, pier alongside the Great Bath

finished off with tile facing, is displayed at one end of the Great Bath. At the same time, the piers lining the bath had to be strengthened to take the extra thrust of the vault; and if you look carefully at them you will see that the middle (original) portion was cut back at this period, and extra masonry added both in front and behind it (fig 30). Additional piers also strengthened the inner and outer corners of the alcoves which face onto the ambulatory. One or two more details may be pointed out: the water-pipe of Charterhouse lead was inserted into the paving in period IV (third-fourth centuries) to take water from the spring direct to a new immersion-bath (see below). Finally, two ornamental features relieved the general austerity of the bath: a fountain rested on the projecting block in the centre of the north side, and a semi-circular, shrine-like structure lay on the slab at the NW corner where the water enters the bath.

From the Great Bath go to the far end where a smaller swimming-bath, the Lucas Bath, and a series of rooms with a complicated history, are reached. A pool built in period I was replaced by a small set of turkish baths in period II, and this set was rebuilt on a much larger scale in period IV, when an immersion-bath was also added in the apse opposite the end of the Lucas Bath (the lead pipe noted above was heading for here). All these changes are now explained by means of lighting-effects which illuminate the various features in their respective phases.

A visit to the Roman Baths would be incomplete without seeing the excellent Museum, which contains a wealth of sculptural and other material. All is carefully labelled and a detailed description here is unnecessary, but a few outstanding exhibits may be mentioned. Most important of all is the famous Medusa head which formed the centre-piece of the temple's pediment (fig 31). The snaky-headed Medusa appeared on Minerva's shield and so is an appropriate subject for the temple, but the native sculptor has turned her into a male, with craggy face, penetrating gaze and luxuriant moustache. It is an odd synthesis, but the effect is striking: 'it represents,' as J M C Toynbee has put it, 'the perfect marriage of classical standards and traditions with Celtic taste and native inventiveness.' Then there are two of the corner slabs of the Great Altar mentioned above (p. 95), and some sculptural fragments and inscriptions belonging to yet another monument in the precinct, the façade of the Four Seasons; where precisely this stood is unknown. Outstanding too is the

31   Bath, the Medusa head

gilt-bronze head of Minerva, now lacking the helmet which
would have fitted onto the top of the head. It may even be part of
the cult-statue of the goddess, executed in a good classical style
which provides such a contrast to the sculptured pediment.
Finally, there is the rich haul of altars and tombstones which tell
us much about the men and women who patronized the
establishment: not only Britons or Roman legionaries centred in
Britain, but foreigners too – a sculptor from the Chartres area of
north France, a lady from Metz and a man from Trier in
Germany. Each stone tells a story of its own. The one illustrated
here (fig 32), found in 1965 beneath the Pump Room, records a
dedication to the goddess Sulis by L. Marcius Memor, who is a
haruspex. This is the only known example in Britain of this
priesthood: his duties would have included the interpretation of
omens and the inspection of sacrificial victims. Note that the
letters VSP have clearly been added later to the centrally-placed
HAR – perhaps nobody could understand what that abbreviation
meant.

Of the rest of Roman Bath, nothing is visible except a feeble
black-and-white mosaic in the basement of the Royal Mineral
Water Hospital (enquire at the entrance). There may have been a
theatre under the Abbey; there was another bathing-
establishment south-west of the main baths; and there was
probably a Roman town-wall on the line of its medieval
successor. But whether Bath was an administrative centre is
uncertain – no trace of a forum has ever been found – and the
town's precise status is obscure.

The status of the two remaining towns in this region is not,
however, in doubt: Gloucester was a *colonia*, a settlement of
retired Roman legionaries and their families, whereas Cirencester
was the tribal capital of the Dobunni. Roman **Gloucester** (SO
8318) need not detain us long, as virtually nothing survives *in situ*.
The early history of the site has been, until recently, baffling: it
was first thought that the early legionary fortress (probably for
the Twentieth Legion) lay under the site of the later *colonia*. Then
it was suggested that its site was Kingsholm, one mile north of
Gloucester, where a great deal of military equipment has been
found, but no defences. It has now been established, however,
that there *was* a legionary fortress under the *colonia*, but coin
evidence firmly indicates that its date cannot be earlier than AD
64. Where, then, was the fortress of AD 49, mentioned by

Tacitus? The likelihood is that its site still remains to be found, in Kingsholm.

Military occupation of the Gloucester site seems to have faded out in the 80's, but the earliest civilians still lived in the military barracks before the site was properly cleared in the second century. Yet the formal settlement as a *colonia* was made under the emperor Nerva (96–98), as we know from an inscription giving its full title as *Colonia Nervia Glevensium*. The peak of the town's prosperity seems to have been in the second century, but its proximity to flourishing Cirencester stunted its growth and it was never as successful as the *colonia* of Lincoln, which doubled in size in the second century.

The visible remains of Gloucester are hardly worth recording: medieval and later development has hit them hard. Inside the walls there is only a fragment of relaid Roman mosaic in the hall of the National Westminster Bank in Eastgate Street, and others in the Market Hall and in the crypt of the Friends' Meeting House in Crypt Lane. Northgate and Southgate Streets are on the site of Roman predecessors. Of the Roman walls, only fragments are visible and most of them are inaccessible. One stretch can, however, be viewed (by prior arrangement) in the basement of the Museum, and another, under the Midlands Electricity Board Centre in King's Square, can be seen through inspection-

32   *Bath, dedication to the goddess*

33   *Gloucester, tombstone of Rufus Sita*

windows and trap-doors. The first town-defences consisted of an earth rampart built in the late second century, with stone interval-towers; the full stone wall was added sometime in the third century and rebuilt at a later period. The first masonry wall seems to have consisted of small facing-stones raised on a massive plinth, but large blocks were used in the rebuilding. Both periods are visible on the Electricity Board site.

The City Museum in Brunswick Street has an especially fine collection of sculpture: you should see the tombstone of Rufus Sita, a cavalryman with a cohort of Thracians from north Greece. It is of a common type, with the officer riding down his barbarian foe (fig 33). How this auxiliary cohort fits into the complicated military history of Gloucester (see above) is far from certain, but an *ala Thraecum* is also attested at Cirencester (perhaps the unit was split). Outstanding too is the mid-first-century male head with huge bulging eyes. Like the Bath pediment, it represents a fusion of Roman and Celtic traditions: the three-dimensional modelling is due to classical influence, but all the details – the lips, the eyeballs, the ears and the hair – are very stylized, in the tradition of pre-Roman art.

Cirencester* (SP 0201), CORINIVM DOBVNNORVM, has the distinction of being the second largest town of Roman Britain after London; but its medieval and modern successor is considerably smaller and so large areas within the walls remain free from buildings. Very little, however, of the Roman town is visible, though rescue excavations over the past decade have contributed an enormous amount to our knowledge. Once again the place had a military origin: a first fort established in the area of the Watermoor Hospital was found to be too close to marshy land, and so another fort was built, about AD 49, on better-drained soil, on a site bounded by the Avenue, Chester Street, Watermoor Road and St Michael's Fields. By the mid-70's, when the military moved on, the civilian settlement which had grown up around this fort became the new administrative centre for the *civitas* of the Dobunni. It was laid out on an ambitious scale with a forum and basilica (only London's was larger), what is possibly a theatre, and later an amphitheatre too. Development continued in the second century, despite a setback to the basilica, which had to be entirely rebuilt: the first building, erected over the filled-in ditches of the early fort, had badly subsided. At the end of the second century Corinium received her first earth defences, and these were faced in stone in the third century, when her prosperity continued. Nor was there any slackening off in the fourth century: the town almost certainly became the capital of Britannia Prima when Britain was divided into four separate Roman provinces. The evidence is an inscription in the museum (see below). Her wealth during the fourth century is manifestly demonstrated by the splendid mosaics (in the Corinium Museum) laid by a school of mosaicists centred in the town. Civic life continued well into the fifth century, when the forum was still kept clean. Finally, however, discipline broke down and the time came when unburied bodies were left rotting in the street-gutters.

The Corinium Museum in Park Street contains a splendid display of material which vividly demonstrates the prosperity of the Roman town (open weekdays 10–4.30, Oct. to Apr.; 10–5.30, May to Sept.; closed 1–2; open Sun. 2–5.30, June to Aug. only). The collection is excellently displayed in a well-lit room. The visitor is immediately struck by the three large mosaics in the centre of the floor. The first depicts hunting-dogs chasing a (lost) prey in the central roundel, with sea-beasts in two of the surrounding half-circles, a head of Medusa in one corner and a head of Oceanus in an intervening space. This and the second mosaic are both of second-century date: the latter is part of an elaborate floor of which five roundels survive complete. Three contain Seasons (Winter is missing) and the other two portray mythological events – Actaeon being torn to pieces by his dogs (for seeing the goddess Diana at her bath) (fig 34), and Silenus, one of Dionysus' attendants, riding on a donkey. The third mosaic was laid in the fourth century and depicts Orpheus with his lyre, charming the birds and animals which proceed in stately fashion round him. The idea of putting the animals and birds in concentric circles around the central figure of Orpheus seems to be peculiar to the Corinium mosaic-school, and the subject appears on several mosaics known from the neighbourhood: Woodchester is one of them, but the rest are covered up or lost.

At the far end of the museum are architectural fragments, sculptures, and inscriptions. Along the back wall are the tomb-stones of soldiers who served at Cirencester in its early years: Genialis of the *Ala Thraecum* and Dannicus of the *Ala Indiana*. In front of these is a huge Corinthian capital with the heads of four native deities, and next to it a dedication to Jupiter by

Septimius, governor of Britannia Prima (PRIMAE PROVINCIAE
RECTOR), evidence which suggests that Corinium was capital of
this new province in the fourth century. Finally, you should not
leave the museum without seeing the famous word-square,
ROTAS|OPERA|TENET|AREPO|SATOR, 'Arepo the sower holds the
wheels as his work', scratched on a piece of wall-plaster. When
the words are set out one above another, the line can be read from
left to right, right to left, top to bottom and bottom to top. The
first words of the Lord's Prayer, *Pater Noster*, are contained
twice over in the formula (with two A's and O's, alpha and omega,
to spare), and so the inscription may attest the presence of
Christians in Corinium.

Apart from the objects in the Museum, Cirencester did not
until recently have much of its Roman past on show. The apse
of the basilica is marked out in modern materials in a cul-de-sac
which opens off the Avenue opposite Tower Street; but nothing
else is at present visible within the walls. An exciting and
spectacular find of a town-house, however, was made in Beeches
Road, south of London Road (A417), in 1971. It contained a
compact bath-house and several mosaics, including one of a

34   Cirencester, mosaic of Actaeon

crouching hare. In 1972 another house was excavated here, and it too was equipped with mosaics and heated rooms. Plans are being made to keep the site open on display (but see p. 360).

The defences are visible as a large bank on much of the east side of the town, running along Beeches Road, and then further south in Watermoor recreation-ground. North of London Road, however, a stretch has been fully excavated and conserved. It is reached from the housing-estate of Corinium Gate, opposite the end of Beeches Road; continue straight on until you come to a footbridge on the right. There was a flood-bank here in the late first century, but the first proper defences, consisting of an earth bank and the (visible) stone internal turret, belong to the second half of the second century. This was subsequently revetted with a stone wall not earlier than AD 220. This was only quite narrow – about four feet wide – but parts of it, as can be seen, were later replaced by a broader wall varying in width from seven to nine feet. Why the narrow wall (visible in the middle section, adjoining the internal tower) was not replaced throughout is unclear, but perhaps only the sectors in danger of collapse were rebuilt. Finally, sometime about AD 330, projecting bastions were added to the wall, and the foundations of two of these, one square and the other polygonal, can be seen. Again the reason for the variation is obscure, though it is likely that the superstructure of both bastions was polygonal.

Finally, the amphitheatre is well worth a visit. Turn left at the end of Querns Road (signposted Somerford Keynes) and right at the fork, along Cotswold Avenue: the amphitheatre is reached by the footpath next to no. 30. It is now a large grassy depression, with entrance-gaps at either end, but the banks still stand to a height of about 25 feet above the arena floor and are an impressive sight. Excavation has shown that the earliest building, of earth and timber, was given retaining-walls of stone in the early second century. It was rebuilt several times and continued in use into the fifth century. No stonework has been left exposed.

The prosperity of Cirencester must have been largely due to the wealth of the surrounding countryside. The town formed the market-centre for the agricultural products of the many villas which are known in the Cotswold region, though the development and economic basis of the area are still largely obscure. Of these known villas, the vast majority have been reburied, but the area covered in this chapter has, in fact, more visible villa-remains than anywhere else in Britain. It is convenient to deal with these in two main groups – those around Bristol, and those around Cirencester.

Bristol itself was not a Roman town, though the City Museum has a superbly-displayed collection of local finds. There was, however, a settlement known as ABONAE in the suburb of **Sea Mills** (ST 5575). It probably began as the *vicus* of an early Roman fort, but by the end of the second century shops and houses in stone had been constructed. The foundations of one building, probably a house, are visible at the junction of Portway (A4) with Roman Way, opposite a bus-shelter about 2m south of Avonmouth. There is a small courtyard with rooms surrounding it.

About 2m NW of Sea Mills is the Roman villa of **King's Weston** (ST 5377). From Avonmouth take the B4054 for $\frac{1}{2}$m, then turn left at the traffic-lights along King's Weston Avenue. The Roman villa lies on the right after another $\frac{1}{2}$m. There are no opening hours, and the key must be obtained from the caretaker at 17, Hopewell Gardens (down Windcliff Crescent, then first left, first right). The part still accessible was built sometime between AD 270 and 300, and saw various alterations before its abandonment towards the end of the fourth century. It was excavated in 1948–50. The entrance leads immediately to the four rooms of the east wing, of which the largest had a hypocaust inserted into the floor sometime later than the original building. The threshold of this room leads to a long corridor which gave access through columns (a few bases are visible) to a gravelled court on the right. The building was entered by a small porch which projects from the south (left-hand) wall of the corridor. The west wing is covered by a wooden shed. The room on the left has a mediocre geometric mosaic, but the floor of the other room had largely perished and the present mosaic comes from another Bristol villa (at Brislington) which was found in 1900. Beyond are the remains of a small bath-suite. The apsidal heated room belonged (with an adjoining room to the right, now destroyed) to the original building, but the other two compartments – on the left an undressing-room, and, in the centre, a room with steps leading down to a cold bath – are of later date.

On the other side of Bristol (to the SE) are two more villa-sites close to one another. Leave Bristol on the Bath Road (A4); at

the roundabout avoid the Keynsham by-pass and take the B-road
for the town itself. After ¼m you will see a cemetery on your left
behind some trees. This is the site of the **Keynsham** (ST 6469)
villa, a spacious example of the courtyard type, as proved by
excavations in 1922–4. Only fragments of the north wing,
consisting of a few columns, are visible today, near the mortuary
chapel. Mosaics from the Keynsham villa, however, are kept at
nearby Somerdale: continue on towards Keynsham, and fork
left by the church. Immediately after bridging the A4 and the
railway-line, you will come to the entrance to Fry's chocolate-
factory at **Somerdale** (ST 6569). Facing the entrance-lodge are
the foundations of a small Roman house, discovered in 1922
when the factory was being built and untidily laid out here 300
yards south of its original position. Finds from the villas are
displayed in the museum at the entrance-lodge (6 a.m.–10 p.m.,
Mondays to Fridays only), but the best mosaics from Keynsham,
including a representation of Europa about to be abducted by
Jupiter disguised as a bull (cf. fig 16), are preserved in a hall in the
factory proper, and can only be visited by prior arrangement.

Of the villas situated around Cirencester, the least worth
visiting is at **Wadfield** (SP 0226). It lies on the left of the
Winchcombe to Andoversford minor road, 2m south of the
former and 200 yards beyond the AM sign to Belas Knap Long
Barrow. The villa is situated in a small enclosure of trees in the
middle of a field, entered by a broken-down gate at a passing-
place on the road. It was first discovered and partly explored in
1863 and again later in the nineteenth century. The ground-plan
of the villa is still traceable, consisting of two wings arranged
round a small courtyard. One room is floored with red *tesserae*,
but the main room, covered by a wooden hut, has a partly-
restored geometric mosaic, of which half is in position. The rest
was presumably lost soon after discovery, for of some mosaic it
was written that 'its speedy removal was found to be absolutely
necessary in order to preserve it from the Winchcombe public,
who in the space of one Sunday afternoon carried off a large
portion, in small pieces, as souvenirs.' Another villa is situated in
Spoonley Wood, only a mile away across the valley, but it is in a
totally-ruined state and not worth a visit (App. I).

Much better preserved is the **Great Witcombe** villa (SO 8914)
[AM; A]. Like so many villas, it is situated in a beautiful position
close to a source of water; but here the water is a little *too* near,

for the whole hillside is riddled with springs, and the owners had great difficulty in preventing these from undermining the whole house and carrying it away down the slope. Most of the visible walls, which belong to rooms arranged round three sides of an open courtyard, were built c. AD 250–70, but alterations were made thereafter, in the period 270–400. Traces have also been found of an earlier dwelling on the site, dating back to the late first century.

The villa is reached by a road on the right (the south) of the A417 (Gloucester–Cirencester) immediately east of the roundabout where it is crossed by the A46 (Cheltenham–Stroud); there is a DOE signpost. First, apply for the key at the farm and walk over to the far corner of the remains to see the bath-house, most of which belongs to the secondary phase. In the hut on the left is a plunge-bath, associated with the hot sweating-room (*sudatorium*) which at present lies under cover on the right of the gangway. The little wooden bridge crosses over the hypocausted *tepidarium*, with its stoke-hole on the left, to the second hut. Note a slab projecting from the hut-wall left of the entrance: it is one of the sides of the doorway built on the skew to link the *tepidarium*

35   *Great Witcombe villa, shrine (?)*

with the *caldarium*, which is the room on the left inside the hut. The main room here, however, is the *frigidarium*, floored with a crude but lively sea-creature mosaic and reached from the *caldarium* by another superbly-preserved doorway. A plan of the villa is displayed on the wall.

The room adjacent to the shed on the uphill side has a central basin and three niches in the walls (fig 35). It is believed to have had a religious function, perhaps the worship of the local water-nymphs, who no doubt needed appeasing to prevent landslides. The end of this wing, at the top of the slope, was the area first planned as the original baths; the two small projecting rooms here were plunge-baths. Turn right along a corridor and note, on the left, a drain and, on the right, a series of buttresses designed to prevent the foundations from settling. In the centre of the corridor, on the left, is an octagonal construction, added in the second period to replace the original rectangular room, visible beneath; its purpose is unknown.

The rest of the villa, first uncovered in 1818–19, is still being excavated and consolidated, and is not yet open to the public. The main feature is the kitchen in the far left-hand corner of the building, with ovens and hearths.

The outstanding Cotswold site, however, is at **Chedworth*** (SP 0513), which is widely regarded as the finest preserved villa in the country. It is certainly one of the most beautiful, lying at the head of the peaceful wooded valley of the Coln in an utterly charming position. The villa is *not* open on Mondays (except Bank Holidays), nor from 1st–15th October, nor any day in January; when it is open the hours are 10–1 and 2–7 (or dusk if earlier).

The villa is best approached from the Fosse Way (A429) 1m south of the crossroads with the A40: take the road to Yarnworth (*not* Chedworth village) and then to the site (sign-posted). The other approach is from the north: take the turning to Withington from the A436, ½m west of Andoversford and then follow sign-posts to the villa. It was discovered accidently in 1864 by a game-keeper digging for a lost ferret, and has been National Trust property since 1924. Only excavations in the 1960's, however, have clarified the history of the site, and four separate phases are now known. In the first, dated to the first half of the second century, the house consisted of two separate buildings on the west and south and a detached bath-suite to the north. In the early third century (phase II) the west and south wings were rebuilt after a fire, the baths were enlarged, and a few rooms were added on their east side (now forming the middle of the north wing). In the early fourth century the villa took on its present appearance: the existing elements were united with a covered verandah, and an inner garden and outer courtyard were created. At the same time the dining-room received its mosaics and the north half of the west wing was converted to take a second set of baths (damp-heat); meanwhile the existing baths were modified into dry-heat sauna-baths. Finally, in phase IV (late-fourth-century), the north wing was further extended by the addition of a new dining-room. Occupation continued to the end of the century.

Begin your tour by turning left out of the ticket-office and seeing what remains of the south wing, most of which still lies buried. Only the rooms as far as the steps belong to the original wing; the rest of the rooms here were all added in the early fourth century. These latter include the 'steward's room' (labelled 2), so called because a large number of coins were found here; the latrine (4) with its usual sewer (now gravel-filled) and channel for running water; and the kitchen (3) with an oven-base. The latter

36   *Chedworth villa, mosaic of Summer*

served the heated dining-room (*triclinium*) (5), which in its present form dates to the first half of the fourth century. The most striking feature is the mosaic floor, laid by the Cirencester workshop. The main portion is partially destroyed, but originally it contained a central octagon (perhaps with a representation of Bacchus) surrounded by eight main panels. These were filled with figures of nymphs and satyrs, and the greater portion of three remain. Perfectly preserved, however, are three of the Seasons, represented as charming little boys: Spring wears only a scarf and holds a bird and flower-basket; Summer, who is completely naked and also winged, holds a garland (fig 36); and Winter, wearing hood, cloak and leggings, holds a twig and a dead hare. This part of the room probably formed an ante-chamber; the dining-room proper lies beyond the projecting piers and has an ordinary geometric floor bordered on two sides by superb floral scrolls springing from vases (fig 37). Note the drain in the far left-hand corner, for swilling rubbish away after a meal.

The next three rooms (6, 7, 8) have nothing of interest and were probably ordinary day-rooms or possibly bedrooms. Next we enter the baths of damp heat, which once again only belong to

37   *Chedworth villa, floral scroll*

the fourth-century expansion of Chedworth. They are a very well-preserved example and give an excellent idea of the Roman bathing system. First (10) is the undressing room; it has a hypocaust underneath and box-shaped flue-tiles in the walls. Visible here is a tree-stump marking the 1864 ground-level. Next (11) is the little *tepidarium*, with flue-tiles and hypocaust *pilae* clearly visible and mosaic floor in position; but the floor of the *caldarium* (12) has gone, leaving just the *pilae*. A semi-circular hot bath opens off it. Then the bather would return to the room where you are now standing, the *frigidarium* (14), to cool off before taking a plunge in the cold bath (15), still complete with its steps and drainage-pipe. He would then go back to 10 to put his clothes on. The cold-room mosaic was repaired with stone slabs at a later period, and parts of both floors are visible; this repair and the heavy wear on the door-sill of 11 show the popularity of these baths with the owner and his guests. The furnace for heating the baths can be studied outside (turn left and left again).

Now cross the grass to see the shrine of the water-nymphs (17) a few yards away. Here wells up the spring which supplied the Roman inhabitants with their water. The shrine has a curved back and an octagonal pool. Parts of its rim were inscribed with Christian monograms, now in the Museum.

The first part of the north wing contains another bath-suite, the original baths of the villa. These were originally quite simple, were then extended in phase II, and then partly demolished. The plan of the demolished rooms is marked out in modern concrete. The final, fourth-century alterations included the building of the colonnade, of which the column-stumps are visible (fig 38), and the conversion of the baths to the dry-heat variety to supplement those in the west wing. Mount the steps into room 21, which was the undressing-room of the final baths (previously the *tepidarium*). On your left you can peer through the glass to see two small hot rooms, originally with apsidal plunge-baths later disused (22). Straight ahead (23) is a large cold plunge-bath and two flanking immersion-baths, all added in the fourth century. Now come down the steps and note on your left (25) two rooms with channelled hypocausts, the larger probably being some kind of reception-room.

The rest of the north wing can be summarily dealt with. Don't, incidentally, be misled by the tiresome modern 'roofs' which the walls have been given here, as elsewhere: they are designed to protect the ancient structure from rain and frost. Rooms 26–29 belong to the early-third-century extension of the north wing. 26 shows its hypocaust *pilae* but the floor has gone. The rest of the wing (30–32) was constructed in the villa's closing years at the end of the fourth century. The very last room was the largest in the villa, heated by a channelled hypocaust. One end was raised on a dais as the hypocaust is on a higher level here: it is probably another dining-room. A visit to the little Museum completes a tour of this lovely site.

Brief mention must also be made of another villa, one of the largest and most luxurious found in Britain, though, as in all cases except Fishbourne, the summit of prosperity was not reached until the fourth century. It lies at **Woodchester** (ST 8403), a village 2m south of Stroud off the A46. 64 rooms grouped round two courtyards were found at the end of the eighteenth century. There is nothing whatever visible today, but the uncovering of its chief mosaic, 49 feet square, every twelve years or so, justifies its inclusion in this book: the last time it was exposed was in 1973. It is a magnificent portrayal of Orpheus charming the birds and animals, a large version of the mosaic in the Corinium Museum

38 Chedworth villa, the north wing

and, like that one, laid by Cirencester mosaicists in the early fourth century AD. It is greatly to be hoped that money can soon be found to keep the Woodchester mosaic open on permanent display.

Further away from the area I have so far dealt with, but still in the Cotswolds, is the villa at **North Leigh** (SP 3915) [AM; A] in Oxfordshire. It was first discovered and excavated in 1813–16 and again before the First World War; further examination and consolidation are currently in progress. In its final fourth-century form, North Leigh is an excellent example of the courtyard type of villa, with wings on three sides and an entrance-gate on the fourth. This was, however, only the last stage in a long and complicated development: the earliest villa, built in the second century, consisted of a small main house, under the later north wing, and a detached bath-house at the NE corner. Further buildings, discovered by aerial photography but as yet unexcavated, lie to the SW of the main villa.

The site is signposted from the A4095, 3m NE of Witney. Although it can be visited at any time, it is best to see the villa at weekends, when a custodian is present and the sheds are

39   North Leigh villa, mosaic

unlocked. You first arrive at the main heated room of the villa. This is floored with a geometric mosaic that was laid by Ciren-cester mosaicists at the beginning of the fourth century, as is known from stylistic comparisons with other mosaics (fig 39). The hypocaust is still in perfect condition, and part of the floor has been cut away to reveal the *pilae* beneath. On the wall of the shed is displayed a plan of the villa, which should be studied before going on. Now walk along the corridor of the north wing, the main living-quarters, towards the modern cottage at the NE corner. On your left is another heated room, this time with a channelled hypocaust, as distinct from the pillared type in the mosaic room. Beyond this the walls of some more living-rooms have been consolidated, but not all the visible remains belong to the same period. Thus the curved wall beyond the heated room and the wall built of stones pitched at an angle both belong to earlier phases in the villa's history, and would have been buried below the floors of the final building. At the NE corner was the main bath-suite, but the only recognizable feature of it at present is the semicircular warm immersion-bath, protected by a stone hut close to the cottage fence. Now walk down towards the river, following the site of the east wing, which contained another set of baths. Turning right, past the site of the gateway leading to the courtyard, you reach the foundations of the west wing, perhaps the servants' quarters. Again, not all the visible walls belong to the same period.

It will have been noted that nearly all the villas mentioned above reached the height of their prosperity during the fourth century. Their owners must clearly have been very wealthy to be able to afford the sumptuous mosaics of which such impressive vestiges remain to this day. An equally rich patronage, presum-ably by the owners of these same villas is implied by the building of an elegant temple-complex at **Lydney** (SO 6102) in the closing years of the fourth century. The site has long been known, but it was only established in excavations of 1928-9 by Sir Mortimer Wheeler that the whole complex was erected after AD 364. The temple itself was dedicated to an otherwise unknown god, Nodens, who was certainly connected with hunting and perhaps also with the sea: the main mosaic in the temple, now lost, depicted sea-monsters and fish and was dedicated by a naval officer. In addition, Nodens appears to be connected with healing, and the discovery of numerous votive figures of dogs in the excavations supports this, as dogs are often associated with healing sanctuaries in the ancient world. In addition to the temple, there was a long building of eleven rooms opening out onto a verandah (apparently for patients to spend the night in the hope of a visitation from the god); a large guest-house with numerous rooms ranged about a courtyard; and a fine set of baths. The sanctuary was clearly built by and for worshippers of some standing. That such a shrine was built at this time, in the closing years of the Roman Empire when Christianity was growing in popularity at the expense of paganism, and the island was becoming increasingly insecure at the threat of barbarian attacks, is truly remarkable.

The existing remains of the Lydney complex, situated within a prehistoric hill-fort amidst the luxuriant foliage of a private deer-park, are very overgrown and are unlikely to prove of great interest except to the enthusiastic visitor. In addition, they can *only* be visited by prior written arrangement with the Lydney Estate Office, Lydney, Glos. Those, then, who have made the effort to obtain permission should ask for directions from the Office, reached by a drive off the A48, immediately east of the village of Aylburton. Remember to wear old clothes and take a torch if you wish to explore the iron-mine (see below). The temple is of unusual plan, being neither strictly classical nor Romano–Celtic in type: it consisted of a rectangular outer wall with bays or 'chapels' and an inner shrine with three small sanctuaries at the far end (nearer the path). In the first building the roof of the inner shrine was supported on six piers, but when one of these subsided, sometime between 367 and 375, with the consequent collapse of the temple, the spaces between the piers were blocked up in the rebuilding to make a continuous wall. In addition, L-shaped walls were built round three of the bays in the ambulatory, but the purpose of these side-chapels is unknown: presumably they were connected with some temple-rite, perhaps healing. The site of the long dormitory building is behind the temple, on the left side of the track, under the trees. The remains of the guest-house, which are also filled in, were found to the right of the track, opposite the bath-house. Most of the latter is still visible, including several heated rooms and stoke-holes. At one point the Roman floor-level is marked by a massive door-sill still in position, linking the *tepidarium* with the large, apsed *caldarium*. The metal covers here close off the entrance to an

exploratory iron-mine, of which a better example will be seen
presently. Continue along the track a little further and you will
see on the left, next to the large tree, the foundations of a water-
tank which supplied the baths. Now strike through the bracken
to the right of the track, over to the ramparts of the prehistoric
hill-fort. These, erected sometime in the first century BC or AD,
are at their most impressive here. With a bit of searching you will
find the metal covers that close off another Roman iron-mine,
which in many ways is the most exciting of the present remains at
Lydney (fig 40). By the light of a torch you can climb down the
steps and examine the walls of the narrow passage, still bearing
the pick-marks of the Roman miners. The mine was never fully
operational: this passage was only a test-dig in the hope of
finding a body of iron-ore rich enough to be worth extracting.
It was probably made in the third century AD when Roman
activity inside the hill-fort prior to the building of the temple
seems to have been at its height.

The Romans exploited iron in many parts of the Forest of
Dean, and the centre of the industry was the small town of
ARICONIVM, now Weston-under-Penyard near Ross-on-Wye

40   *Lydney, iron mine*

(nothing visible). The road which linked Weston with Lydney is unusual in being paved with stone slabs in its course through the Forest of Dean. One piece of this road is kept preserved at **Blackpool Bridge** (SO 6508); it is only eight feet wide, very narrow for a Roman road, but it is carefully built with kerb-stones on either side. At one point a different line of kerb-stones can be seen joining the main portion at an angle, for here a loop road crossed the stream by a bridge, whereas the main stretch used a ford. Blocks from it are still lying about in the stream-bed next to the modern bridge. The spot is reached by taking the Colesford road, the B4431, just west of Blakeney on the A48, and turning right after two miles, at the signpost to 'Soudley, scenic road'. The Roman road is on the left after the railway-bridge and cattle-grid.

Chapter 4

East Anglia

Buckinghamshire, Cambridgeshire, Essex, Hertfordshire,
Norfolk and Suffolk

In about AD 10 Cunobelinus, better known as the Cymbeline
of Shakespeare's play, became king of the Trinovantes, the tribe
occupying the area of modern Essex. Very rapidly his influence
extended over the whole of SE England, and his capital at
Colchester became the most important centre of pre-Roman
Britain, defended by a complicated series of dykes still traceable
to the west and south of the modern town. It is not surprising,
therefore, that the Roman invading army under Aulus Plautius
in AD 43, three years or so after Cunobelinus' death, made for
Colchester after crossing the Thames. Before advancing on the
capital, Plautius sent for the Emperor Claudius, and the triumph

over Camulodunum, 'the fortress of Camulos' (a war-god), was duly completed in imperial company.

The first Roman occupation of **Colchester*** (TL 9925) took the form of a legionary fortress situated, almost certainly, on North Hill, under the western half of the later town. Here pits and timber buildings associated with a legionary dagger and other equipment were found in 1965, but no trace of military defences has yet been located. Then, in AD 49–50, the first town was founded at CAMVLODVNVM. It was, as the historian Tacitus tells us 'a strong *colonia* of ex-soldiers established on conquered territory, to provide a protection against rebels and a centre for instructing the provincials in the procedures of the law'. Its official title was COLONIA CLAVDIA VICTRICENSIS. The first buildings were of good construction, with masonry footings, wall-plaster, roofing-tiles, and a piped water-supply. This earliest settlement, according to Tacitus, was undefended, but the military ramparts, even if neglected, may still have been visible. Outside this town to the east was a vast classical-style temple raised on a lofty *podium* and approached by a flight of steps. It was dedicated to the Emperor Claudius and was viewed, in British eyes, as the *arx aeternae dominationis*, 'the stronghold of everlasting domination', according to Tacitus. The presence of this symbol and the alleged rapacity of the imperial financial administrator Catus Decianus were enough to spark off the famous revolt of the Iceni under their queen Boudicca (Boadicea) in AD 60 or 61. The portents in Colchester immediately before the revolt are described by Tacitus in a graphic passage: 'the statue of Victory fell down, its back turned as though in retreat from the enemy. Women roused into frenzy chanted of approaching destruction, and declared that the cries of barbarians had been heard in the council-chamber, that the theatre had re-echoed with shrieks, that a reflection of the *colonia*, overthrown, had been seen in the Thames estuary. The sea appeared blood-red, and spectres of human corpses were left behind as the tide went out.' When the revolt broke, there was no hope for the Roman inhabitants of the *colonia*. 'In the attack,' says Tacitus, 'everything was broken down and burnt. The temple where the soldiers had congregated was besieged for two days and then sacked.' Archaeological evidence of Boudicca's attack has been encountered usually in the area west of the Temple of Claudius, suggesting that the earliest *colonia* was confined to this western half of the later city. The evidence is generally a thick layer of ash and burnt wattle-and-daub, but in 1927 blackened Samian pots, stacked together waiting to be sold, together with molten fragments of glass vessels which had fused into them, provided an even more vivid illustration of Tacitus' words.

Our knowledge of the later development of Roman Colchester is less complete. Recovery after the Boudiccan fire seems to have been slow, but by the beginning of the second century occupation had spread into most of the 108 acres later enclosed by the town-wall. When the latter was erected is still a matter of debate: excavations in 1951 showed that the stone wall and the banks behind it were contemporary, probably belonging to the middle of the second century, but a section cut in 1970 near the Balkerne Gate produced a different and unexpected result. Here the wall was free-standing *before* the addition of a bank behind it, and this sequence was confirmed by further excavation in 1972 along the south defences, when the wall was tentatively dated to AD 120–50 and the rampart behind it to 150–75. The surviving parts of the circuit are described in detail below.

The best starting-place for a tour of Roman Colchester is the Museum, situated in the castle which the Normans built on the foundations of the Temple of Claudius (weekdays 10–5; Sun., Apr.–Sept. only, 2.30–5). There are many splendid objects displayed here and some must be singled out for comment. On the right of the entrance-passageway is the Beryfield pavement, the best-preserved mosaic so far to have come from the Roman town. Inside the main hall, along the left-hand wall, are some fine second-century geometric mosaics. They were found in a Roman town-house on North Hill, built over the early military buildings mentioned above. At the top of the stairs is the peculiar group of 'face-urns', second-century funeral pots with crude but amusing faces decorating their sides (fig 41). Other finds from the Roman cemeteries are displayed in cases nearby: note especially the group of charming objects from a child's grave of c. AD 50, including terracotta toys in the shape of a boar, a bull and other animals, caricatures of reclining and reciting figures, and a drinking-bottle. More important are the finds arranged along the end wall. In the right-hand corner is one of the best bronze statuettes to survive from Roman Britain, an imported figure of Mercury made about AD 200. In the centre is the gladiator vase, of the same date, produced by a local workshop and depicting a combat between Memnon and Valentinus, as the inscription round the top informs us. Near it is another funerary monument – the Colchester Sphinx, a vigorous rendering in British stone, with a man's head (no doubt the deceased) between her paws. Finally, magnificently displayed against a rich blue curtain, are two famous military tombstones from the early days of Roman Colchester. One is that of Marcus Favonius Facilis, centurion of the Twentieth Legion, and it contains a superb full-length portrait of the dead man (fig 42). Great attention has been paid to the details of his uniform, including his sword, his dagger and the vine-staff, the symbol of his rank, which he holds in his right hand. The other tombstone depicts an auxiliary cavalryman from Bulgaria, wearing a metal-plated jerkin. He is called Longinus, and his father goes by the delightful name of Sdapezematycus. The inscription has been broken, and the face of the deceased mutilated, while that of the grotesque barbarian under his feet survives intact. It is reasonable to assume that this damage was done by Boudicca's followers in the sack of Colchester in AD 60 or 61.

When you have finished looking at the Museum, ask a

41   Colchester, a 'face-urn' in a cremation-burial

42   Colchester, tombstone of Facilis

custodian to take you down to the vaults. They belong to the
substructures of the massive Temple of Claudius, and form one
of the earliest and most impressive monuments of Roman Britain.
The superstructure was entirely swept away by the Normans
when they built their castle at the end of the eleventh century,
but a model of the temple is on show near the entrance to the
Museum. You may think this is fanciful, but Roman temples of
the classical type, rare in Britain, are sufficiently stereotyped to
allow a high degree of confidence in their reconstruction. The
vaults still visible were designed purely to support the weight of
the temple above; there was no access to them in Roman times,
and they were filled with rammed sand until the seventeenth
century, though the Roman date of the work was not recognized
until 1919. The plan consists of two parallel vaults with one cross-
wall off-centre. At one point the joint between the Roman and
the Norman masonry can be seen.

A few other Roman remnants can be traced in the castle
grounds. On leaving the Museum turn right and follow the path
running alongside the castle wall, which here, as elsewhere,
displays plenty of re-used Roman tile. Near the NW corner, the
path slopes down and cuts through a flint wall. This is a tiny
fragment of one of the walls which enclosed the temple-precinct.
Nearby, over in the shrubbery to the left of the path, near the

43   Colchester, south part of Balkerne Gate (from inside)

fence, a section of Roman drain is preserved behind railings. Next to the bandstand, a little further on, are some red tessellated pavements belonging to a town-house excavated over fifty years ago. Finally, two further portions of Roman drain are visible through grilles in the grass east of the castle, near the children's playground.

Nothing else of Roman Colchester is visible within the walls, but the latter survive for much of their original course; a walk round them takes about $1\frac{1}{4}$ hours. The Roman work is at its best on the west side of the town near the mighty Balkerne Gate. This is reached from the Museum by turning right along High Street and going down the narrow lane at the end by the 'Waggon and Horses'. The ruins of the gateway, though much mutilated, are still impressive, and can be understood with the help of the plan displayed on the modern wall below the inn. The gate, a massive 107 feet wide, consisted of two central carriage-ways for wheeled traffic and two smaller passageways for pedestrians; and the whole was flanked by D-shaped bastions containing guard-chambers. One of the pedestrian tunnels and the entrance to the adjacent guard-chamber survive intact (fig 43) and can be viewed from the grounds of the Mercury Theatre. The middle portion of the gate is mostly invisible, but part of the central pier, rebuilt at some stage in the Roman period when the carriageways were made narrower, can be seen through the grille below the inn. Later still, probably at the close of the Roman period, the gate was entirely blocked with a rough wall, also visible. To the left the north bastion still stands 20 feet high, and from here the Roman wall can be followed down Balkerne Hill. Only rubble-core is visible, and the stretch is at present very overgrown with foliage, but nowhere else at Colchester does pure Roman work stand to such a height. The problem of the date of the gateway and the town-wall is discussed above (p. 121).

From the foot of Balkerne Hill to the traffic-lights the wall is largely repatched with later material, but the tile bonding-courses which occasionally appear make it easy to spot the little Roman work that still remains visible here. Cross straight over at the traffic-lights and walk along St Peter's Street, where the wall is not visible. At the end of this is the entrance to Castle Park, where the wall reappears, though again much re-faced with later material. After a while you come to the railed-in remains of Duncan's Gate, named after its discoverer in 1853. It consists of a

single passageway set back a little from the line of the wall, which
turns in to meet it. Behind, at present totally overgrown, is some
fallen masonry from the superstructure of the gate, including
part of the arches of two windows. Continue following the wall
to the NE corner, where you can observe it curving round into
Dobson's Meadow, and then retrace your steps for a few yards
to pass through a modern arched opening into Roman Road.
At the end of this is East Hill. Cross the road, turn left and then
immediately right down an alley bordering the church. Here you
will see a good stretch of the Roman wall, with bonding-courses
clearly visible at the far end. The site of the east gate, demolished
in 1675, lies near here under East Hill. Continue down this and
turn right into Priory Street. The wall again becomes visible
rounding the SE corner and running along the car-park on the
south side. After a breach filled with seventeenth-century
brickwork, the Roman tile bonding-courses are again visible near
the top of the wall. The bastions here are all medieval, though
incorporating Roman materials: thus bastion V, near the end of
the car-park, uses Roman tiles at its top. There is no evidence at
present that the Roman wall had external bastions, but it had the
usual internal turrets at intervals, some of which have been
excavated.

On the left at the end of Priory Street is the eleventh-century
St Botolph's Priory, built largely of Roman stones and tiles
[AM; A]. Cross now into Vinyard Street, where the wall is again
visible, much mutilated, along another car-park. This stretch
is due to be bisected soon by a service-road; at present,
half way along, a well-preserved Roman arched drain can be
seen issuing from the wall at ground-level. Thereafter the wall
disappears for a long time, though there is a small fragment
visible down the corridor on the right of 37 Crouch Street (cross
Head Street and keep straight on). Then turn right down
Balkerne Lane, soon to be replaced by a relief-road; a fine stretch
of the Roman wall is visible below St Mary's Church. It is then
only a short distance to the Balkerne Gate.

Three other monuments to the west of the modern town may
be mentioned in conclusion, one pre-Roman, one Roman and
one dubiously Roman. Take the old A12 out of Colchester for
about 1½m and turn left down Fitzwalter Road. The low mound
in the field on the left next to No. 38 was excavated in 1924 and
found to contain an exceptionally rich group of grave-goods,

dated to the first half of the first century AD and now displayed in Colchester Museum. Clearly a native royal prince was buried here, possibly Cunobelinus himself. Much more impressive structurally, but less exciting in that it lacks any possible historical connections, is another *tumulus* a short distance away. Continue along the A12 to the village of Lexden, and turn left along Church Lane. Then take the first turning on the right (Shakespeare Road) and right again down Thomson Avenue, then first left (Masefield Drive) and right (Wordsworth Road). The steep-sided burial-mound, this time of Roman date (second half of first century), lies in the back garden of the first house on the left beyond Marlowe Way. Partial exploration in 1910 yielded nothing of any note. Return once more to the A12 and continue to the traffic-lights, where you should turn left along Straight Road (signposted Mersea). After 250 yards, on the left-hand side of the road is the so-called Lexden Triple Dyke [AM; A]. Excavation in 1961 apparently showed this to be of Roman date, but its purpose is unknown. Perhaps it was intended to provide temporary cover for the invading army before it built its fortress. But since it continues the line of a known pre-Roman defence, it seems more likely that it was thrown up immediately before Roman armies reached Colchester, and that it forms part of the complicated defences of the British settlement.

Another Roman town which, like Colchester, was both founded near a pre-Roman settlement and sacked by Boudicca, is one of the outstanding sites of Roman Britain. It is VERVLAMIVM near the modern **St Albans*** (TL 1307), the third largest Romano–British city and still largely free from later buildings. About one third of the 200 acres within the walls has been excavated, mainly in the campaigns of Sir Mortimer Wheeler between 1930 and 1934 and of Professor Sheppard Frere between 1955 and 1961. Thanks to these excavations, and especially to the latter, a very great deal is known about the development, prosperity and decline of this great Roman city.

The capital of the British tribe which inhabited this area, the Catuvellauni, lay to the west of the Roman city, in Prae Wood. Coins inscribed VERLAMIO were issued under King Tasciovanus, the predecessor of the great Cunobelinus, and even when the latter shifted his capital to Colchester, the Prae Wood settlement continued to flourish and still minted coins. A fragment of coin-mould can be seen in the Museum.

The first Roman occupation of the site was a small military post in the area occupied by the village of St Michaels, guarding the crossing of the river Ver. This phase was short, and in AD 49 or 50 the first Roman town was laid out. This was a *municipium*, according to Tacitus, ie a self-governing community, the magistrates of which were given the privilege of Roman citizenship. In 1955 a first-century defence-circuit was located well inside the area later enclosed by the city-walls, and it is likely that this delineated the *municipium* from the time of its foundation. Many of the streets and a row of rectangular timber-framed shops belonging to this first town have been found by excavation, but Boudicca and her followers saw to it in AD 60 or 61 that the entire settlement was razed to the ground.

Recovery from this attack was slow, and rebuilding on a large scale was not in progress until the late 70's. The new forum and basilica were dedicated in 79, during the governorship of Tacitus' father-in-law Agricola, whose name partly survives on a fragmentary inscription found in 1955. By the beginning of the second century the town had overspilled the early defence-circuit, which had been filled in, and many of the public buildings had been erected in stone. Private dwellings, however, remained in timber until another fire destroyed the city in about AD 155. Whether this was accidental or caused by enemy action is uncertain, but it does not seem to have greatly interrupted the prosperity of Verulamium. Town houses were now built in stone for the first time, and many were floored with splendid mosaics: it is clear from finds here and at surrounding villa-sites that a school of mosaicists was operating in the town at this period. The theatre was built now, and about the end of the second century, too, an earthwork defence, known as the Fosse, was thrown up at the west corner of the city. This appears to be unfinished, but why is unknown. If it was begun at a time of crisis (see p. 21), maybe construction was still in progress when the danger passed, and it was thought unnecessary to continue. The monumental gateways on Watling Street, one facing London and the other Chester, probably belong to the end of the second century also. In the early third century, the visible stone defences with earth bank behind and internal turrets were erected to enclose a different area from that of the Fosse. The projecting bastions were probably added, as elsewhere, in the fourth century.

No mosaics and not many structural alterations can be

attributed to the third century, but we need not assume from this
that the city was in decline. A burst of renewed activity in both
private and public building points to continued prosperity in the
fourth century, and the abandonment of the theatre and the
temples c. 380–390 was probably more for religious reasons (the
advance of Christianity which disapproved of pagan ritual and
barbaric games) than for economic ones. Private buildings
continued to flourish in the fifth century, and dramatic evidence
for the continuance of organized life well after the legions had
left Britain was found by Professor Frere. Mosaics were still
being laid c. 390, and one very large house, was built from
scratch after 380. One of its mosaics was used long enough for a
worn area to be repatched, before the construction of a corn-
drying oven destroyed it. This too was used for some time, for its
stoke-hole was rebuilt. Only then was the house demolished, and
a substantial barn built on its site. Even when that was
demolished, a wooden water-pipe with iron joints at six-foot
intervals was laid, testifying to the remarkable survival of both
constructional skills and civic discipline. In the absence of
coinage, which ceased about 430, the date of this pipe-laying
cannot be established, but it must be around the middle of the
fifth century. The story speaks for itself: the hoary myth of
Britain dramatically perishing by fire and sword before a Saxon
advance has clearly been exploded.

Verulamium lies to the west of the modern town of St Albans,
which grew up around the shrine of Alban, executed for his
Christian beliefs, perhaps in AD 304, on the hill where the Abbey
now stands. You should start your visit to the Roman city by
seeing the Verulamium Museum, which is signposted from the
A414 (St Albans–Hemel Hempstead) [weekdays, Apr.–Oct.
10–5.30; Nov.–March, 10–4; Sun. 2–4 or 5.30]. It is one of the
most outstanding Roman collections in the country, both for the
quality of the display and the beauty of the objects, which amply
demonstrate the taste and elegance of the people of Verulamium.
Nearly every object deserves a paragraph to itself and I can do no
more here than mention the best exhibits. Taking pride of place
at the entrance to the main hall is the little bronze statuette of
Venus, with flowing drapery gathered round her hips. It was made
in the second century, perhaps in Gaul, and was found in 1959
in a cellar below one of the shops near the theatre. Mercifully it
was for some reason saved, together with other bronze vessels,

from the melting-pot for which it was destined. Beyond Venus is a model of the London gate, with two passageways for vehicles and two for pedestrians; its site will be visited presently. Along the left-hand wall a series of showcases illustrates the development of the city from its earliest origins. Note in particular, half-way along, the curious 'lamp-chimney' from one of the temples excavated by Wheeler. But your eye will have already caught the three superb floor-mosaics displayed against the end wall. The earliest and most unusual is the Scallop Shell mosaic, laid between AD 130 and 150, brilliantly designed and executed with subtle and pleasing use of colour. The two mosaics on either side, one entirely geometric and the other depicting at the centre a rugged sea-god with beard and claws sprouting from his head, belong to the later second century. A little earlier in date, but far less skilled, is the dolphin mosaic on the floor. Before seeing the rest of the main hall, move into the annexe on the left, which houses the chief finds of the 1955–61 excavations. The mosaic here, also perfectly preserved, is another extremely competent and pleasing piece laid in the second century. The central panel depicts a powerfully-drawn lion making off with the head and antlers of a stag. Equally impressive are the reconstructed panels of painted wall-plaster and, in one case, ceiling-plaster. These are finds which have added enormously to our knowledge of Romano–British interior-decorating. The best pieces are in the British Museum (fig 138). The other important exhibit is the fragmentary basilica-inscription, dated to AD 79. The suggested restoration of the lost parts is not fanciful, as Roman epigraphy follows strict conventions and the gaps can be filled from other stones. One of the fragments contains part of the name of Agricola, governor of Britain from 78 to 85 and immortalized in Tacitus' biography. Only two other epigraphic records of his activity in Britain are known (both at Chester).

Turn right on leaving the Museum and a three-minute walk will bring you to the Roman theatre, the only visible example in Britain (except for fragments at Canterbury). Discovered in 1847 and excavated in 1934, it is open every day from 10 a.m. to dusk. It was built in the middle of the second century, after the fire of 155, on a site previously reserved for it, as no earlier structures were found beneath. The first building had only a tiny timber stage and the entertainment must have taken place mainly in the *orchestra*. This area was used as the dance floor in the ancient

Greek theatre (*orchester* = dancer) and the modern use of the
term is therefore misleading. The nature of the entertainment at
this period is uncertain, but its close association with a large
temple to the south (buried) suggests that the theatre was sometimes used in religious ceremonies. At a later period in the
second century the stage was enlarged and rebuilt in stone. But
the most important alteration took place in the early fourth
century when the theatre was enlarged by the addition of a
massive outer wall. The building continued in use until the last
quarter of the century.

Passing the ticket-office and turning left in front of the
'dressing-room', go up the steps to the mound which surrounds
the remains : this is merely the excavation 'dump', made into a
viewing platform, and is no part of the original design. You will
see at once that the theatre consists of a stage and an *orchestra* ;
the latter is encircled with earth banks, partially re-erected, which
carried timber seating (fig 44). The stage displays three periods
of work : originally it was wooden, and the posts which supported
it have been replaced by modern timbers. Then, before the end of
the second century (phase II), it was rebuilt in stone on a more

44   *St Albans, the Roman theatre*

impressive scale and given a back-drop of columns; one has been
reconstructed in modern materials, based on ancient fragments,
to give some idea of the height of the stage-building. Then, about
AD 200, another wall was added in front of the stage, forming a
narrow slot into which the curtain was lowered and raised (the
reverse of modern procedure). The wooden cross in the centre
of the *orchestra* marks the position of what was probably some
kind of pole. Perhaps it was a sort of maypole and had a religious
significance, or else animals were tied to it in blood-sports.
In phase II, timber seats were built in part of the *orchestra*; but in
the early fourth-century rebuilding they were removed, and the
area of the *orchestra* reduced a little by the addition of a curved
wall in front of the previous one retaining the seating-banks. The
banks would then have been enlarged to take more seats, but the
retaining-walls of both periods are now visible. The *orchestra*
was entered by the three wide passageways which interrupt the
seating-banks, but these entrances would have originally been
vaulted and the seats carried over them. Finally, there are the
outer walls of the theatre, at the foot of the bank on which you are
standing. The inner, buttressed wall was the outer wall when the

45   St Albans, reconstruction-drawing of the theatre

theatre was first built in the second century. It is clearly visible in the reconstruction-drawing (fig 45), which represents the building in its third-century state, after the addition of the curtain-slot c. 200, but before the major alterations of c. 300. In these latter, the buttresses of the original wall were demolished to floor-level and a massive new outer wall was built, forming a corridor round the whole of the back of the theatre, and increasing its capacity still further as more seats would have been built above it. The path leads behind the stage and back to the ticket-office again, passing the base of one pier of a triumphal arch, built over Watling Street in the fourth century.

Between the theatre and the A414 some of the buildings excavated in 1957–60 remain exposed. On the left, marked out in concrete, is the plan of some timber-framed shops belonging to the original foundation of c. AD 50 and destroyed by Boudicca ten years or so later. This is the earliest ground-plan of a Roman building to be seen in Britain. The stark regularity of the plan and the timber-framed construction were far in advance of anything Britain had previously known, and it is likely that military construction-experts supervised the laying-out of the earliest town. The shops were separated from Watling Street, now under Gorhambury Drive, by a covered pavement-walk. This is not visible, as it lies buried beneath a flint wall of c. 300, which belongs to the last series of shops on the site. The shops themselves consist of a working-area in front and living-quarters (the part nearer you) behind. The labels here give the various trades of the occupants as suggested by finds from the excavations. After the destruction of AD 60, the area lay idle until redevelopment c. 75, but constant use until the fire of 155 entailed the rebuilding of the shops on four occasions in that period, resulting in a build-up of layers. This can be seen by comparing the left-hand part of this site, which represents the timber shops erected after 155, with the level of the pre-Boudiccan building, about $3\frac{1}{2}$ feet below.

A little further on, to the right of the path, are the foundations of part of a town-house built in stone after the fire of 155. An earlier timber house, which yielded the dolphin mosaic and the imitation-marble wall-plaster (both in the Museum), was found below. The only features of note in the visible remains are the pipes in one room belonging to a hypocaust, and the apse of a shrine, the rest of which lies under the road. The apse was

presumably intended for a statue and the side-niche for a lamp,
but the shrine does not appear to have been finished and it was
used as a cellar until the late fourth century.

   Now retrace your steps to the Museum and go into the car-
park beyond. Laid out in the grass on the left of the entrance are
some of the offices belonging to the basilica, which lies under St
Michael's Church; the forum lay beyond, in the area of the
vicarage. From the car-park follow the signs across the grass to
the 'Hypocaust' (same hours as the museum, but closed Mon.–
Fri., Nov.–Feb.). Here a modern bungalow covers the *tepidarium*
of the bath-suite of a second-century town-house. Part of the floor
has been cut away to reveal the hypocaust beneath. The geometric mosaic consists of four rows of four motifs arranged in
pairs. Stand on the long side of the room and note the third
(horizontal) row away from you. The first and third panels,
though identical in design, look different because they have been
set on a different orientation: this was clearly due to a fault in the
laying and provides evidence that the individual panels were
manufactured elsewhere and merely assembled here by less
competent craftsmen.

   Bear right on leaving the bungalow, making in the direction of
the Abbey. Soon you will come to the railed-in remains of a
fragment of city-wall (fig 46). Turn right and follow the bump in
the ground as far as the massive London gate, the plan of which
has been marked out. It consists of two passageways for vehicles
and two for pedestrians, with flanking towers on either side; a
model is in the Museum. The date of this gateway and the defences
as a whole has been discussed above (p. 128). From here stretches
a long section of the stone wall, with the bank behind it, and the
ditch, now overgrown, on the left [AM; A]. The facing-stones of
the wall have gone and the core is much battered, but it still
stands 8–10 feet high, about half its original height. Half-way
along are the foundations of a projecting bastion, and another
stands to a good height at the corner. Here you should clamber
up onto the top of the wall to see the remains of an internal tower.
This is contemporary with the stone wall of the early third
century, but the projecting bastion is probably a fourth-century
addition, though, if so, its junction with the wall has been skilfully
bonded in. The line of the defences, with occasional flintwork
showing, continues in the wood beyond (walk along King
Harry's Lane and then through the fence into the field on your

right). You will soon reach the A414 again and so back to the theatre and Museum. The Fosse earthwork lies on private land beyond the A414: it can be traced with the help of the map on sale in the Museum, provided permission has been obtained from the Gorhambury Estate Office.

When Boudicca's revolt had been crushed and her tribe, the Iceni, had been reconciled to the idea of Roman occupation, a small Roman town was founded for them as their tribal capital. It was VENTA ICENORVM near the village of **Caistor St Edmund** (TG 2303), some 3m south of Norwich. The site is reached by taking the Ipswich road (A140) out of Norwich and turning to the left (signposted Caistor St Edmund) just after the junction with the B1113. Turn right at the next cross-roads, and, after 200 yards, look out on the right for the gates to the parish church. The path to the latter crosses the nettle-filled ditch and then cuts through the prominent mound which formed the east defences of VENTA. From here (see the plan displayed near the path), you can survey the interior of the Roman town, now entirely under cultivation. If, however, you are lucky enough to visit the site in July or early August, as I was, you should be able to see the street-

46   St Albans, Roman city-wall and the abbey

grid of the city clearly marked as parched lines in the ripening corn. The clarity with which these appeared on an air-photograph of 1928 caused some excitement, and funds were raised which enabled the excavation of some of the internal buildings in 1929–35. These have been filled in (see p. 360).

The street-plan of VENTA was laid out about AD 70, but buildings remained very modest until the second century. Then a forum and basilica were built, but nothing is known of its plan: the one recovered from the excavations belongs to the middle of the century, and the bath-house near the west gate is of a similar date. There were repairs to both after burning at the end of the second century, and the forum was totally rebuilt on a smaller and simpler scale c. 270–90. Two stone temples were also found, but private dwellings were very humble and even in the third century were still not constructed of stone. Air-photographs have revealed a defence-system of earlier date on the south side of the town, but when the town-walls were finally built, c. 200, they enclosed a smaller area than that envisaged by the street-grid. All this points to only a moderately-successful town, and the 34 acres enclosed within the final defences make it one of the smallest tribal capitals in Roman Britain, smaller even than distant Caerwent in South Wales (44 acres).

Though nothing is visible within the defences, the latter are still prominent in their entire circuit. They comprised an external ditch and a stone wall, backed by an internal bank and strengthened by bastions. Presumably there were the usual two or three phases in the development of these defences, but excavation has yet to prove it.

Walk through the churchyard, keeping the church on your right (note Roman tiles built into the porch), and go through the gap in the hedge to the field beyond. You are soon at the SE corner. Flints poke out of the grass along the entire length of the south rampart and there is an impressive drop to the ditch below. A depression half-way along marks the site of the south gate, which consisted of a single portal and two guardrooms. It soon became choked with rubbish and the guardrooms were deliberately filled in before AD 300. Near the SW angle you must make the hazardous descent down the steep bank on the left and aim for the gate in the corner of the field. Turn right on passing through this, and you will soon pick up the line of the west rampart, now only a low mound. The ditch was omitted on this side as the river Tas flows nearby. A depression and a wooden fence mark the site of the west gate. Just beyond this, by a clump of trees, an isolated bastion still stands to an impressive height of 10 feet, displaying four courses of triple bonding-tiles. Another lump of stone core appears at the NW angle and again at the beginning of the north wall. Climb over the wall at this point and follow the defences on the inside. After a gap for the north gate, the rampart-mound becomes very impressive and is largely free from nettles and trees. In places considerable stretches of flint wall can be seen, still 20 feet high; this must be virtually its original height except for the parapet. But these stretches cannot be properly viewed from ground-level outside because thick undergrowth, nettles and trees obscure them. Keep inside the defences and round the NE angle. You are then back at the fence bordering the church-path.

Each of the three towns so far described in this chapter had a different administrative status: *colonia*, *municipium*, and tribal capital. The fourth and last town is different again, for although it would have had some degree of self-government it came under the wider control of the tribal capital (cf. 'county-town') of VENTA. It is **Caister-on-Sea** (TG 5212) [AM ; S], 3m north of Great Yarmouth on the north side of the road to Acle (A1064), on the western outskirts of the village. The coastline has changed a great deal since Roman times: Caister was then at the mouth of a large estuary stretching some way inland, and where Yarmouth now is would have been sea. The Roman town was therefore founded primarily as a trading port about AD 125. It may have had a semi-military importance in the early third century, when its stone wall was built, but if so this must have transferred to Burgh Castle (see below) when the latter was constructed. The town was still flourishing in the fourth century, and a Saxon settlement is represented by over 150 burials. The site was excavated in the 1950's. Its Roman name is not known.

Immediately inside the entrance-gate to the remains are two concrete circles and a long wiggly concrete line. The circles mark the site of post-holes for the timbers which carried a wooden bridge over the ditch outside the defences. The concrete line represents the timber palisade which surrounded the town from its foundation. This was replaced by the stone wall, originally backed by a clay rampart, which was erected to defend the town in the first half of the third century. It enclosed a square area of

9–10 acres, but only this portion of the south defences, and the western guardroom of the south gate, are visible now.

Inside the town-wall are the remains of the south wing of a large courtyard-building identified as a seamen's hostel. It was built at the end of the second century, went through several modifications, and was still in use in the fourth century. At this time the fine cobbled corridor on the south had been filled in. The small curved wall in one corner of the first room (end nearest the Roman guardroom) is believed to have been a latrine. There is a hearth in the centre of the next room. A little further on is an unusual hypocaust, with the channelled type in the centre and *pilae* set round the edges. The room is curiously labelled 'granary'; but although the hypocaust was filled with rammed clay mixed with quantities of wheat when it fell into disuse, there seems no reason to doubt that the chamber was originally built as a normal heated room. Its furnace was in the adjoining cubicle, in one corner of which is a water-tank. The rest of the building is now largely buried. The only other features to note on the site are two depressions, the sites of Saxon huts, and the pebbled main street leading down to the south gate and so out to the harbour.

47   *Burgh Castle, the south wall*

In the second half of the third century the threat of attacks on
SE England by Saxon pirates increased. The towns such as
Caister-on-Sea were safe behind their stone walls, but the
countryside and the smaller settlements needed protection. To
co-ordinate resistance to these attacks, a series of strong forts,
known as the Forts of the Saxon Shore, was built. Several have
already been described in Chapter One and another in Chapter
Two, and there were three more on the East Anglian coast. Those
at Brancaster, near Hunstanton in Norfolk, and at Bradwell-on-
Sea, in Essex, have left little trace above ground (see App. I), but
the site at **Burgh Castle*** (TG 4704) [AM ; A] is very fine. This was
the GARIANNONVM of the Romans, and the garrison was a
detachment of Stablesian cavalry from what is now Yugoslavia.
The fort lies on the river Waveney only a short distance from the
remains of Caister-on-Sea, but in Roman times the two sites lay
on opposite sides of a large estuary. Take the Lowestoft road
(A12) for about two miles out of Great Yarmouth, until a roundabout is reached ; Burgh Castle is signposted from there. The footpath leads to the SE corner bastion and the short but
picturesque portion of the south wall, part standing, part
toppling, part fallen (fig 47). The standing part retains all its
facing-flints, separated by rows of tile bonding-courses (at
Burgh only surface-deep), and forms a magnificent stretch of
Roman masonry, eight feet thick at base and 15 feet high –
probably its original height except for a parapet. The fallen
bastion here displays two features of interest. In the middle of its
top is a circular socket for anchoring a Roman *ballista*, which
hurled stone balls and other weapons onto the attacker ; and the
base shows traces of the timber framework used in the foundations of the wall. The use of timber posts is also implied by a
series of vertical square holes which can be seen on the inside of
the stretch of south wall nearest the river. From here you can
walk round the inside of the three remaining fort-walls : that on
the west has totally vanished, but what was presumably a timber
wharf was found in the nineteenth century at the foot of the low
cliff facing the river. The thickness of the wall was reduced on the
inside face by a series of offsets, which can be seen (partially
restored) in the eastern portion of the south wall. The main gate
of the fort was in the long east wall, but only a simple gap remains
today. Eventually you reach the centre of the north wall and its
leaning bastion. This originally protected a narrow postern-gate,

but hardly anything remains of it now. The particular interest of this bastion lies in the curving profile of its back, and in the matching mortar curve of the main body of the wall from which it has fallen. The reason for this is as follows. When the decision to build Burgh Castle was taken, the plan was to have the conventional internal turrets and no projecting bastions: two such turrets have been found in excavations but are not now visible. After about seven feet of the curtain-wall had been built, the order went out that bastions were to be added. For this reason, only the top half of each bastion is bonded into the wall; the lower half merely stands up against it. The curving portion marks the joint between the bonded and unbonded parts of each bastion, and, having observed it with ease in this example on the north, you can examine the rest of the standing bastions (fig 48) for this feature as you make your way round the outside of the walls, back to the SE corner. Throughout, the walls stand to a spectacular height, even though many of the facing-stones have been robbed. The construction of the bastions as an afterthought gives a clue to the dating of GARIANNONVM. It is later than the early examples of the series, such as Reculver, which have no bastions, but is earlier than the late Saxon Shore forts such as Richborough, Portchester and Pevensey, where bastions are an integral part of the scheme. A date around AD 275 is the most likely for the building of Burgh Castle. It was occupied up to the close of the fourth century.

The comparative lack of prosperity in the Icenian tribal capital is reflected by a similar situation in the surrounding countryside, where villas never reached the size or degree of romanized luxury displayed by those of the south-west. It is not surprising, there-fore, to find no villa-site visible today in the territory of the Iceni. Further west, the Fens were drained for the first time by the Romans and the area extensively cultivated, but villa-estates are non-existent here and it has been suggested that the area may have been an imperial estate. The system of canals, however, remains to bear witness to Roman engineering skills in this region. The main canal is the Car Dyke, which excavation has shown to have been eight feet deep, 30 feet wide at the bottom and 50 feet at the top. It was probably cut at the beginning of the second century (some think a little earlier), and was clearly used partly for drainage and partly for transporting grain to the garrisons serving in the north, for the network existed as far as

Lincoln and possibly beyond. Long stretches of the Car Dyke can be traced both in Cambridgeshire and Lincolnshire with the help of OS maps, but it is rarely more than a wet ditch and hardly likely to rouse much excitement. One convenient place to view the Cambridgeshire Car Dyke is near **Waterbeach** (TL 4867), a few miles north of Cambridge. From the latter follow the Ely road (A10) for six miles, until you reach a turning to the left (just past the airfield) signposted 'Landbeach 1, Cottenham 3'. Park here but continue walking along the A10 for a few yards until you come to some white railings near a 'Parking $\frac{1}{2}$ mile' sign. The Roman canal shows as a wet ditch below and beyond the railings.

Villas become more plentiful and more imposing in the territory of the Catuvellauni, especially around Verulamium, but at the time of writing no worthwhile remains are visible. Two recently-excavated sites, however, will deserve a visit soon. One is the **Latimer** villa (SU 9998), partly explored in 1864 and 1910–12, and fully excavated in 1964–71 by selective trenching in the grounds of Latimer Park Farm. There was a timber building here in the first century, but the first stone villa was built about AD

48 *Burgh Castle, a bastion on the east wall*

150–60. A few rooms and a corridor were added in phase two, in the first half of the third century, but for a short time c. 270–90 the villa was abandoned except for squatter-occupation. At the beginning of the fourth century it was rebuilt and new wings added to enclose a courtyard, but by the middle of the century decay had set in. Bit by bit, areas of the villa were abandoned, until only a tiny portion of the whole building was inhabited. Even when this was deserted, at the end of the fourth century, timber buildings were erected in and around the former court-yard, and habitation of some sort continued on the site well into the fifth century.

Only a small part of the villa will be preserved – two living-rooms, one large (referred to as 1 below) and one small (2), an L-shaped corridor (3), and part of a long corridor (4) on one side. The walls of these rooms are about three feet high, but at the time of writing (1972) they are overgrown and crumbling. The owner of the site intends to have them consolidated and erect a timber shed, and the situation may therefore have changed by the time this book appears in print. Rooms 1, 2 and 3 belong to the original villa, when 1 had a concrete and 2 a wooden floor. In phase two the long corridor (4) was added, a channelled hypo-caust inserted in room 1, and this and room 2 given new floors of crushed brick. In the fourth-century repairs, plain red tessellated floors were laid in rooms 1 and 2, but corridor 4 was given a patterned mosaic of red diamonds on a white background. Corridor 3 had a concrete floor throughout phases two and three. All this area remained inhabited until the very end of the villa-occupation, at the close of the fourth century. The entrance to Latimer Park Farm is clearly marked on the north side of the B485 Chesham to Rickmansworth road, $1\frac{1}{2}$m west of Chenies. The site lies between the drive and the road.

The other villa is at Dicket Mead, **Welwyn** (TL 2315), on the west bank of the river Mimram. Two sets of long buildings with front and rear corridors have been excavated here; they are over 300 yards apart but connected by an enclosure-wall. Neither was well preserved and they are not now visible. The end of one of these buildings, however, contained a small bath-house with walls still four to five feet high. It consists of three rooms each about eight feet square – *frigidarium*, *tepidarium*, and *caldarium*. The cold and hot rooms have plunge-baths attached to them, and there is a tank over the stoke-hole to the hot room. The arch of this stoke-hole is excellently preserved. The bath-house (which was excavated in 1970–1) was built in the middle of the third century but had a short life, as it was partially robbed c. AD 300. It lies in the path of the new A1 (M) motorway, but it has been decided to preserve it *in situ* in a concrete vault beneath the road. At the time of writing the bath-house is not yet open to the public.

But if the East Anglian countryside does not bristle with remains of villas, the area is rich in Roman funerary monuments. Most of these are in the form of earth burial-mounds, or *tumuli*, but an exception is the stone mausoleum at **Harpenden** (TL 1113). It lies in the private grounds of the Rothampstead Experimental Station, which is signposted to the right (west) of the St Albans road (A6) just south of the town. Casual visitors during working hours on Mondays to Fridays are usually not unwelcome, but it is best to write first if you know you are going on a particular day. Enquire at the reception-desk in the entrance and you will be escorted to the site. Here you will see the foundations of a circular building 11 feet in diameter, with a plinth in the centre and a cross-wall making an alcove. Fragments of a statue, presumably of the dead person, were found during excavations in 1937, and this probably stood in the alcove, while the plinth served as the base of an altar. The thickness of the external walls suggests that the superstructure of the mausoleum was quite substantial, perhaps 20 feet high. It stood in the middle of an enclosure, about 100 feet square, in which two cremation-burials dating to the first half of the second century were found. One side and two corners of the enclosure-wall remain exposed.

Of the many sites in East Anglia where Romano–British *tumuli* are visible I will describe only four here; one near Colchester has already been mentioned, and the rest are listed in Appendix I. The most interesting barrow is perhaps that on **Mersea Island** (TM 0214), the sole British example where it is possible to go underneath the earth mound to inspect the site of the burial-chamber. Immediately after the B1025 crosses the causeway onto the island, turn left along the East Mersea road. The barrow lies behind railings on the left just beyond a road to the right (Dawes Lane). The keys are obtainable from a house 200 yards further on ('Bower Haven'). A concrete tunnel made by the excavators of 1912 leads to the middle of the barrow; the site of the burial is marked by some tiles in the floor of the last chamber. These Roman tiles formed a cavity 18 inches high, and

inside was a lead casket containing a glass bowl with ashes of
human bones. These finds, probably belonging to the second
half of the first century AD, are now in Colchester Museum. The
earth mound raised over the burial is 110 feet in diameter and
over 20 feet high, and since 1966 has been cleared of undergrowth
and carefully maintained.

The Mersea example is an isolated barrow, but *tumuli* also
occur in groups. At **Thornborough** (SP 7333) in Buckinghamshire
two are found side by side. They are quite well preserved, one
16 feet high and 120 feet in diameter, and the other a little smaller.
When opened about 1840, the larger barrow yielded second-
century samian pottery, bronze jugs, a glass vessel and other
finds; these are now in the Museum of Archaeology and
Ethnology at Cambridge. From Buckingham follow the
Bletchley road (B4304) for about two miles until you reach a
heavily-signposted narrow bridge (roadworks to be carried out
in 1972–3 may alter this), and you will see the two *tumuli* in the
field on the left beyond the bridge.

A larger group, this time of six barrows arranged in a single
row, can be seen at **Stevenage** (TL 2323) in Hertfordshire. Each is
60 feet in diameter and now about 10 feet high. One was dug into
in 1741 when 'wood and iron' were found, but otherwise they
have not been explored. The *tumuli* are situated by a roundabout
with a filling-station on the south side of Stevenage, but the town
is full of roundabouts and I despair of giving further details. Ask
locally for the Six Hills.

The largest and most famous group of Romano–British *tumuli*
is at **Bartlow** (TL 5844), on the border of Essex and Cambridgeshire. Here there were two rows of three and four barrows
respectively, but the former was destroyed in the nineteenth
century. The surviving four are excellently preserved, but they
are at present sadly overgrown. They were explored in 1832–40,
when many fine grave-goods were found. These indicated that
the barrows were erected between the end of the first and the
middle of the second century AD. Most of the objects
unfortunately perished in a fire in 1847, but some remnants are in
Saffron Walden museum (weekdays 11–1, 2–4 or 5; Sun.,
summer only, 2.30–5).

Bartlow is signposted from the A604 (Colchester road) just
east of the village of Linton, 10m SE of Cambridge. Turn right
at the first crossroads and go straight over the second. The foot-

path to the Bartlow Hills, the name by which the barrows are
known, is signposted on the left immediately after the former
railway-bridge. On the left of the path is barrow 2, 25 feet high
and the least overgrown. In it were found a lamp and mid-
second-century pottery, and a wooden chest which contained a
pot and cremated bones in a glass jug. Barrow 3, on the right, is
the largest extant *tumulus* in Roman Britain, a massive heap 144
feet in diameter and 45 feet high. It is very steep, but can be
climbed with the help of the trees growing on one side. Its grave-
goods were elaborate – a wooden chest containing glass vessels
(for holding perfumes, food and the cremated bones), an
enamelled bowl, and a folding stool with bronze fittings and a
leather seat. The adjacent barrow 4, which is 35 feet high, is totally
overgrown and at present inaccessible, for it lies outside the
fence surrounding barrow 3; it is almost invisible even from the
top of the latter. It produced finds similar to those of barrow 2.
Finally there is barrow 1, the northernmost of the row, which
lies in private grounds on the other side of the former railway. It
can, therefore, only be visited with the permission of the owner,
but one side of it, rising steeply, can be seen from the railway-
footbridge. A bronze bowl, an iron lamp and a toilet-instrument
were found inside.

Chapter 5

Central England

Leicestershire, Lincolnshire, Rutland, Shropshire, Staffordshire and Warwickshire

(Appendix I only – Derbyshire, Huntingdonshire and Northamptonshire)

With the capture of Colchester in AD 43 and the establishment of a base there for the Twentieth Legion, the invading army split up. The Second Legion made for the West Country (see Chapter Two), the Ninth advanced northwards towards Lincoln, and the Fourteenth aimed for the Shropshire area. The precise movements of these legions in the period AD 44–60 are still far from certain, but a vast addition to our knowledge has been made by aerial discoveries and excavation during the last two decades. It is now known that the Ninth Legion was not established in its Lincoln fortress until about AD 60; before that it was divided between a 28-acre ('half-legionary') fortress at Longthorpe near Peterborough, and another of similar size at Newton-on-Trent near Lincoln. Smaller forts, garrisoned by auxiliary soldiers with some legionary detachments, are known to have existed at several places in the same area, but no trace of any of these early forts is visible on the ground today.

Less is known about the progress of the Fourteenth Legion. One part may have advanced through Cambridge and Godmanchester (near Huntingdon) to Leicester, where the size of the early fort is still undetermined but is possibly legionary in character. Another part of the Fourteenth may have followed the line later taken by Watling Street. In the 50's, when a temporary frontier had been adopted along the course of the Fosse Way, the legion's bases lay NW of this line, perhaps at Kinvaston near Penkridge (Staffs.), and at Wall. At both these places enclosures of 'half-legionary' size are known but are not visible on the ground. Eventually, about AD 58, the separated detachments were brought together and a fortress for the full Fourteenth Legion was established at Wroxeter.

The only one of these first-century forts worth visiting is that at the Lunt, **Baginton*** (SP 344752). Here an ambitious reconstruction-scheme, started in 1966, has turned a flat field into one of the most interesting and instructive sites of Roman Britain. The village of Baginton lies 2m due south of Coventry and is best reached by the minor road to Coventry airport. This leaves the roundabout joining the Coventry by-pass (A45) with the A423, SE of the city. At present the fort is closed except on Saturday afternoons and Sundays, but from 1974 it should be open every day. The site was occupied only between AD 60 and 74, but within that period its history is extremely complex. It was apparently constructed in the aftermath of the Boudiccan rebellion, for no finds at present point to the existence of a fort here in the earliest invasion-period. The first fort was much larger than the visible enclosure and its exact size has not yet been established. In the second phase the internal buildings were rebuilt on a different alignment. Then a curious circular structure was erected, covering in part two barrack buildings of the second stage of the fort. The original fort was then reduced in size, and the new eastern defences made a curious detour to avoid the circular structure. Finally, in period III, the size of the fort was apparently reduced once again, with a pair of ditches cutting through the *via principalis* of the period-II fort. In AD 74, when the coin-series from the site ends, the fort was abandoned, the defences dismantled, and the timber carried away for use elsewhere.

The most impressive feature at the Lunt at present is the magnificent east gateway to the period-II fort and the section of earth-and-timber defences rebuilt on either side of it (figs 49–50). The plan of the gateway was learnt from excavation in 1966–7; its elevation is based on evidence of a similar structure represented on Trajan's Column in Rome. It was prefabricated in modern army-workshops and erected by the Royal Engineers during three days in September 1970. No modern equipment was used to haul the pieces of the gateway into position.

From here to the centre of the fort ran the *via principalis*, but this was removed when the two period-III ditches, here visible, reduced the size of the fort for the second time. In the centre, the plan of the period-II HQ building has been marked out. It lacks a cross-hall but has the usual central courtyard and five administrative rooms along the back. The room in the middle was the shrine for the standards, and sunk into its floor is a strong-room, a common feature of later stone forts (cf. Chesters and Chesterholm, Chapter 8). But the headquarters was presumably no longer used after the odd reduction of period III, for the fort's new south gateway, twin-portalled like the reconstructed one, was built over part of the HQ courtyard. The post-holes of this gate have been marked out as six concrete circles. Near here will be the site-museum, due to be housed in a reconstructed timber granary by 1974.

The whole of the northern half of the period-II fort had been excavated by 1972 and the plan of the barracks and granaries marked out in concrete. One structure calls for special comment. It lies between the *principia* and the eastern defences, which bulge out to avoid it, and consists of a circular arena 107 feet in diameter, dug out to a depth of $2\frac{1}{2}$ feet below the rest of the interior of the fort, and surrounded by a timber stockade, perhaps six feet high. The structure is unique and its purpose therefore uncertain; the most convincing hypothesis is that it is a *gyrus*, or special training-ground for horses.

The Lunt is therefore an impressive and fascinating site, but it is important to bear in mind that it is not typical of a Roman fort. Having puzzled over the circular structure, do not go away thinking that every Roman fort had one. And having admired the splendid reconstructions of the gateway and portions of the earth-and-timber defences, remember that the sinuous course taken by the eastern rampart is a feature unique in Britain and very rare on the continent. Roman forts are almost always built to a regular playing-card shape with rounded corners and straight sides; and it is perhaps a pity that of all the Roman forts in Britain where such reconstruction could have taken place, it has been done at the most untypical example of all!

At five other fort-sites in central England something can be seen of the surrounding rampart-mounds, but at none of them are the remains impressive and they are therefore relegated to Appendix I. Metchley was a large fort built soon after the conquest and burnt down c. 55–65; reconstruction was attempted here some years ago but it was vandalized, and only a burnt timber tower and an overgrown mound remain visible. Of a smaller, late-first-century fort nothing is visible. The other four were semi-permanent forts belonging to the garrisoned zone of Roman Britain. The two Derbyshire ones belong to the southern edge of the Pennine chain of forts (Chapter 7), while Greensforge and Wall Town are on the fringes of Wales. Most of central England, however, became civilian in character after the military had moved northwards and westwards in the last quarter of the first century AD, and many of the places which started life as forts were rebuilt as towns. The two legionary fortresses, Lincoln and Wroxeter, were no exception.

*49 Baginton,
on the rampart-walk*

50 Baginton, reconstructed fort-gateway (from outside)

The fortress at **Lincoln*** (SK 9771) was founded, as we saw above, in about AD 60 or 61 for the Ninth Legion, though there may well have been a smaller auxiliary fort on the site before that. About ten years later the Ninth was moved forward to Yorkshire, and its place at Lincoln was taken by a legion newly brought to Britain, the Second Adiutrix. The earth-and-timber defences of this fortress have been found in excavations, but little is yet known of its internal lay-out. In about AD 77 *Legio* II *Adiutrix* moved to Chester, and the military phase at Lincoln was over.

As with all the short-term legionary fortresses in Britain except for Wroxeter, the site was resettled as a *colonia*, a town for retired legionaries and their families. This first town clung to the hill-top and when stone defences were erected in the early second century, they followed the same line as the legionary ramparts, and in fact used the latter to form the core of the bank behind the wall. The *colonia* of LINDVM was a flourishing town, and occupation also increased on the slope facing the river. Before very long, probably in the middle of the second century, this area too was walled, and the size of the town was thus increased from 41 to 97 acres. The defences of the upper town

51   Lincoln, the East Gate

were rebuilt on a more massive scale at the end of the second or
beginning of the third century, and most of the visible remnants
of the wall belong to this period, while the strengthening of the
lower town was carried out in the first half of the fourth century.
Much less is known about the interior of Roman Lincoln, but an
impressive sewerage-system and mosaic pavements point to a
comfortable standard of living.

Many fine stretches of the defences of LINDVM still exist, but
its chief pride are the three magnificent Roman gateways. A
convenient place to start a tour of the Roman remains is at the
Eastgate Hotel, opposite the Cathedral. Here, in the forecourt of
the hotel, the north tower of the Roman east gate stands to a
spectacular height (fig 51). The entrance-door, the jamb from
which the arch sprang, and the staircase giving access to an upper
level, are all impressively preserved. This semicircular bastion
was matched by another (buried beneath the pavement and part
of the cathedral green) which flanked the double carriageway of
the gate proper, now under the road. These massive remains,
however, only belong to the last phase of the gateway, in the late
second or early third century. Excavation within the tower in
1959–66 revealed the post-holes of the gateway of the timber
legionary fortress of AD 61–77 and also the narrow stone wall, $4\frac{1}{2}$
feet wide, which was built to front the timber gateway soon after
the founding of the *colonia*. Both these earlier periods, labelled 1
and 2, are also visible and can be understood with the help of
the plan displayed on the retaining-wall.

In the grounds of the hotel is a picturesque stretch of the
Roman wall, part of which can be seen from the extreme northern
end of the hotel car-park. Now walk down the narrow lane
adjoining the remains of the east gate. After turning the corner,
in private grounds behind railings on the right of the road, you
will see a massive lump of wall-core, 10 feet thick. It is backed by a
large platform which formed the foundation for a water storage
tank. The water came from a spring $1\frac{1}{4}$ miles to the north, whence
it was pumped uphill in a sealed pipe-line. Next to it, attached to a
piece of the original (narrow) gauge of stone wall, is an internal
tower. The lane soon leads to the famous Newport Arch, the
north gate of the town and the only Roman archway still
standing in Britain (fig 52). Until a lorry crashed into it in 1964
it had survived unharmed since its building at the close of the
second or beginning of the third century; it has now been faith-

fully restored. It is a fine relic, looking a little squat because of a build-up in road-levels, and consists of a main arch and a smaller one for pedestrians on one side, originally matched by a similar small arch on the other. Only the inner part of the gate is Roman; the rest of the masonry, including the pedestrian tunnel, belongs to the medieval structure. Like the east gate, it was flanked by projecting towers, and the lowest courses of one of these, overlain by medieval work, can be seen laid out on the left (west) of the road. (If you want to be thorough, you may like to see a large but overgrown section of the ditch accompanying the wall. It lies on private property in the back garden of Fosse House, on the corner of Church Lane; go outside the Arch and turn right.)

When you have had your fill of the Newport Arch, walk down Bailgate, turn right along Westgate and then right again into West Bight. On the right, at the point where the lane becomes a footpath, is a garage yard. Here, on the right, forming the back wall of a lean-to, and supporting a varied assortment of engine-parts, is the Mint Wall, 70 feet long and 18 feet high, and for all its griminess an impressive enough piece of Roman masonry. It belongs to part of a massive complex of buildings inside the town,

52   Lincoln, the Newport Arch

but its precise purpose is still not clear. It was connected with a large colonnade, 275 feet long, which gives some idea of the scale on which this particular building was planned. The sites of some of the column-bases are marked by the circular granite sets in the middle of Bailgate.

Continue now to the end of Bailgate and down Steep Hill. On the right, between a snack-bar and an antique shop, is a piece of mellowed stone. This fragment is part of the south gate of the upper town; when the walls were extended in the mid-second century, there was of course another south gate, at the foot of High Street, facing the river. The upper gate, even before this, can hardly have been important, for the gradient here is too steep for wheeled traffic and difficult enough for pedestrians.

Now retrace your steps a little and turn right into the Cathedral precinct. Under a stairway leading off the NE corner of the cloisters is a portion of Roman mosaic, found nearby in 1793. On the south side of the Cathedral are the remains of the Bishop's Palace [AM], at present under consolidation but soon to be opened to the public. For the moment, therefore, a good stretch of Roman town-wall at the extreme south end of this, bordering what was once the Palace garden, is inaccessible. It is still 14 feet high and formed part of the eastern defences of the lower town. Apart from this piece of wall, and the splendid exception described in the next paragraph, very little is visible of the lower *colonia*. A shapeless fragment of wall-ditch, also on the line of the eastern defences, and a flue-arch found in 1925 and perhaps belonging to a bath-building, are all that can be mentioned. The former is in the grounds of the Usher Art Gallery, Lindum Road, and the latter can be seen, with the manager's permission, in the basement of Messrs. Boots, on the corner of High Street and Clasketgate.

Until the important excavations of 1970–1 very little was known of the walls of the lower Roman town, and none of its gates had been found. Now, however, a superb stretch, including the west gate (fig 53), has been excavated and consolidated in the forecourt of the new Municipal Offices in Orchard Street. More of these defences were located in 1971 a few yards further north, on the site of the new Police Headquarters, but these have been destroyed. As a result of this work we now know that the first wall surrounding the lower *colonia* was built in the middle of the second century and was only five feet thick. It was, however, well constructed and seems to have stood unrepaired until the fourth century. Then, about AD 330–40, a massive new gateway with projecting rectangular towers, defending a single passageway 16 feet wide, was erected. The backs of these towers still stand to a considerable height, and here can be seen the rear portion of the two guard-chambers which each contained. The fronts of the towers are less well preserved, but it can be seen that their foundations incorporate material which has been pirated from other buildings in the town. One piece built into the south side of the north tower is a superb second-century frieze, perhaps from a temple.

Sometime after this gateway was built, in the later fourth century, the defences were strengthened still further. North of the gate the old wall was completely replaced at this time, but to the south new masonry was tacked onto the back of the early wall, and to save material the width was reduced by a series of offsets, thus creating the present step-like effect. The wall here stands to a spectacular height of 15 feet; the stonework was not robbed in medieval times, because it was protected by the clay mound which backed the wall and which was increased to a width of 80 feet in these late-fourth-century changes. It has now been removed, of course, to display the splendid masonry of the rear face of the wall. Coins on the road-surface indicate that the gate remained in use into the fifth century. Finally, a visit can be made to the small but well-arranged City and County Museum in Broadgate (10–5.30; Sun. 2–5.30). It is next to the church of St Swithin's, where a Roman altar is displayed.

Whereas the legionary fortress at Lincoln became a *colonia*, that at **Wroxeter*** (SJ 5608) [AM; S] was turned into the tribal capital of the Cornovii, VIROCONIVM CORNOVIORVM. Part of the ditches of the military fortress has been identified from the air, and timber buildings belonging to it have been excavated beneath the later bath-site. Finds indicate that the military phase lasted from about AD 58 to 75. The civilian settlement which must have grown up during this period then expanded and flourished, and when the city was eventually provided with defences these enclosed about 170 acres, making VIROCONIVM the fourth largest town in Roman Britain. Most of this area is still farmland, and excavation has been largely confined to the central sector of the town.

The site is best reached by turning off the A5 5m east of

53   Lincoln, the West Gate (lower colonia) during excavation

Shrewsbury, following the B4380 to Ironbridge, and turning right
at the first crossroads. The entrance to the ticket-office and
museum is on the left, but first look over the fence on the right of
the road a little further on and you will see a long line of column-
stumps which form part of a portico on the east side of the forum.
The whole of the latter was excavated in the 1920's but only this
part has been left exposed. The excavations produced one of the
largest and finest inscriptions from Roman Britain, recording
the erection of the building by the *civitas Cornoviorum* under the
emperor Hadrian in AD 130. The original (fig 54) is in Rowley's
House Museum, Shrewsbury (weekdays 10–1, 2–5), but there is a
cast in the site-museum. The excavations also showed that a
bath-building had been planned for the forum area, but that it
was demolished before completion.

Now enter the main site and visit the new museum. Apart from
the cast of the forum stone, another inscription of great interest
is displayed here. It reads: 'Cunorix, son of Maqqos-Colini' (Son
of the Holly), and is dated on linguistic grounds to AD 460–75.
Macus and Maqqos mean 'son' in ancient Irish, and Cunorix is
probably an Irishman settled by the Romans in Britain to help
stave off other invaders; such men were known as *foederati*,
'allied'.

54   Wroxeter, the forum inscription

When you have finished visiting the museum, go out onto the verandah and look over the rest of the site. The most conspicuous feature is the fine upstanding piece of masonry known as the Old Work, which has miraculously survived medieval stone-robbing and over 1800 years of British weather. It is part of the south wall of a large aisled building which occupied all the area between the museum and the rest of the site, and which formed an exercise-hall (*palaestra*) for the baths. About AD 350 it collapsed, and in the building-rubble several timber structures, some of considerable pretensions, have been traced. Dating evidence is lacking, but life must have continued here into the fifth and possibly even the sixth century before Wroxeter was abandoned.

The *palaestra* excavations are still in progress (1973) and it is not yet clear how much, if any, of the remains can be consolidated and left open on permanent display. For the moment, therefore, a temporary walk-way leads to the rest of the site and the tour begins at its western end, near the road. On the right of the path is a small market-hall, consisting of a series of small rooms ranged about a courtyard; only the north wing is at present visible, but the rest is under excavation. On the left of the path are two square rooms of unknown purpose, a narrow corridor, and then a public latrine. This can be recognized by the sewer, originally

covered by wooden seats, which runs along the back wall of the
building.

The rest of the remains on the site belong to the public baths.
Unfortunately they have been left exposed since 1863 and a
detailed history of their development cannot now be recovered.
The *piscina*, however, has only recently been found. The baths
themselves were not erected until the second half of the second
century, and many of the visible walls belong to this period, but
beneath there was an earlier civic building which was never
completed. It is conceivable that the vast *palaestra* was built as the
basilica of the new town, while the forum, planned for the site now
occupied by the baths, was never completed and, in reorganization at the beginning of the second century, baths and forum
changed places.

The bath-house was entered from the *palaestra* through the
double doors which partially filled the present gap in the Old
Work. On the underside of this gap can be seen the two rounded
impressions left by the relieving-arches (now vanished) which
lay above the lintels of the two doors; the doors were not, therefore, as high as the present gap in the structure. Higher up are
three great tile arches which form deep recesses and were
originally supported by pilasters. All these features can be better
understood by a glance at the drawing of the suggested reconstruction (fig 55).

Now turn your back on the Old Work and examine the rest of

55   *Wroxeter, the Old Work reconstructed*

the bath-complex. You are now standing in the *frigidarium*. On the left and right are cold plunge-baths and in front of you are the worn thresholds which led into the *tepidarium*. From here onwards you are walking below the original floor-level, for none of the baths' floors have survived. The *tepidarium* appears to be divided into two parts by a cross-wall. On the left are two smaller rooms, one with a few *pilae*-bases and an adjoining stoke-hole. These were subsidiary rooms of intense dry heat and were matched by a similar set on the right. Ignore the latter for the moment and move from the second (main) part of the *tepidarium* into the *caldarium* (moist heat), on either side of which are recesses for hot baths. All the *pilae* here are modern, as all the original tiles had been robbed and only their impressions remained. The original walls of these rooms had also disappeared, and they too are marked out in modern materials. At some stage in the history of the baths, an outer wall of grey sandstone partly encased the *caldarium*, and this survives to its original height on the left (east) side. Probably cracks developed in the inner wall, and the new wall was then built to prevent heat-loss. At the end of the *caldarium* is the stoke-hole (fig 56); this was probably originally intended to heat both the warm rooms, but later the *tepidarium* was given a separate furnace, and part of its internal flue is represented by the lump of Roman masonry visible on the floor of that room.

Now turn right across the grass to see the small swimming-bath (*piscina*) with an apse at each end. This was not a regular feature of Roman baths, and it is in fact the only visible example in Britain, apart from the Great Bath at Bath. The latter was, however, enclosed in a hall and fed by natural hot springs; the Wroxeter example was open to the sky. It was in fact never used: the paving is unfinished and the *piscina* was filled with rubbish including late-second-century pottery. The British weather may have been the reason for abandoning the scheme, or else the decision to build an extension to the main bath-suite, thus preventing convenient access to the swimming-pool. The *caldarium* of this extension is clearly recognizable by the semi-circular wall north of the *piscina*. Its stoke-hole is represented by the two large blocks to the left, while the room on the right, with another furnace-chamber approached by steps, was the *tepidarium* of the extension. This room was originally intended, however, to be one of a pair of dry-heat rooms flanking the

tepidarium of the main suite, and matched by the similar pair of
rooms mentioned earlier. The reason for building the extension
is not known for certain, but it may have become an independent
set of baths reserved for women.

The other tribal capital in central England was **Leicester***
(SK 5804), which was RATAE CORITANORVM, the capital town of
the Coritani. There was pre-Roman occupation of the site and a
military post, possibly legionary, in the early years of the Roman
conquest, but as yet very little is known of either phase. The later
town-walls enclosed about 100 acres, but no scrap of them
remains visible. One area inside the town has, however, been left
exposed; like Wroxeter, it is the site of the public baths and, again
like Wroxeter, it preserves a magnificent stretch of Roman
masonry 30 feet high, the Jewry Wall (fig 58).

The site, which lies in the western half of the modern town
near the church of St Nicholas, was excavated in 1936–9. The
intention had been to erect modern swimming-baths on the site,
but as it was believed at the time that the Jewry Wall was part of
the basilica and that the supposed adjacent forum was later
covered by public baths, it was decided to preserve what was
thought to be the earliest administrative centre of Leicester. It is
now known, however, that the forum and basilica lay on an
adjacent site partly under St Nicholas' Circle, and that the Jewry

56   Wroxeter, the baths and the Old Work

Wall, like the Old Work at Wroxeter, is part of the *palaestra*, or exercise-hall, of the baths.

It is best to visit first the excellent Jewry Wall Museum (10.30–7, Sat. from 9.30, Sun. 2–5), which overlooks the Roman remains. The most spectacular exhibits are the two stretches of wall-plaster, recovered from a Roman town-house in 1958, which depict human figures, birds, garlands, etc. set in an architectural background (fig 57). There are also some notable mosaics, especially the second-century Peacock floor. Outstanding among other finds are the weathered stone head of a boy, from Hinkley, and a Roman milestone of AD 119–20 recording a distance of two miles from Leicester – A RATIS II.

On leaving the museum, take a look at the plan of the Roman baths which is displayed on the terrace. It will be seen from this that the visible remains belong to two periods, the first about AD 125 (red labels), when the Jewry Wall itself and the rooms nearest to it were put up, and the second about 135–40, when the central area, including the three large halls in front of you, was built. The apsed hot baths and furnaces marked on the plan were filled in when the museum was constructed. Keep to the right and make for the superb Roman drain with a single capstone *in situ*. This marks Roman ground-level: all the remains here except for the Jewry Wall are reduced to foundations only. Beyond the drain, at a higher level, is part of a town-house. Now walk over to the impressive Jewry Wall, which may owe its preservation to the fact that it was incorporated into a Saxon church. The origin of the present name is unknown. It is an imposing stretch, with tile bonding-courses and one of the two arches in a fine state of preservation (fig 58). The square holes were designed to hold wooden scaffolding during construction, and would have been plugged with other material which has now fallen out. Below the Jewry Wall is another section of drain. At the far end, close to the metal staircase, is an outfall-channel leading into another drain from a tiny room at a higher level. This was a latrine. Now turn and face the museum. On the small mound in front of you are the bases of hypocaust *pilae*. Finally, at a lower level beyond, there are three rooms with apses for plunge-baths on either side (blue-stained grass). The precise sequence of rooms which the bather would have followed is not clearly understood, and the Leicester site is not, therefore, as good an example of a public bath-suite as that at Wroxeter.

After you have left the site, take a look at the other side of the Jewry Wall. Four arches are visible here, and a niche, presumably for a statue, in the middle. One of the piers which supported a row of columns belonging to the *palaestra* can be seen by looking over the brick wall at the north (College) end of the footpath.

Finally, two other remains of Roman Leicester should be mentioned. One is a good geometric mosaic of second-century date which is preserved *in situ* under the railway-embankment in Bath Lane. At present (1972) the site is closed because of a lack of illumination, but one hopes that this situation may soon be remedied (enquire at the museum). The other is a stretch of fairly impressive earthwork known as the Raw Dykes, usually inter-preted as part of an aqueduct but perhaps more likely to have been connected with a docks-installation alongside a Roman canal. It lies about 1 m south of the Jewry Wall site. Take the Rugby road (A426) out of Leicester and stop just after the B5366 to South Wigston goes off to the left (Saffron Lane). The earth-work is on the right of Aylestone Road before the railway-bridge.

The rest of the Roman towns in central England were much smaller in size, and some of those situated on the trunk-roads

57   Leicester, Roman wall-plaster

58   *Leicester, the Jewry Wall*

served as 'posting-stations', where a traveller could expect to find a hotel and a stable for his horses. One of those on Watling Street was LETOCETVM, now the village of **Wall** (SK 0906) [AM; S] near Lichfield in Staffordshire. The earliest occupation at Wall was military, but the full details of a complex series of forts have yet to be unravelled. The earliest was about 30 acres in size and was presumably the base, from about AD 50–58, for part of the Fourteenth Legion. Finds however indicate that the same site continued in use until about AD 70. In the second century there was a small fort on the crest of the hill by the church. The importance of Wall as a military site would have attracted civilians to settle along Watling Street. The resulting town was a sprawling one and does not seem to have been enclosed by defences until the fourth century, and even then they did not include the bath-house. Only this last building, compact and well-preserved, can be seen at Wall today.

The bath-house was excavated in 1912–14 together with an adjacent building identified as a *mansio*, or inn; if this is correct, then it is very odd that two such important buildings should have been left outside the fourth-century town-walls. The *mansio* was filled in but is currently being re-excavated. The bath-house is extremely complicated in its present, final form, in which five separate phases have been recognized. The first building, revealed by excavation in 1956 but not now visible, belonged to the first century and was presumably military. The phase-II bath-house, perhaps early second-century, occupies about one third of the area of the final building and is the part first reached from the custodian's hut. In phase III (third-century) a new undressing-room and cold plunge were added. In phase IV there were internal changes, and in phase V (perhaps at the same time as IV) the main stoke-hole was rebuilt. Visitors who want to try and work out all these phases on the site should study the plan displayed in the adjacent museum, where a small collection of finds has been arranged.

The path leads to the *tepidarium* and *caldarium*, built in phase II. The floor has gone but many *pilae* are visible (fig 59). At first a small rectangular alcove projected from the exterior wall in front of you, and the broken ends of it are visible at the foot of the path-steps; it was demolished in phase IV and the wall made continuous. Turn right towards the hedge. The room next to the one with the *pilae* was the entrance-hall and cold room of the

phase-II baths. Next comes a tiny hot bath with stone seat and
lead outflow-pipe, and a small room for dry heat beyond. The
bath was inserted in phase IV; in the phase-II building this had
been a single room, and was in fact the southern limit of the bath-
house at this stage. The date of the room next to the hedge is
unknown. It has a stoke-hole to warm the adjacent hot room, but
the presence of four *pilae*-bases indicate that it too was heated at
some stage.

Now return to the other end of the bath-house and go round the
projecting stoke-yard which supplied heat to the main rooms with
the *pilae*. You can now examine the wall running down the
middle of the building, which was the outer wall of the phase-II
bath-house. Traces of three of its external buttresses, designed to
take the thrust of the vaulted roof, can be seen here. The one
nearest the path is the most conspicuous, and another will have
been noted projecting into the path on the other side. The wall
here has been much altered in later phases, and a new stoke-hole
was inserted in phase V. Now make towards the hedge again,
crossing three walls in the process. Two belong to a verandah of
the large adjoining exercise-courtyard, added in phase IV, while

59   *Wall, the bath-house*

the third wall is part of an earlier building underlying the court-yard. Three rooms will be noted in succession from here, all added in phase III and all excellently preserved. The first, which has its floor in position and a slab lying on top of it, was a room of dry heat (*laconicum*): the hypocaust-flues are visible beneath. The next room also retains its original floor and is the undressing-room. In phase IV a niche was inserted, presumably for a statue; it is still covered with salmon-pink plaster. At the same time also, the drain visible in this room was inserted to take away water from the small hot bath already noted. Lastly, between the undressing-room and the hedge is the fine cold plunge-bath with an inlet and two outlets for filling and emptying it with water.

Another posting-station on a great trunk-road is the village of **Great Casterton** (TF 0009) on Ermine Street. It lies in Rutland, a few miles NW of Stamford. It is now by-passed by the A1; so if you are heading north, turn off for the Nottingham road (A606), and if you are going southwards, take the B1081 for Stamford. In the village, follow a lane signposted to Ryall and Essendine, and you will see on your right, just after the farm, the surprisingly impressive remains of the town's defences (fig 60). No stonework is now exposed, but the mound of the rampart is here five feet high and the enormous shallow ditch in front of it is 60 feet wide. Elsewhere the rampart has been largely ploughed away but the great ditch can be followed all the way down the east side of the town. Beyond the field wall, where it swings away to the right, it is much fainter. Excavations in the 1950's revealed that the town

60   Great Casterton, remains of defences

wall was first built, with a bank behind it, at the close of the second century, and that there was a deep V-shaped ditch seven feet in front of it. These walls enclosed about 18 acres but, of the buildings within, apart from a late-first-century bath-house, nothing is known. Soon after the middle of the fourth century the defences were drastically reorganized, and it was then that the wide ditch visible today was dug. The second-century ditch, which lay much closer to the wall, was then filled with the material excavated from the new ditch. The filling provided a foundation for rectangular projecting bastions which were added to the wall at this time. These were designed to carry the Roman catapult machines, *ballistae*, which hurled stone balls and iron-tipped bolts at the enemy. The purpose of the new broad ditch, cut out of solid rock, was to keep the enemy at a range suited to the *ballistae*.

Outside the town, but close to the corner where the defences are visible, a temporary fort was discovered from the air in 1959. Excavation showed that it was built soon after the conquest and occupied until about AD 80, after a slight reduction in size c. 70. It is not visible from the ground. Further away to the east a villa has been excavated, now also filled in. It was built as late as c. AD 350–65, enlarged c. 370–80 and burnt at the very end of the fourth century. There is evidence that even then agricultural activity continued at the site, and it is likely that life went on behind the shelter of the town-walls well into the fifth century.

The next town of any size on Ermine Street north of Great Casterton was situated at **Ancaster** (SK 9843), and the course of the Roman road between the two is followed by modern highways. For the first 12 miles north of Great Casterton, Ermine Street is represented by the dual carriageway of the A1, but then you should turn off along the B6403, and keep straight on for Ancaster. For the last six miles the road is very straight: it is a fine piece of highway, with the B-road running on top of an *agger* about four feet high.

At Ancaster, Ermine Street is crossed by the A153 (Grantham-Sleaford). Beyond this crossroads, in the field on the right of the B-road, is the SE corner of the defences of the Roman town, here represented by a mound and a broad ditch, less impressive than at Great Casterton. The history of the rampart is not fully known, but is probably similar to that of Great Casterton. A stone wall was built at the end of the second century and defended by one or more ditches, but the visible broad ditch is probably later. Two bastions have been discovered at Ancaster and there was no doubt a series of these, presumably of fourth-century date.

The line of the western defences can be gauged by going into the churchyard on the other side of Ermine Street. Beyond the tower there is a drop in ground-level and the path cuts through the site of the rampart. The change in levels is also clear in the garden adjoining the churchyard on the south. Little is known of buildings within the town, which was preceded, as so often, by a military fort in the middle of the first century. Some finds from Ancaster, including a representation of the Mother Goddesses and other sculpture, are in Grantham Museum.

The last two towns to be mentioned in this chapter, Caistor and Horncastle, lie in NE Lincolnshire. The status of both is uncertain, but the presence of defensive stone walls, which constitute the visible remains at both places, implies that the towns were of some importance. They were probably market-centres for the local produce, though a semi-military role has also been suggested because of their walls and their relative proximity to an exposed coastline. Limited excavation at both has failed to date the defensive circuits, but they most probably belong to the late third or early fourth centuries, if, as seems likely, the bastions were part of the original scheme.

The remains of the walls at **Caistor** (TA 1101) are insignificant and hardly worth recording. The most substantial fragment lies on the south side of the churchyard. At the point where the brick wall of a house leaves the path, the top of the Roman wall can be seen by leaning over the fence. But the fragment can only be properly viewed, with the owner's permission, from the back-yard of the house. It is about seven feet high, of rubble-core only, and includes the slight remains of a bastion projecting three feet from the wall. This is part of the south defences of Roman Caistor. More insignificant is the tiny fragment of bastion on the north wall, possibly flanking the north gate. From Market Square, the centre of the modern town, go down the narrow Bank Lane and then turn right down Chapel Street. At the gap between houses on the left (next to No. 6), go into the yard and turn sharply round to your left. Between two projecting outhouses, and forming the base of a modern brick wall, a piece of Roman wall about three feet high can be seen. On the right, now obscured by plants, the wall projects a little and this marks the beginning of the bastion.

For the sake of completeness, it may be added that a chunk of rubble-core, hidden by ivy, exists at the west end of the Grammar School grounds in Church Street and marks the line of the west defences; and what may be part of the east gate exists in the cellar of a private house on the south corner of Bank Lane with Market Square.

The walls of Roman **Horncastle** (TF 2569) have left more numerous and more interesting fragments. The walk round these only takes about 20 minutes, as the area enclosed by the defences is very small (seven acres, about one less than at Caistor). There does seem, however, to have been Roman settlement outside the walled area, especially to the south. A convenient starting-point is Market Place, where a plan of the modern town marking the Roman remains can be studied. Now walk down nearly to the end of Church Street; on the left, at present in a derelict yard, opposite the churchyard steps, is a piece of wall-core forming the base of a modern brick wall. Turn left along Wharf Road. A fine stretch, 20 feet long and four feet high, including part of the inner face, is displayed in the vestibule of a new Branch Library on the left. Go up Bull Ring, turn left into High Street and so back to

61   *Horncastle, a bastion*

Market Place. Turn right down St Lawrence Street. On the right, immediately beyond a public toilet, is a yard from which the fine north corner bastion (fig 61) can be seen. But demolition is in progress in the yard, and the view of the bastion from here may be obscured. It is about 10 feet high, and the lowest courses of an adjoining stretch of wall are also visible. The remains are situated in the back garden of a private house. Now return to Market Place, turn left by Woolworths down Manor House Street, and along a gated private road. In a field on the left a fenced-off fishpond and bits of Roman core mark the position of the west angle. Another scrap of wall is meant to be visible in the yard-complex on the right of the private road, but my trespassing was not thorough enough to find it. Continue on down to the end of Manor House Street, where another stretch of wall, six feet high, can be seen at the entrance to the health centre. Now return along this street and go into the churchyard, keeping straight along the path to the other side. On the right, opposite house no. 1, is a side-gate giving access to the longest and highest stretch of wall at Horncastle, though once again only core is visible. At present (1972) the door has collapsed and so the wall is visible from the street. With the permission of the respective owners, it is possible to follow this piece of wall, past a short brick interruption and through another gate into another back-yard, and see the wall rounding the south corner. The lowest course of the Roman wall is also visible on the left of the road, before disappearing under the churchyard wall.

Chapter 6

Wales

including Cheshire

Wales was something of a problem for the Roman administration: the area was too hostile to be left alone, as it provided a
threat to the security of the towns and villas of the peaceful lowlands. It had therefore to be conquered and garrisoned, and the
cost of this can hardly have been offset by the minerals, especially
gold and copper, which the Romans exploited. Even after its
final pacification, Wales remained a garrisoned zone, and
although romanization in the form of villas and a couple of towns

reached the extreme south and south-west, life for the natives in most places must have been little changed by the Roman conquest.

We know a fair amount about the military campaigns against the Welsh tribes from the pages of the historian Tacitus, but he gives no place-names and few geographical details, and it is therefore impossible to reconstruct each campaign with precision. The first attempts were made by Ostorius Scapula, governor between AD 47 and 52, with further advances under Veranius in 57 and Suetonius Paulinus in 58–9 until the latter was halted by the rebellion of Boudicca in East Anglia. We do not hear of any further campaigns until AD 74, when Julius Frontinus finally subdued the Silures, the tribe occupying most of South Wales except the SW corner; and the Ordovices of North Wales were not quelled until 78 by Frontinus' successor, Julius Agricola.

The archaeological record for these campaigns is sparse. Until quite recently only three marching-camps had been known in Wales, but many more have now been discovered by aerial photography and fieldwork. Most or perhaps all of those mentioned later in this chapter, or listed in Appendix I, belong to this early period, So too does the site at **Clyro** (SO 2243), which lies between Hay-on-Wye and the village of Clyro, in the field beyond the yard of Boatside Farm. Take the first turning on the right on the B4351 after crossing the Wye, ½m from Hay, and turn right again when the track forks. Permission to visit should be sought at the farm on arrival, but visitors are not welcome; so only go if you are keen and feel you have a good excuse to offer. There is not a great deal to see – just the earth ramparts on the NE and SE sides of what was a very large fort, covering 26 acres. The strategic importance of the site, and the finds of pottery, which indicate that occupation had ceased before c. 75, make it clear that here was a base for large expeditionary forces in their attacks on the Silures.

With the final pacification of Wales in 78, our literary sources dry up, and the rest of its history under the Roman occupation has to come from archaeology. The whole area was controlled by a carefully-designed network of forts, fortlets and roads. Much work remains to be done both in the discovery of new sites and in the elucidation of their history, so that many of the dates given below may have to be revised in the light of future research.

The two corner-stones for the garrison of Wales were the

legionary fortresses at Caerleon and Chester, which, together
with York, formed the three permanent bases of the legions in
Roman Britain. **Caerleon*** (ST 3490) was ISCA, the home of the
Second Augustan Legion, situated 3m NE of Newport, or 1½m
from intersection 25 on the M4. The fortress was established by
Frontinus in AD 74 or 75 with an earth rampart and timber
buildings. An inscription of AD 100 shows that there was some
rebuilding in stone about this time, but it is also clear from
excavation that at least some of the barracks were still wooden
in the middle of the second century. The earth rampart appears
to have been given a stone facing not in the initial rebuilding c. 100
but about 20 years later. There was extensive reconstruction
in the early third century, but before the beginning of the fourth,
as excavations in 1968–9 have proved, the fortress was no longer
garrisoned: part of the legion either now or later was transferred
to Richborough in Kent. Regular excavations since 1926 have
provided many details of the lay-out of the 50-acre fortress, but
only one small portion, the west corner [AM; A], is visible today.

To reach it, take the road by the church signposted 'Roman
Amphitheatre', which partially runs along the *via principalis* and

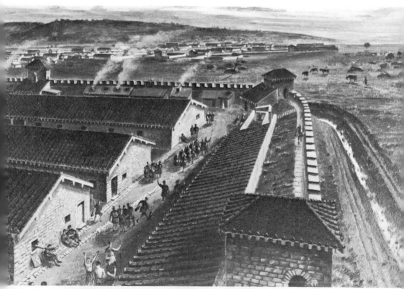

62   *Caerleon, reconstruction-drawing of a corner of the fortress*

passes through the site of the SW gateway, marked by a modern
plaque. You are now outside the fortress, with the amphitheatre
on your left. Ignore that for the moment, and take the path on
your right which runs adjacent to the fortress-ditch and passes
the site of the parade-ground and civil settlement under the
playing-fields on the left. After 150 yards, cross a plank bridge
and you find yourself in the west corner of ISCA. What you first
see as you walk down to the far end are the circular oven-bases
which back onto the rampart. These were once domed structures
of tiles and masonry, probably covered by wooden sheds. They
belong to the original fortress of AD 75 but were superseded about
150 by more substantial square stone structures, with furnaces
and built-in flues. Two of these cookhouses are visible, built up
against already existing stone turrets which are also visible; one
is half-way along the fortress-bank here, the other is at the corner.
Also at the corner, adjoining the cookhouse and contemporary
with it, is a latrine. The most prominent feature is its stone-built
sewer running below floor-level on three sides; it would have been
surmounted by a row of wooden seats.

The interior of the fortress at this corner was occupied by rows
of barrack-blocks arranged in pairs facing each other (fig 62).
Only one is visible now, the plans of three others being mis-
leadingly laid out at a higher level in modern materials. This is
only a fraction of the total: to get some idea of the fortress' size,
you have to imagine 24 of them stretching in a row from here to
the north corner; then there were 24 more at the other end, and

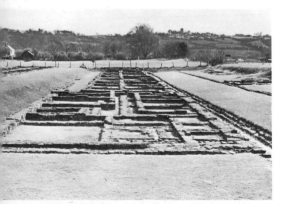

63   *Caerleon, a legionary barrack-block*   64   *Caerleon, the amphithe*

a further 16 in the centre, flanking the headquarters building:
Caerleon church, the tower of which is visible from here, overlies
part of the HQ and thus roughly marks the central point of ISCA.
As can be seen from the plan before you (fig 63), a barrack-block
consists of spacious quarters at one end of the building (that
nearer you) for the officer, a centurion, and perhaps his junior
staff, and twelve pairs of rooms for the rest of his company. The
larger room of each pair provided the living- and sleeping-
quarters for about six men, while the smaller was used for
storing their arms and equipment; each barrack was thus
designed to hold a *centuria* of 80 men. The barracks here were
built in the second century to replace earlier ones of timber, but
various modifications were made in the third century to the
centurion's quarters; not all the dividing walls visible today
belong to one period.

The outstanding Roman monument at Caerleon, however, is
the amphitheatre [AM; S], dug by Sir Mortimer Wheeler in
1926-7 and still the only completely excavated example in
Britain. It was constructed about AD 80 and is therefore
contemporary with the most famous amphitheatre of all, the
Colosseum. But whereas the latter was designed purely for the
gratification and enjoyment of the Roman masses, its com-
paratively humble counterpart in distant Caerleon was primarily
used for military exercises and displays, though no doubt blood-
sports and gladiatorial combat were also staged here. There
were various modifications in the middle of the second and at the
beginning of the third century, until its final abandonment on the
departure of the garrison.

On passing the custodian's hut and moving round anti-clockwise, you can see that the amphitheatre has been hollowed out to
create the arena, the upcast earth being used to form banks on
which timber seating was erected. These banks were encased in
masonry both internally and externally, where buttresses give
added support. The stoke-hole for heating a small bath-
building is visible close to the outer wall on this west side: it
preceded the amphitheatre by a few years but was not used after
c. AD 125. From here you can use the broad flight of steps in the
adjoining entrance (fig 64) to reach the arena, passing through a
small room where competitors waited their turn. Over it was
suspended a 'royal box' for top-ranking officers, access to which
(as well as to adjoining seats) was provided by the stairs on either

side of the little room : those on the right, reached through a perfect brick arch, are still substantially complete. The companies
which built the amphitheatre inscribed their names on some
stones in the arena wall, even though the latter was soon to be
covered with mortar. Four casts are still in position, but they are
difficult to locate and still more difficult to decipher. The two
easiest to find are a short distance on either side of the entrance
you have just passed through, that on your right being six courses
above ground-level, and that on your left seven. Continuing
anti-clockwise, you will follow the arena wall round to the south
entrance. This, and its better-preserved counterpart on the north,
were the principal entrances to the arena and were originally
vaulted to carry an upper tier of seats. Continue round the arena,
past one of the four narrow stairways giving access to the seating,
until you reach another of the competitors' 'waiting-rooms', this
time complete with stone benches. There is also a domed recess
here, perhaps for a statuette of Nemesis, the goddess of Fate.
From here you can complete your tour of the amphitheatre with a
visit to the north entrance, which displays massive external piers
of masonry with sockets for the bars barricading the arena. The
arena wall near here still bears substantial traces of its mortar
facing.

  Before leaving Caerleon, a visit should be made to the
excellent little Museum, with its classical-style portico, situated
on the main road close to the church. It is open from April to the
end of September (weekdays 11–5, Sun. 2–5), and on application
to the caretaker at other times (address on wall). There is plenty
to enjoy here – soldiers' weapons and everyday objects ; an
amphitheatre stone (> RVFIN = company, or *centuria*, of
Rufinus) ; a cremation in a lead canister with a pipe protruding
above ground (this was for pouring libations to the dead person) ;
a stone head from a grave-monument, found in 1972, and other
sculptures ; a maze mosaic in the basement (not open at present),
one of very few British mosaics from military sites ; and above all
the inscriptions on the end wall which help to reconstruct the
history of ISCA. The central one was dedicated to Trajan (TRAIANO
in the second line) in AD 100, as we know from the number of
consulships he had held by that year (COS III in line 5) ; note how
the third stroke has clearly been added later, showing that the
stone was carved in 99, when Trajan was COS II, but not erected
until the following year (fig 65).

Caerleon's sister fortress at **Chester*** (SJ 4066), the Roman
DEVA, is even more built over. With the outstanding exceptions
of the north wall and the amphitheatre, its surviving remains are
isolated fragments which require a good deal of patience to track
down. This is hardly surprising in a city like Chester; its strategic
position, first recognized by the Romans, has ensured its continued importance to the present day. There may have been a
small fort here around AD 60, but the first fortress, in earth and
timber like Caerleon but a little larger (60 acres compared with
50), was built in AD 76–8, and two lead water-pipes bearing the
name Agricola show that the finishing touches had been put by
79. The initial garrison, as we know from tombstones, was the
Second Adiutrix Legion, but this was replaced, in 87 or a little
later, by the Twentieth Valeria Victrix, which then remained at
Chester throughout. Rebuilding in stone, first of the defences and
probably of the internal buildings soon afterwards, started at the
beginning of the second century. Chester apparently escaped
destruction in c. 196, but not the troubles of a hundred years later,
for there was rebuilding of the defences on a large scale in the
early fourth century. The final withdrawal of the garrison

65   Caerleon, a building-inscription

probably occurred about 380.

Rescue excavation, especially during the past decade, has recovered much of the plan of the fortress' buildings, but little is now to be seen. Many of the surviving fragments are on private property, and prior permission is needed to visit them. Only the most interesting have been included here, while the rest are listed in Appendix I.

The best place to start your tour is at the Eastgate, which lies on the site of a Roman predecessor. Immediately north of this, a fine portion of Roman fortress-wall can be seen by looking over the medieval wall just before reaching the car-park steps. King Charles Tower stands on the Roman NE corner, but from here to the north gate you are walking not on the foundations but on the very substance of the Roman wall, still preserved to an amazing height of 15 feet and only lacking its wall-walk. It is best, therefore, to get off the walls at Northgate and go into George Street to examine the Roman work (turn right at the foot of the steps, and then first right). In its present form (fig 66) it dates largely from the fourth-century rebuilding, as a large number of earlier tombstones robbed from an adjacent cemetery were found

66   Chester, the north wall

in the core of the wall during repairs between 1883 and 1892; they are now in the Museum. In the stretch nearest the Northgate the Roman moulded cornice is very clear, marking the top of the Roman work and the beginning of the modern. Recent excavations (1964–5) also found the NW corner standing 15 feet high, but this had to give way to the inner ring-road; its plan is outlined on the pavement below St Martin's Gate. From here onwards the medieval and Roman walls part company: the Roman west wall followed the line of the inner ring-road, while the medieval circuit embraced a wider area to the west and south.

Return to Northgate and enter the street of the same name, which was the Roman *via decumana*. Between the Town Hall and the central cross of the Rows lies the site of the *Principia*, the HQ of the fortress, of which two fragments are accessible. One, excavated in 1970 and soon to be visible from Hamilton Place (turn right beyond 'The Forum'), is part of the row of offices along the north range of the building, including the shrine where the legionary standards were kept (*sacellum*), and, below it, the rock-cut strong-room (*aerarium*). The other is a massive base for one of the columns of the cross-hall, together with two ends of column-shafts projecting out of the cellar walls, in the basement of a lady's gown shop, Nola Ltd, at 23, Northgate Row. At no. 14, Quaintways' shop, the uninspiring remains of an isolated hypocaust may be viewed. The area around St Michael's Row was occupied by a large internal bath-building, of which a very well-preserved hypocaust is on show in Messrs. Lawleys' china shop at 39, Bridge Street: part of the floor and its supporting *pilae* are visible. From here, turn left along Pepper Street in order to reach Newgate, from which the SE angle tower of the fortress can be seen, and, opposite, a public garden containing some re-erected Roman columns and a hypocaust from the bath-building mentioned above. Just north of the angle tower, in an inspection-chamber which can be visited during office-hours in the yard of Messrs. Jolliffe's premises in St John Street, is another stretch of the fortress-wall.

The most interesting monument of Roman Chester is undoubtedly the amphitheatre, which was opened to the public in 1972 [AM; A]. Only the north half is visible, as the rest lies buried under a convent: it cannot therefore rival the Caerleon example, even though Chester's is substantially larger – the largest, in fact, known in Roman Britain. Its site, just outside

Newgate, has been known since 1929 but proper excavation
began only in 1960. This showed that a timber amphitheatre,
with an arena of the same size but only half the seating capacity,
was replaced in stone after a few years, perhaps c. AD 86. Its outer
wall, supported by massive buttresses, has been robbed, but the
arena wall is well preserved. Two main entrances are visible, on
the north and the east. That on the north was closed by large
wooden doors hung on the stone gate-posts which are visible on
either side, next to the arena wall; behind were flights of steps
leading up to the seats, but only those on the right survive.
Adjoining this entrance on the west is a small room which was
clearly used as a shrine of Nemesis, the goddess of Fate (fig 67):
an altar to her (replaced on the site by a replica), and two
column-bases, perhaps once supporting dedications, were placed
here c. AD 300. The east entrance consists of a level passage and
then a few steps down to a room at arena-level. Stairs on either
side of it led to the seats and also to an officers' box raised above
this room; those on one side, much worn, are still visible (fig 68).
The superbly-preserved door-jambs leading to the arena will also
be noticed. The position of the subsidiary staircases giving
access to the seating (which was wooden, supported on banks of
sand) has been marked out on the grass, together with the plan of
the outer, buttressed wall. The arena floor showed traces of
repair in about AD 300 after a long period of disuse, and also of a
curious timber platform in the centre, carefully avoided by a
drain which ran from the north entrance right through the centre
of the arena, but which is not now visible.

Two other extra-mural monuments complete this survey of
Roman Chester. Part of the Roman quay wall, badly displayed
and overgrown, is situated behind a ladies' toilet on the race-
course, opposite the end of Blackfriars. It is partly visible from
the Roodee itself, but a closer look can only be obtained with the
permission of the course manager. The other is a Roman quarry-
face and a much-weathered figure of Minerva visible in a public
garden called Edgar's Field, on the south side of the river, on the
right immediately after crossing Dee bridge. Finally, no visit to
Chester is complete without seeing the Grosvenor Museum in
Grosvenor Street, which has one of the finest displays of Roman
military remains and sculptural material in the country (weekdays 10–5; Sun. 2–5).

These two fortresses of ISCA and DEVA were, as I have said, the cornerstones for the control of Wales, though the Chester command no doubt had responsibilities too in northern England. Wales itself was studded with carefully-sited forts, and to some of these I will now turn.

In the south the fort at **Brecon Gaer*** (SO 0029) [AM ; A] was one of the largest and most important, as it lay at the junction of several roads. It is best reached by following the A40 west of Brecon for four miles and taking the first road on the right, to Aberbran. Turn right at the T-junction in this village, and continue straight on for two miles. Immediately after the second turning to the left, after crossing a stream, you will come to an unsignposted cross-roads. (This point can also be reached by taking a minor road from Brecon to Battle and turning left in Cradoc.) Here you must turn back hard on your right, along a metalled but heavily-grassed track which leads to Y Gaer farm. The fort lies in the field beyond the farm. It was built c. AD 80 with earth ramparts and timber buildings. Its garrison at the turn of the century was a Spanish cavalry regiment of Vettones, 500 strong. A stone wall was added to the defences in about 140, and the principal internal buildings were also rebuilt in stone at

67   *Chester, the shrine of Nemesis in the amphitheatre*

about the same time. The gates seem to have been rebuilt at the end of the second century, perhaps after destruction, but the fort was evacuated soon afterwards. There was a brief reoccupation at the end of the third century when the south gate was repaired. A trickle of finds goes on into the fourth century, and the fort was probably held by a caretaker garrison of just a few men during this period. It was excavated by Sir Mortimer Wheeler in 1924–5, but only three gateways, an angle turret, and part of the fort-wall remain visible today.

You enter the fort close to the barn, which covers the site of the north gate. On the left is a fine stretch of the stone defences, 10 feet or so high. Turning left and following the walls clockwise, you will pass an angle tower and then arrive at the east gate. Just one guardroom with its entrance is now visible; the carriageway and the other guardroom have gone. Move on now to the fine south gate (fig. 69): both guard-chambers are excellently preserved, together with the two carriageways separated by a central pier which is pierced by a doorway. Two of the pivot-holes for hanging the gates can be seen, as well as a drain under one of the carriageways. The stone sill across the front of the

68   Chester, east entrance to the amphitheatre

69 *Brecon Gaer, the south gate*

western carriageway was inserted later when the road-level was raised. The front wall of the eastern guard-chamber was roughly repaired at the end of the third century: the tattiness of the work is in strong contrast with the fine workmanship of the rest of the masonry. Finally, you will come to the west gate, which is less well preserved but unusual in having projecting rectangular guard-chambers. Once again there are two carriageways, the central pier, and the pivot-holes for the gates. It should in theory have been the fort's main gate as the *principia* faces it, but the steepness of the slope outside probably meant that it was used less than the more accessible north gate.

At least five Roman roads centred on Brecon Gaer: (i) followed the river Usk SE to Caerleon with intermediate forts at Pen-y-Gaer (App. I), Abergavenny, and Usk (App. I); (ii) ran south to Cardiff via Pen-y-Darren (Merthyr Tydfil), Gelligaer and Caerphilly; (iii) ran SW to Neath through a fort at Coelbren (App. I); (iv) went north to Castell Collen; and (v) ran west to Llandovery and beyond. I will now describe the forts in this network where there is still something worth seeing, though the remains are hardly spectacular at any of them.

The fort at **Gelligaer** (ST 1397), on road (ii) above, lies just west of the church on the north side of the B4254. The mounds of the ramparts are mostly followed by field boundaries, except on the side nearest the road which is the most conspicuous. If you want to examine the banks in detail, ask permission at Gelligaer House (first house on the right). The fort was built in stone early in the second century (as we know from an inscription), was evacuated at the end of the century, but reoccupied from the late third to fourth centuries. The entire plan of its buildings was recovered by excavations at the close of the nineteenth century, but no stonework is visible today. On its east (right-hand side when looking from the B4254) was an annexe, also defended, which contained the regimental bath-house. The annexe stretched as far as the churchyard, but hardly any trace is visible now. This stone fort was not, however, the earliest at Gelligaer: a larger fort, with earth ramparts and timber buildings, lay on a completely different, though adjacent, site to the west, on the other side of Rectory Road. Virtually nothing is traceable of this fort on the ground today. Further north, on Gelligaer Common, five practice camps are known; two of these can be traced quite easily with the help of a 1″ OS Map (sheet 154 (new series 171), ST 1399).

The fort at **Neath** (SS 7497), the terminal point of Roman road (iii) from Brecon, was not identified until 1949, although it had long been known that the Roman NIDVM must have been at or close to the present town. The strategic importance of its position, accessible by sea, guarding an important river-crossing on the east-west coastal road, and controlling a valley which penetrates far inland, was obvious. Yet the occupation seems to have been brief: from about AD 75 for a few years, then a stone rebuilding c. 120 after a short gap, and then a final abandonment apparently about 130. Two gates (south and east) of the stone reconstruction, both with double carriageways and guardrooms, have been preserved in a housing-estate served by a road appropriately called Roman Way. To reach this from the centre of Neath, take the road to Swansea (A48). Roman Way is the first side-road on the left after the roundabout reached immediately after crossing the river.

The road running due north from Brecon Gaer (iv above) aimed for **Castell Collen** (SO 0562), which overlooks a large bend in the river Ithon just north of Llandrindod Wells. The fort-platform is reached by a road which leaves the A4081 (Llan-drindod to Rhyader) on the right, immediately after crossing the river. Follow this road as far as the red-brick farmhouse: the Roman site lies in the field beyond it. The banks and ditches of a square fort are impressively visible in their entire circuit, with an apparently isolated bank and ditch lying to the west of it (nearest the farmhouse). In fact the latter was part of the defences of an original large fort, holding an infantry garrison about 1,000 strong, which was built in turf and timber c. 75–8 and faced in stone about 140. But in the early third century the area of the fort was reduced by the building of a cross-wall, and the outer defences (the now isolated bank and ditch) were no longer used. There were further repairs to the defences in the late third century and occupation continued into the fourth, though these periods were separated by spells when the fort was empty. Some traces of the stone buildings in the centre of the fort, excavated in 1911–13, still remain, though in a very dilapidated condition. They comprise an HQ building in the centre, a granary to the north and a commandant's house to the south.

Llandrindod Wells also has the distinction of having the largest known group of military practice camps in the whole Roman Empire. The troops stationed at Castell Collen were responsible for digging, presumably at various times, no less than 18 of these small camps, roughly 100 feet square. Very little of them is left, but if you have the time or the enthusiasm, you can trace some of them on Llandrindod Common, south of the town to the west of the A483 (see bibliography). The one I found easiest to locate is reached by a lane leaving the A-road on the right, 600 yards south of a filling-station; the camp is situated on the crest of the field to the right, opposite the entrance to 'Castalia'.

The course of the Roman road running west from Brecon Gaer (v above, p. 184) is not clear until the village of Trecastle on the A40. Here you can take the minor road to the left and then after ½m branch right along a modern track which roughly follows the Roman alignment. After three miles it passes the fine Roman marching-camps of **Y Pigwn** (SN 8231), in a wild and desolate position 1,350 feet high. A less arduous approach for the motorist is from the west. Continue along the A40 for four miles beyond Trecastle and take the narrow unsignposted road on the left immediately before Halfway Inn. Keep along this for two miles, through a metal gate, past a farmhouse on the left, and up a steep twisting hill, until you reach a T-junction. Turn left here (signposted 'No Through Road') and leave your car by the farm after ½m. It is then 20 minutes' walk to the camps.

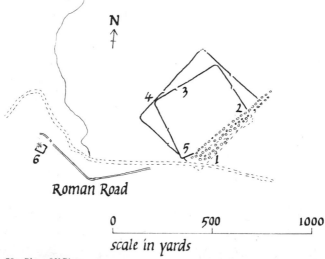

70   Plan of Y Pigwn

The camps are temporary ones belonging to the early years of
the Roman conquest and occupied at the most for a few
campaigns. There are two camps here, one inside the other (plan,
fig 70); the inner one, as will be seen, is later in date, but only by a
few years, as both must fall within the period AD 47–78. Keep
walking until you see on the left the large series of lead-working
mounds which have destroyed the south ramparts of both camps.
Leave the track at this point (1 on fig 70) and follow the north
edge of the workings for about 350 yards, looking out on the left
for the rampart of the inner camp. This can be easily spotted by
the coarser, browner grass which grows in its accompanying
ditch (2). From here, with the help of the plan, you should be able
to trace the ramparts of both camps. Their north sides are
particularly fine (over the crest and down the slope beyond), with
the north gate of the smaller camp (3) in an excellent state of
preservation, its *clavicula* boldly visible (fig. 71). Note also how
the ramparts come very close to touching at the NW corner (4).
By now your eye should be in and you will be able to see that at the
SW corner (5) the inner rampart actually projects over the line
of the outer as the former rounds the corner, and this proves that
the smaller camp was constructed after the larger one. The camps
were superseded by a permanent fortlet 500 yards to the west on
the other side of the track (6), with a superb view down towards
Llandovery, where there was a fort (App. I). The fortlet is about
120 feet square and its north corner is obscured by a low medieval
motte, but it is extremely hard to trace on the ground today.

The Roman road running NW from Llandovery passed the
site of the only known gold mine in Roman Britain, at **Dolaucothi**
(SN 6640). I mention it more for its uniqueness than for the
spectacular nature of the surviving remains, and if you want to
trace these in detail, you should read the works cited in the
Bibliography. To reach the site, which is owned by the National
Trust, take the first turning to the left after crossing the bridge at
Pumpsaint on the Lampeter-Llandovery road (A482), and then
turn left again at the crossroads. The main opencast area lies
almost immediately on the right, where camping facilities are
available. The primary interest lies in the complexity of the
Roman activity. Gold-bearing pyrites were extracted by means
of opencast workings and underground galleries, traced to a
depth of 145 feet at one point and drained by a timber water-
wheel (a fragment found here is in the National Museum at

Cardiff). Water was brought to the site by means of three aqueducts, one of them seven miles long; these were simple channels cut into the hillside. The water was used partly for washing the ore after crushing, and partly for breaking down soft beds of pyrites. Of the settlement associated with these mines little is at present known: what has been taken for a pit-head bath-house probably belonged to a fort situated under Pump-saint village, and part of this fort was excavated in 1972. Most of the visible features at Dolaucothi are probably of Roman date, though it is not yet clear to what extent nineteenth-century workings and even a brief probe in the 1930's have left their marks. After exploring the main opencast area near the camping-site, climb up to the highest part of the hill behind, passing over a fenced track en route (wooden steps provided to cross it). Here are some further mining entrances (fig 72), which are certainly Roman in date. To the right of the spot where the photograph was taken is the earth supporting-bank of a water-tank, the water here being used to wash the ore over a series of stepped washing-tables down the hillside. From this point, walk straight across the open field along the site of an aqueduct-channel now completely invisible, cross the fence at the other side by the wooden steps, and you will come at once to a large depression in the hillside. This is the tank which formed the terminal reservoir of the main aqueduct. These and other remains, which can be traced most easily in winter or early spring before they are obscured by bracken growth, give us an interesting insight into Roman industrial activity in Britain.

71   Y Pigwn; the north gate, inner camp

Our knowledge of the road-system and its accompanying
forts is less complete for North Wales than it is for the south; in
particular there is a wide area to the west and south of Chester
where there is almost a complete gap. There was a road running
west to the coast along the Upper Severn from the town at
Wroxeter, and fort-platforms are visible along this route at
Forden Gaer and Caersws (both App. I). There are also two fortlets in this part of Wales: one on a deserted hilltop at Pen-y-
crogbren and another, seven miles due south, in an isolated
position at Cae Gaer (both App. I). The earth ramparts of the
latter are impressively preserved, but as the site lies in Forestry
Commission property, prior permission to visit must be obtained.

Moving further into the NW corner of Wales, we come to an
important fort at **Tomen-y-Mur** (SH 7038), near Trawsfynydd
in Merionethshire. Even if there was nothing to see, the site
would be worth visiting for the wild beauty of its natural setting,
with superb command of the surrounding countryside in nearly
every direction. The wind usually blows here, so exposed is the
position, and we can sympathize with the soldiers whose lot it
was to serve in this remote spot. Yet its very remoteness has

72 Dolaucothi, entrances to mining tunnels

ensured the good state of preservation of the surviving earthworks, and there is much of interest. I must confess that mist and
torrential rain have twice prevented me from examining the site
in detail, but I hope that some, at least, of the surviving earthworks can be traced with the help of fig 73.

Tomen-y-Mur is reached by a minor road on the east side of
the A487 immediately south of its junction with the Ffestiniog
road (A4108) about 2½m north of Trawsfynydd village. Follow
this road until you cross a cattle-grid and you will see on your
right (A on the plan) a unique monument: it is the only known
amphitheatre attached to an auxiliary fort in Roman Britain.
The arena is now marshy and the surrounding banks are much
depleted, but its character is clear. Its primary purpose was
surely to provide amusements for the garrison of this remote
outpost, though it may have been used in military training as well.
Next make towards the fort itself (just beyond the ruined farm-
buildings), crossing on your way a gate warning against tres-
passers – so ask permission locally. The most conspicuous feature
at the fort is the large circular Norman *motte* which, as the plan
shows (B), sits on the middle of the Roman rampart belonging

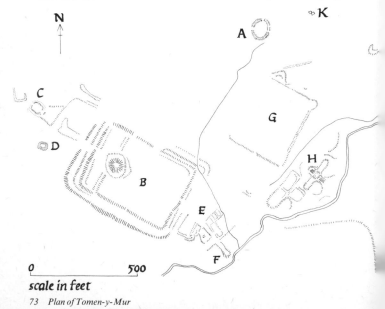

73   Plan of Tomen-y-Mur

to the second phase of the site. For here, as at Castell Collen, the original earth-and-timber fort, built by Agricola in about 78, was reduced in size at a later date. In this instance it probably occurred early in Hadrian's reign, c. 110, when the new, reduced fort was given a stone wall. No stonework is visible now, most of it having been robbed to build the many confusing field-walls here which crown the earth banks on all sides except the NW. Occupation at Tomen-y-Mur seems to have ceased about 140.

Of particular interest are the earthworks which lie outside the fort-walls, though not all of them are fully understood. About 100 yards beyond the NW gate, if you can surmount the fence in your way, can be found a small earthwork (C) with two gates and a *titulum*: it is a practice camp built by the troops as part of their training. Another earthwork to the south (D) may also be an example. SE of the fort, where the ground falls steeply towards the stream, are some stone buildings (E), now represented by a series of grass mounds about one foot high, which were explored in the nineteenth century. The fort bath-house and civil settlement lay here. A little beyond (F), is an embankment eight feet high, which formed an abutment for a wooden bridge carrying the Roman road from here to Caer Gai; the corresponding abutment on the other side has presumably been completely eroded by the stream. Between here and the amphitheatre is the parade-ground (G), now very marshy. As it was unfinished you can see the method employed in its construction: banks were made round three sides, increasing in height down the slope so that the top was level throughout. The intention was then to excavate earth just north of the area and cart it down the slope until the ground was level with the banks, but this was only half completed and so the delimiting banks and the excavation-pits to the north are still visible. Hillock (H), with flanking terraces, and earthwork (J) are both of unknown purpose. Two mounds (K), close to the amphitheatre and the start of this tour, are probably small tombs.

This, however, by no means exhausts the list of Roman earthworks in the vicinity of Tomen-y-Mur, and visitors with plenty of time may like to explore further by crossing the stream and proceeding SE on the alignment of the Roman road (set by the SE gate to the bridge abutment, F): some more disfigured mounds, probably tombs, lie 500 yards SE of the SE gate, midway between the two streams. An OS map will be needed if you want to find two practice camps further afield. Llwyn-Crwn (SH 713382)

measures about 122 by 112 feet and is two feet high in parts;
Braich-ddu (SH 717383), near a disused slate-quarry, is about 75
feet square with four gates and internal *claviculae* almost touching. Another group of five practice camps is known further east
at Doldinnas (SH 734378), but their remains are so slight that
they are almost invisible except to a trained eye.

The Roman road which passes all these earthworks was heading over the mountains for the fort at **Caer Gai** (SH 8731), which
lies at the SW corner of Bala Lake. It is reached by a farm-track
on the north side of the A494 ¾m north of Llanuwchllyn. It was
occupied in the period c. 78–125, the original turf rampart being
revetted in stone presumably at the beginning of the second
century. The garrison at this time was the First Cohort of Nervii
from Belgium, as we know from an inscription found in 1885 and
now at Cardiff. A farm obscures the northern corner (enquire
here for permission), but the earth rampart and ditch are impressive at the west and south corners and along the SW side. On the
SE, parallel to the main road, part of the Roman stone core has
been incorporated into a modern wall running the whole length
of the rampart. Two practice camps are known nearby, one of
them still visible (Pont Rhyd Sarn, App. I).

The road north from Tomen-y-Mur led to **Caerhun** (SH 7770)
in the Conway valley, after an intermediate station near Betws-y-
Coed (Bryn-y-gefeiliau, App. I). The fort at Caerhun, KANOVIVM
as we can read on a milestone in the British Museum (p. 332), is
situated 4½m due south of Conway and is reached by a lane on the
left (east) of the B5106 immediately after its junction with a minor
road to Rowaen. The lane is unsignposted but flanked by two
massive stone gate-piers. The history of the place holds some
puzzles: the usual earth-and-timber fort of c. 78 was replaced in
stone probably c. 140. The entire plan of the latter, except for the
NE corner underlying the church and churchyard, was recovered
in excavations in 1926–9. But coins, pottery and the milestone
mentioned above indicate that occupation lasted into the fourth
century, although no trace of structures of this date was found
inside the fort. All the excavations have been filled in, and only
the mound of the rampart, very well-preserved on the south
where the lane bisects it, can be seen on the site today, with
occasionally a bit of stonework peeping through the turf. If you
want to leave the lane and explore further, permission should be
obtained from the farm on the opposite side of the B-road.

A road running west from Caerhun, and another striking NW from Tomen-y-Mur, met at **Caernarvon*** (SH 4862) [AM ; S], a place of the utmost strategic importance not only in Roman times but later too, as the famous Edwardian castle at the river mouth demonstrates. The Roman name, SEGONTIVM, means 'the forceful river'. The remains of the fort lie in the outskirts of the town on the A4085 to Beddgelert. The main phases of its history were revealed in excavations of 1920–3 by Sir Mortimer Wheeler, but the precise dating of these phases is still not certain. It started life, as usual, in earth-and-timber form c. 78, probably for a part-mounted cohort 1000 strong. Stone rebuilding took place in stages during the second half of the second century – the NW gate c. 155, the other gates, the stone wall and the internal buildings somewhat later. The Twentieth Legion from Chester helped in this, bringing with it the red Cheshire sandstone. The fort was probably destroyed by a native uprising in 197 coinciding with the general unrest in Britain at the time of Albinus' revolt : an inscription in the museum refers to the rebuilding of an aqueduct 'collapsed through age', probably a euphemism for enemy destruction. The inscription also tells us that the garrison at this time was the First Cohort of Sunici from Germany. Occupation seems to have continued throughout the third and fourth centuries, with a final reconstruction after a fire, probably connected with the disaster which brought the emperor Constans to Britain in 343. The garrison was finally removed in 383 by Magnus Maximus in his attempt to become emperor.

The entrance to the site is close to the SE gate (underneath the road) and an adjoining section of fort-wall. First the excellent little museum should be visited, where the main finds from the fort are exhibited ; everything is carefully labelled and a description here is unnecessary. Leaving the museum, and keeping close to the boundary-wall skirting the reservoir, you will see the foundations of several barrack-buildings which fill up the whole of the rear portion of the fort : these consist of quarters for officers at one end and a long section, originally divided by partitions, for the men. Most of the visible masonry belongs to the fourth-century rebuilding, except for the buttressed construction half-covered by the reservoir, which is a second-century granary. Next to this are the paltry remains of the NE gate with twin roadways and guard-chambers. Following the rampart-bank from here, you round the north corner (traces of a turret) and arrive at the NW gate, which is a little confusing as it displays masonry of several periods. It started with the normal twin passages and guard-chambers, but in the fourth century the gate was reduced to a single carriageway and the other (on the left) was converted into a new guardroom; the original guard-room here was then filled up, but it has been cleared out again now. Walking in a straight line from here to the modern houses, you are on the line of the *via principalis*. The area on your right between here and the road has been excavated but is not now visible. On the left, first of all, is a long shed with a large adjoining yard – the fort's *fabrica*, or workshop. Beyond the yard is the commandant's house, as it appeared in its final fourth-century form of four ranges of rooms around a central courtyard; the far right-hand corner, however, has a few blocks of red sandstone used in the first stone building of the second century. An isolated masonry plinth in a room at the far end was perhaps the base for an altar. Finally, you come to the central building of the fort and the most interesting of all, the *principia*, or HQ. The front part consists of a courtyard, of which the well and some paving-flags are visible; the central part was a roofed assembly-hall later subdivided for office use; and the rear range consisted of five rooms (two under the modern house) of which the central one was the chapel where the military standard was kept; under it, originally vaulted, a strong-room was built in the third century with steps leading down to it (fig 74). At the same time a heated room was tacked on rather crudely at the rear. It is sometimes claimed, on the strength of an inscription (cast in museum), to be the record-office of the quartermaster. The channels for hot air to circulate below floor-level can be seen.

The rest of SEGONTIVM lies on the other side of the A4085 and although plans have been made to excavate it nothing has yet been done. The SW gate, however, is visible and can be reached by a path almost opposite the entrance to the museum. The path runs outside the fort-wall, here masked by modern refacing as far as the south angle, which displays the Roman core. Following this round, through a children's playground, you will come to the SW gate, now regrettably used as a rubbish dump.

Building operations around the fort have revealed traces of a large civilian settlement, including a temple of Mithras. None of this is now visible. There is, however, an impressive enclosure-wall known as Hen Waliau situated 150 yards west of the fort.

To reach it from the SW gate, continue along the footpath, cross the road and go down Hendre Street; then turn right at the A-road. Some of it is hidden behind houses, but a fine stretch on its south side, still standing 19 feet above Roman ground-level, can be seen in the Ministry of Health car-park adjoining the A487/A499 (to Pwllheli). A gateway, blocked up with modern material, is also visible here, but as there is no sign of gate-towers or other bastions it is best to regard this as a stores-compound rather than a late fort (it was probably built in the early third century). Even so, it reflects the growing insecurity that must have been felt at the time, an insecurity emphasized by two important additions to the Welsh defences at Holyhead and Cardiff. The forts so far described all belong to the detailed Roman plan, worked out in the first century, of garrisoning Wales by means of regularly-placed forts. The new forts, however, at Holyhead and Cardiff belong to the late third or early fourth century and were clearly designed, like the Saxon Shore forts of SE England, to combat an enemy expected from the sea, not from the Welsh mountains.

The fort at Holyhead, known as **Caer Gybi*** (SH 2482), owes its preservation to the church of St Gybi which stands inside its walls.

74 *Caernarvon, the strong-room*

Fork left for the town-centre and you will see the rebuilt south
gate on your right, by the telephone-boxes at the top of the hill.
The small cliff on which the fort stands was originally much less
steep and the walls continued down to the beach, with the shore-
side left open: it is, therefore, a defended beaching-point for the
navy using Holyhead harbour. The walls are $5\frac{1}{2}$ feet thick, built
of small stones partly laid in herringbone pattern, and still
13–15 feet high where best preserved, on the north and west sides.
Even details of the rampart-walk are clearly visible, especially on
the north when viewed from the churchyard. Four round towers
can be seen, but only that at the NW corner is substantially
Roman: the rest have suffered in various degrees from medieval
and modern rebuilding. The original entrance, on the south, is
now much obscured by later work; the gap in the north wall is not
of Roman origin. The date of Caer Gybi is not precisely known,
but it probably belongs to the late fourth century. Why other
similar structures are not known on the Welsh coasts is something
of a mystery: perhaps the copper mines of Anglesey were believed
to merit special protection.

The fort at **Cardiff Castle*** (ST 1876) is a much more massive
affair, closely similar to the Saxon Shore forts of SE England. It
was built on or near the site of an earlier fort in the late third or
early fourth century, with semi-octagonal bastions and two
single-arched gates each protected by guard-towers. It was
occupied until at least 367. The fort is particularly striking for the
reconstruction of the north, east and part of the south walls,
carried out at the turn of the century: the north gate is especially
fine (fig 75). We can thus gain a clear idea of what a Saxon Shore
fort may have looked like in the fourth century. The original
Roman facing is visible at the foot of the walls, especially on the
south; it is separated from the reconstruction above by a row of
pink stones. On the north stretch, five openings near ground-level
give a glimpse of the Roman core which lies behind. The National
Museum of Wales, which has an archaeological section, is
nearby: it is open weekdays 10 a.m.–5 p.m. (6 p.m. April–
October).

Cardiff cannot have stood alone and must have been linked
with a series of signal-posts to give warnings of imminent
pirate raids. It was designed especially to protect the civilian
population of the Glamorgan plain and the Severn estuary. Only
in this part of Wales was there the spread of romanization in the

form of towns and villas so familiar in the English lowlands. Or
rather not quite. Until 1968, Caerwent (between Newport and
Chepstow) was the only known Roman town in our area, but a
totally new light has been shed on the romanization of SW Wales
by the recent discovery of a walled town-site at **Carmarthen** (SN
4120). Presumably the Demetae, the tribe which occupied this
corner, were rewarded for a lack of resistance to Roman arms by
the creation of a tribal capital. Excavations in 1968 and following
years suggested that the town was properly laid out in the second
century, probably developing from a civilian sprawl around an
earlier fort. It was given clay-bank defences at this time, revetted
in stone at some later date. Inside were found buildings of timber

75   *Cardiff, reconstructed north gate*

and stone (including tessellated floors and hypocausts) which
continued in use to the end of the fourth century at least. The
only feature of Roman date visible today, however, is part of the
mound of the amphitheatre, situated immediately north of the
A40 in the northern outskirts of the modern town. It is reached
by an alleyway between houses, 200 yards east of the junction of
the A40 with Old Oak Lane, and close to a path leading to a
housing-estate. There is nothing exciting to see: the south bank
is much eroded, but that on the north is preserved to its original
height, and excavations in 1971 found traces of the timber beams
which supported the seating, as well as a complex drainage-
system. It is to be hoped that the Borough Council's scheme
(1971) for conserving the amphitheatre as a monument is carried
out, for it is a remarkable witness to the extent of the penetration
of Roman influence in this far corner of the province, itself so far
from the heart of the Roman Empire. The county Museum in
Quay Street also deserves a visit (Mon.–Fri. 10–1, 2–5; Sat.
10–12).

The other town at **Caerwent*** (ST 4690) [AM; A] is one of the
most impressive sites not only in this chapter but in the whole of
Roman Britain. It was VENTA SILVRVM, the market-town of the
Silures tribe which proved so hostile to successive Roman armies
in the first century. It was only a small place of 44 acres, hardly
more than what we would call a village, but it had all the usual
buildings – forum, basilica, temples and baths – that we expect of
a tribal capital. It was founded at the close of the first century and
given an earth rampart and ditch not earlier than 130. The visible
stone wall was built in the late second or early third century, and
polygonal bastions to provide extra cover were added to the
north and south walls sometime after about 340.

Your tour of the defences can conveniently begin at the 'Coach
and Horses' close to the east gate. This, like its counterpart on the
west, probably had a double carriageway and flanking towers, a
fragment of which can be seen on the south of the road. It is not
bonded with the rest of the wall and so is earlier in date – perhaps
contemporary with the earth rampart. The wall that stretches
southwards from here is on average 10 feet high, though only the
core is visible as most of the facing-stones have been robbed.
Now cross a stile and round the SE corner (the mound is a
Norman *motte*); after a short while two fences will interrupt
your path. Some wooden steps on the other side of these give

access to the top of the wall, and here, where the earth bank makes a detour, are the remains of the south gate, a single arched passageway in a fine state of preservation. The piers on either side are still complete, together with the springers and even some voussoirs of the arch. Sometime in the fourth century – a reflection of the growing troubles which had caused the new fort at Cardiff to be built – the gate was entirely blocked up (except for an opening left for drainage at the bottom), and this blocking-wall remains in position. From here you can either walk along the wall or return to ground-level to admire the superb stretch of walling and bastion which are in their best-preserved state at this point (fig 76). Note how the bastion sits up against the wall without being bonded into it. Going on you pass other bastions in varying stages of completeness; the last before the SW angle has a (blocked) postern door for defenders to slip out. Then, rounding the angle and following the west wall, you reach the modern road again and the site of the west gate.

Next, walk along the road to Pound Lane (on the left), where are the foundations of a couple of VENTA's houses. The patch of gravel nearest the wall marks the site of the Roman street, which was much wider than its modern counterpart. Its side gutter and part of the drain into which it discharged are visible. The house nearest the road started life in about AD 100 as two long buildings with shops facing the street and living-quarters behind;

76   *Caerwent, Roman town-wall and bastion*

then in the second century the east one was demolished and the
survivor was given two more wings, on the north and later on the
east, to enclose a courtyard (now buried under the adjacent
garden). Occupation continued into the fourth century when part
of it was used for iron-working. The masonry of the other house
belongs to the second quarter of the second century, but only
part of one wing, and the fragment of another peeping out from
the grass, are visible. At the end of the fourth century both houses
were taken over by squatters, who built stone hearths over the
ruined walls and dug pits into the floors.

A little further on is the war-memorial which marks the centre
of the Roman town. It stands at the SW corner of the site of the
forum and basilica, and on the other side of the street, adjacent
to the church, the public baths lie buried. The church porch
contains two Roman inscribed stones (if locked, ask at the cottage
facing the war-memorial). The larger (fig 77) is a record of a
dedication to a certain Paulinus who, having commanded the
Second Augustan Legion at Caerleon, went on to become the
governor of two of the Roman provinces of what is now France,
Narbonensis (capital at Narbonne) and Lugdunensis (Lyon). The

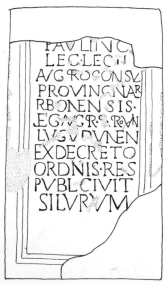

77   *Caerwent, inscription in the church*

end of the inscription reads EX DECRETO ORDINIS RES PVBL
CIVIT SILVRVM, 'by decree of the local senate (*ordo*) the
Community of the Silures (set this up)'. It is an interesting
illustration of the machinery of self-government accorded to the
tribal system in Britain, a system which Rome allowed to
continue in a new romanized form. The other stone is a dedication
to Mars Ocelus, a war-god.

Apart from the houses mentioned above, the only other
Roman building at present exposed within the walls is the little
temple of the normal Romano–Celtic type with the central shrine
(here with an apse) and surrounding ambulatory. It lies, over-
looked by caravans, on the left of the modern road as you return
towards the 'Coach and Horses', and is reached through a large
iron gate opposite the bus-stop.

Visitors may now like to return to their cars and, coming back
to the war-memorial, take the right fork out towards the by-pass.
Before joining the latter, turn right to the Northgate Inn and you
will see, obscured by flower-pots, the structure of the north gate.
It is very similar to the better-preserved south gate, with late
blocking-wall and some voussoirs of the right-hand arch still
visible. Of the rest of the north wall, quite a lot can be seen
running along the back gardens of private houses. More
accessible is a well-preserved bastion near the NW corner (being
excavated in 1972), and the foundations of three more emerging
from the grass on the NE. Finds from Caerwent are in the
Newport Museum (weekdays 10–5.30).

Apart from a few farms around Caerwent and a scattering of
villas on the Glamorgan plain, civilian life continued in Wales in
much the same way as it had before the Roman conquest. There
is, therefore, a whole host of native sites built or adapted in the
Roman period which could be mentioned. In contrast to southern
Britain, many pre-Roman hill-forts continued to be occupied and
even re-fortified. The most famous and impressive is **Tre'r Ceiri**
(SH 3744) in the Lleyn peninsula. It is approached by a public
footpath signposted on the right of the B4417, 1m SW of
Llanaelhaern (on the A499). It is an exhausting climb, 900 feet
or so above the road. The path enters the enclosure by its SW
entrance, which has traces of external bastions on each side. The
whole girdle of its dry-stone walls is still in an amazing state of
preservation, 13 feet high on the outer face. The wall-walk is still
visible in the best-preserved stretches on the north and west.

There are traces too of an additional wall built further down the slope on the north and west sides where the approach is the least difficult. Inside are about 150 huts of various shapes and sizes, some circular, some D-shaped, some rectangular, many with subdivisions. Undivided circular huts are probably the earliest and some may be pre-Roman. The few objects found indicate that the main occupation was from about AD 150–400. The walls clearly owe something to the Roman model of defences, but they were not as strong: they could have kept brigands out, but not the Roman army, should they have been turned to such a use. Two Anglesey hill-forts also have stone ramparts erected during the Roman period: Caer y Twr on Holyhead Mountain (SH 218830) [AM; A], and Din Sylwy in the NE corner of the island (SH 5881). You will need an OS map if you wish to find them.

But not all the native inhabitants lived on hill-tops during the Roman period: open villages of circular or rectangular huts also occur, often in large groups. Again there are many of these, and three Anglesey examples [all AM; A] will have to suffice. Twenty huts are still visible of a settlement occupied from the second to fourth centuries on the SW slope of **Holyhead Mountain** (SH 212820). A rectangular and a circular hut inhabited in the third century were found at **Caer Leb** (SH 4767) in 1866; the double banks which surrounded them are still very prominent, on the left-hand side of the first road on the right of the A4080, west of Bryn-Siencyn. The third site is **Din Lligwy** (SH 4986), which is signposted from the Llanallgo roundabout (junction of the A5025 with the A5108 to Moelfre). This charming site is the fortified residence of (probably) a native chieftain, and consists of two circular and four rectangular huts enclosed by stone walls in the shape of a pentagon. The buildings still stand to a maximum height of six feet, and appear to have been built in the late fourth century. It is a far cry from the civilized luxury of the villas of southern Britain.

Chapter 7

The Pennines and the Lakes

Cumberland, Durham (except South Shields), Lancashire,
Northumberland (south of Hadrian's Wall), Westmorland and
Yorkshire

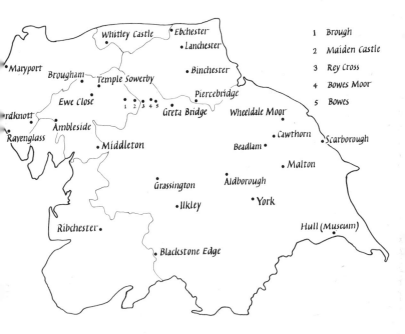

Nearly the whole of the large area covered by this chapter was
inhabited by the Brigantes before the Roman conquest. Their
queen, Cartimandua, was friendly towards the new invaders,
but she ruled uneasily and civil war broke out on a number of
occasions. This resulted in the first official Roman contact with
the north of England, for in 48, c. 57 and 69, Roman arms came
to the help of the queen. The last of these interventions was only
moderately successful, and Tacitus pithily comments: 'the throne
was left to Venutius, the war to us.' Venutius was the divorced
husband of Cartimandua. In AD 71, therefore, the new governor
of Britain, Petillius Cerialis, took the Ninth Legion from Lincoln

and advanced northwards, bent on final conquest. It was in this year or the next that the huge native fortress of Stanwick was taken and stormed. A small section of its stone wall and ditch has been restored [AM; A], part of a circuit which in its final phase enclosed some 600 acres. The site lies close to the hamlet of Forcett, 2m SW of Piercebridge and about 5m NW of Scotch Corner on the A66.

The founding of the legionary fortress for the Ninth at **York*** (SE 6052) is usually attributed to Cerialis in 71. Other large sites, however, suitable for at least half a legion, are known at Malton and at Rossington near Doncaster, and so it is unlikely that the Ninth was brought together in the full legionary fortress at York before the governorship of Agricola (AD 78–85). There was, however, almost certainly a smaller fort on the site under Cerialis or even earlier, but its dimensions are unknown.

From the end of the first century onwards, York was the military capital of Britain and the hub of the northern fort-system. The Agricolan rampart of clay and turf with timber breastwork and towers was rebuilt in stone in AD 107–8. This we know from an inscription which also records the last appearance in Britain of *Legio* IX *Hispana*. Soon afterwards it was transferred to the East where it was disbanded after a disaster sometime before AD 165. Its place at York was taken by the Sixth Legion Victrix, which came to Britain in 122.

The next rebuilding of the defences occurred in the early third century. The weak foundations of the wall of 107–8 had caused partial collapse, and total rebuilding on a more imposing scale was necessary. This work was carried out either by the emperor Severus, who died in York in 211, or by his son Caracalla (emperor 211–7). Further reconstruction was done by Constantius I after barbarian destruction in 296. The east corner of the fortress remained untouched, but the whole of the river front was given a grandiose series of polygonal towers. This was clearly designed to impress, and the elaboration may be connected with the new commander of land forces in Britain, the *Dux Britanniarum*, whose headquarters it was. Constantius died in York in 306, and his son, the famous Constantine the Great, was proclaimed emperor here. The Constantian rebuilding remained the basis of York's defences until the Danes built an earth bank and stockade in the late ninth century. Various repairs and additions were made in the interim period, including the so-

78   *York, fortress-wall near Multangular Tower*

called 'Anglian' Tower (see below).

Of the buildings inside this great legionary fortress of
EBVRACVM, little is known except for an internal bath-house and
the headquarters building, both described below. But York was
more than a military centre in Roman times. The civil settlement
which grew up and flourished on the south bank of the Ouse was
given walls of its own, and acquired the honorary status of *colonia*
in the third century. From 208–11 it was the seat of the Imperial
Court while Severus and Caracalla were engaged on their
Scottish campaigns, and in 213, when Britain was divided into
two provinces, it became the capital of *Britannia Inferior*.
Unfortunately, very little is known about the town's buildings,
but objects found there are displayed in the Museum.

This Museum, and the most spectacular portion of the
fortress' defences, are to be found in the public gardens on the
north side of the river. To the right of the main entrance (near
Lendal Bridge), under a stone archway, are several Roman
coffins, and the conduit-head of a public water-supply found in
the *colonia*. Nearby, the foundations of a polygonal bastion
emerge from the grass: it was one of the series added to the
fortress on this side c. AD 300. From here onwards, shrouded by
trees, is a superb stretch of the fourth-century fortress-wall,
standing virtually to wall-walk height with all its facing stones
and a row of bonding-bricks intact (fig 78). The stretch ends at
the west corner of the 50-acre fortress, known as the Multangular
Tower and one of the best-preserved Roman structures in Britain.
Parts of the exterior have been patched with later material, but
the join between the Roman work and the top 11 feet of medieval
masonry is obvious. Before going inside the walls it is convenient
to visit the archaeological Museum which lies in the gardens
nearby. This collection is one of the richest in the country, and it
must be hoped that a new building can be raised soon to give the
material the presentation it deserves.

The main museum (10–5, Sun. 1–5) contains the most
important finds. In the entrance-hall is a statue of Mars and two
reconstructed panels of wall-plaster from Catterick. In the chief
Roman room the important items to notice are: the stone head
of Constantine the Great, twice life-size (right-hand long wall);
the King's Square inscription in the middle of the left-hand long
wall, which dates the first stone fortress to 107–8 (note the fine
quality of the lettering); below this inscription is a dedication

recording a temple of the Egyptian god Serapis (the temple itself has not been found); and finally, the tombstone on one of the short walls. The most interesting (fig 79) portrays the Augustinus family – mother and father and two sons, all wearing cloaks. The inscription records that both boys died before the age of two, and so the carving represents them a little too old. There are more, equally interesting, exhibits in the museum annexe, the 'Hospitium', which is situated nearby. This is dark, dusty and overcrowded. A coffin on the ground floor, in the middle of the left-hand wall, reads, touchingly: 'For Simplicia Florentina, a most innocent soul, who lived 10 months, Felicius Simplex, her father, of the Sixth Legion Victrix, made this.' Upstairs are some dull mosaics and smaller finds. One is the rare and fascinating survival of a young girl's hair, found in a lead coffin under the Station in 1875.

Now you should return to the Multangular Tower, pass through the narrow gate beside it and so enter the Roman

79 York, tombstone of Augustinus
and his family

80 York, fortress-wall from
Anglian to Multangular Towers

legionary fortress. The interior of the bastion can be seen to be in a fine state of preservation, 19 feet high. Scaffolding holes, an internal partition-wall, Roman coffins and the medieval apertures above are all very clear. On the left of the Tower is an oven-base, excavated in 1925 under the Public Library and reset here. Its floor contained one tile stamped *Leg.IX Hisp.*, and so it is presumably of first-century date. Beyond is the inside face of wall noted earlier. To the right of the Multangular Tower is another fine stretch of fourth-century curtain-wall, excavated in 1969–70. First, walk along by the rough inside face which would have been covered by an earth bank. (The wall on the right is of thirteenth-century date.) Half-way along are the fragmentary remains of an interval-tower, which is believed from the different quality of the masonry to belong to an earlier phase of the defences, of either the second or the third century. Then comes the peculiar 'Anglian' tower, a barrel-vaulted structure built of roughly-dressed stones to fill a breach in the Roman wall. It is unique in Britain and probably in Europe, and it cannot be dated more closely than AD 400–870. Some believe that it is late-Roman, others that it was part of the reorganization of the defences in the seventh century. Beyond, the fine sequence of rampart-banks behind the wall has been carefully displayed – four successive levels from Roman to medieval. Finally, you can go through the Anglian Tower to examine the outer face of the fourth-century wall. Not all of it has been exposed: more lies beneath the path.

Leave the gardens near the Public Library, turn left, and then left again at the traffic-lights. Another fragment of fourth-century wall lies near the bus-shelter on the left. Once again only the top portion is visible, and excavation in 1835 and 1928 showed that another 11 feet lie buried below ground-level. It is worth climbing the mound here for a splendid view of the long stretch of Roman wall already described, from the Anglian to the Multangular Towers (fig 80). Now cross the road and climb the steps to the top of Bootham Bar, which sits on the site of the Roman NW gate (a fragment of it is preserved in a room below the public lavatory; write to the Museum if you are interested). From here you should walk along the walls as far as Monk Bar, following the line of the Roman defences all the way, and passing over the site of the NE gate. Descend to street-level at Monk Bar and cross to the yard opposite to see a long stretch of Roman defences, including an interval-tower and the east angle tower. These are a century

earlier than the remains so far described, as they belong to the
early third-century rebuilding which was untouched in the
Constantian reorganization. This corner tower is on a much
smaller scale and does not project from the wall. The clay lump
in the bottom is part of the bank of the first-century legionary
fortress and is thus the oldest portion of EBVRACVM still on show.
The foundations of the first stone tower, on a slightly different
alignment, were also found during excavations in 1926. In front,
the Roman curtain-wall still stands to a spectacular height of
16 feet, and even the moulded slab on which the parapet rested
survives. The masonry is similar to the fourth-century work, but
there are no brick bonding-courses, and the inner side is properly
faced even where it would have been covered by rampart-mound.
One of the stones on the outer face of the wall at the corner tower
still bears an inscription COH X recording that the tenth cohort
(of the Sixth Legion) built this section of wall.

Now retrace your steps to Monk Bar. Turn left and then right
down Ogleforth. Past a corner the Treasurer's House will be seen
on the right (daily Apr.–Oct., 10.30–6). Here an isolated Roman
column-base is preserved *in situ*, together with part of a Roman
street-surface. You have now arrived at the Minster and the site
of the *Principia*, the Headquarters Building. Until 1966, when it
was announced that the Minster was in serious danger of collapse,
virtually nothing was known about the Roman building, but
excavations carried out during the strengthening of the Minster's
fabric have revealed a great deal, and some Roman walling has
been preserved *in situ* in the magnificently-displayed Undercroft,
opened in 1972. Most of the excavated remains are of fourth-
century date, including several column-bases belonging to the
great cross-hall. One of these, 22 feet long and three feet in
diameter, was found virtually complete, and it has been re-erected
opposite the south door of the Minster. What is particularly
interesting is the date at which it fell: pottery sealed beneath the
destruction rubble of the Roman cross-hall indicates that these
columns were still standing in the ninth century, 400 years after
the Sixth Legion had left York. Detailed description of the
remains displayed in the Undercroft is unnecessary, as labels
indicate how the various walls fit into the plan of the HQ. One
special exhibit, however, must be mentioned. An administrative
room added at the back of the building in the fourth century had
decorated walls, and the surviving fragments have now been

reassembled to form one of the best and largest examples of Roman painted plaster in Britain. High up on the left is a superb theatrical mask, in centre-left birds are depicted; at top right even a window-light survives, and further to the right is a male human figure. The rest is filled up with architectural details and abstract panels in brilliant colour.

Before this museum was opened, only a solitary Roman column-base was visible inside the Minster. This can still be seen in the Old Crypt, on application to a verger. It must belong to a building north of the HQ.

The only other Roman structure at present (1972) visible within the fortress is the bath-house in St Sampson's Square. Leave the Minster by the west door and go down Minster Gates opposite (this and Stonegate follow the line of a Roman street). Turn left at Low Petergate and right at the traffic-lights along Church Street. The remains are preserved beneath 'Roman Bath Inn', and the main feature, the *pilae*-bases of a large apse forming part of the *caldarium*, is now visible through a glass panel in the Saloon Bar. If the landlord is not busy you may be allowed to see the remains at close-quarters. Part of the tiled cold plunge-bath belonging to the *frigidarium* has also been preserved (far right-hand corner). Excavations in 1930–1 established a fourth-century date for the bath-house, but what earlier building occupied the site is unknown.

In November 1972, part of the sewer-system which served the fortress was discovered on a building-site at the corner of Swinegate and Church Street. This structure, some 4–5 feet high and excellently preserved, was traced for over 150 feet. At the time of writing, the developers propose to leave a trap-door in the basement of the new building to allow access to this splendid monument of Roman hygiene; but visits will only be permitted if prior arrangements have been made, in writing, with the Museum.

Apart from a fragment of wall-core visible in the cellar of the Yorkshire Insurance Company's building in Lendal, no other remains of the fortress are now visible (but see p. 360). Of the town across the river, nothing has been preserved *in situ*, except for an uninteresting stone wall probably of Roman date incorporated in the base of a modern wall in Carrs Lane (off Bishophill Senior opposite Victor Street). Of scraps not *in situ* a column-base kept at the back of Holy Trinity Church, Micklegate, a tombstone in St Martin's Church (also Micklegate), and the tombstone of Baebius Crescens, a soldier of the Sixth, in the Mount School (off The Mount), may be mentioned. A unique burial-bault with coffin and skeleton still in position exists under 104, The Mount, but it is bricked up and inaccessible to visitors.

The legionary soldiers based at York were responsible for digging, as part of their training, two series of practice camps in Yorkshire. The first, a couple of camps on Bootham Stray 1½m north of the fortress, has been largely obliterated, but the camps at **Cawthorn** (SE 7890) are the best-preserved examples of their type in Britain. You are urged, however, to visit the site in winter or early spring, as all the camps except D (plan, fig 81) were totally obscured by luxuriant bracken growth when I was there in August 1972. The path I followed then through the bracken is marked by the dotted line on the plan. Turn off the A170 at Wrelton, 2m west of Pickering, signposted Cropton, Harcoft and Rosedale. Then turn right at the end of Cropton village, signposted 'Cawthorn 2'. Keep going until you reach a T-junction at the end of this road, where you should turn right. The track you want is the second on the left after the turning to Keldy; it is a well-defined one between a break in the trees (no signpost). This leads to the south gate of D, the best-preserved of the four camps. The south rampart and double ditches separated by a flat mound are especially fine. The polygonal shape of the next camp, A, is unusual. The rampart is slight and interrupted by three gates on

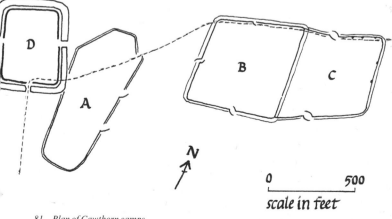

the east side, two with external *claviculae*. After a gap comes camp
B. Its rampart is still 10 feet above the bottom of the ditch outside.
From here its superb command of the North York Moors can
be appreciated. Finally comes camp C, which was tacked onto B
but had ramparts of only half the scale. Excavation has revealed
that the camps are of two different periods, about AD 90 and AD
100. They are the work of the Ninth Legion, as one of the finds
implies the presence of a *ballista*, not used by auxiliary soldiers
at this time. These troops came here to practise the building not
of camps but of forts, for the form and substantial nature of B
and D are not characteristic of temporary works (cf. D with
Hod Hill). In phase I they threw up camp A to protect their tents
and baggage while they were engaged on constructing B. In phase
II, the new troops demolished the east rampart of B and modified
its gates to provide both internal and external *claviculae*, and then
tacked on C. Then, while occupying both camps B and C, they
set about building the substantial camp D, the ditches of which
cut through the rampart of A at one point and so prove that D is
later than A.

The site at Cawthorn lies on a Roman road known as Wade's
Causeway, which ran from Malton to Whitby. Wade is a giant in
local legends and he is alleged to have built the causeway for his
wife who kept cattle on the moor. A 1¼-mile stretch of this road
has been excavated and preserved on **Wheeldale Moor*** (SE
8097) [AM ; A] and is the most impressive piece of original
Roman highway in Britain (fig 82). From Goathland, a village
west of the A169 (Pickering-Whitby), take the road leading
southwards and then follow the AM signs: you have the choice
of walking to one end of the exposed sector, or taking your car
by a very roundabout route to the other end. The present uneven
appearance of the road is misleading: the large slabs which form
the most impressive part of the remains were only intended to act
as the foundation layer for a final surface of gravel or small
stones, long since washed away. In places kerb-stones still
remain, and there are several drainage-culverts with large
cover-stones, particularly near the eastern end of the exposed
stretch.

The road on Wheeldale Moor headed southwards for the fort
at **Malton** (SE 7971), DERVENTIO. This was a very large fort (8½
acres), but little of it remains. From the centre of Malton take the
Scarborough road, and where it makes a 90° turn to the right,

keep straight on (signposted 'No Through Road'). The fort lies
in the field on the left where this road ends. Take the right-hand
footpath, which passes the east corner of the fort. The NE
rampart-mound is well preserved, the SE one less so. The fort
was occupied from c. AD 79 (Agricolan) to the end of the fourth
century, with rebuilding in stone c. 108 and 180. Excavation has
also revealed a very large semi-permanent fortress of at least 22
acres beneath and beyond the fort, and this was probably the base
for half the Ninth Legion in the campaigns of Petillius Cerialis
c. 71–2. Outside the fort was a substantial civil settlement, with
stone buildings, partly excavated in 1949–52 in advance of hous-
ing development. Finds from the area are displayed in the Roman
Malton Museum (daily, except Thurs., 2–4), which lies in the
town-centre opposite the church, to the left of the Milton Rooms.

Several Roman roads radiated from York. The east-coast road
via Malton and Wheeldale Moor has been mentioned. South-
westwards a road ran across the Pennines to Manchester (App. I);
en route the fort-platform at Castleshaw (also App. I) is still
visible. From Tadcaster, 10m SW of York, another road headed
towards Ribchester on the western trunk-road, passing through
forts at Ilkley and Elslack (App. I). **Ilkley** (SE 1148), probably the
Roman OLICANA, has a small museum, and a section of stone
fort-wall is also visible. The Manor House Museum (daily,

82   Wheeldale Moor, Roman road

except Mon., 2–5; May–Sept., 10.30–12.30 as well), is situated on
the north side of the A65 (Skipton Road), next to the church by
the traffic-lights in the centre of the town. Inside are two interesting tombstones, one showing a seated woman with long tresses,
the other (uninscribed) portraying a man, his wife and their little
boy. Behind the museum, and always accessible, is part of the
fort's west wall, four feet high, including the NW corner. The
fort was founded by Agricola c. 80, evacuated peacefully c. 120,
reoccupied in the middle of the second century, and destroyed in
197. The first stone wall and stone internal buildings were then
erected, in the early third century. At first the stone wall had a
clay bank behind it, but in fourth-century alterations it was made
free-standing as it is today. The second-century garrison was
part-mounted, probably the second cohort of Lingones from
east France.

A branch-road joined Ilkley with Manchester, and part of it,
on **Blackstone Edge** near Rochdale (SD 9616), is remarkable for
being paved with large stone setts. This fine monument, unique in
Britain, deserves better treatment than it has received, for some of
the stones have been ripped up by vandals and much of it is
obscured by vegetation. 1m east of Littleborough the A58 makes
a large U-bend. At the bottom of the U, as the road swings due
north, a public footpath is signposted to the right (east) of the
road and a light-green strip can be seen going straight up the
moorland to the top of the hill. It is near the top that the stone
paving becomes visible, 16 feet wide, with a central groove (fig 83).
This is much worn, presumably by the brake-pole of carts as
they tried to descend the hill without going out of control. At
the top, where the road becomes level, the central slab flattens
out. Not surprisingly, the steepness of the gradient was found to
be impractical, for it was bypassed in later Roman times by a road
of normal construction. This is now visible as a light-green zig-
zag to the north of the paved section.

As mentioned above, the east-west road on which Ilkley stood
was heading for **Ribchester** (SD 6535), the BREMETENNACVM of
the Romans and now a village on the B6245 6m north of Black-
burn. The main item of interest here is the little museum near the
church (weekdays 2–5 or 5.30; closed on Fridays in Sep., Nov.,
and Feb.–Apr.; closed entirely Dec. and Jan.). This is crammed
full of inscriptions, reliefs and other smaller material. Outstanding is the pedestal in the centre, which bears reliefs of Apollo

and two female figures and an inscription to the god recording
both the name of the fort (BREMETENN) and its garrison, a regiment
of Sarmatian horsemen from the Danube. The inscription also
mentions the emperor Gordian, thus dating the stone to AD
238–44. Nearby is a late-first or early second-century tombstone
with a cavalryman riding down his barbarian foe. In the annexe
at the back are some more inscriptions, including one with fine
lettering in honour of Caracalla and his mother Julia Domna.
His brother Geta was murdered in 212 and that name has been
erased at the bottom of the stone. The most beautiful find from
Ribchester is now one of the treasures of the British Museum: it
is the decorated cavalry parade-helmet, of which there is a replica
at the site.

In the garden at the back of the museum are the front ends of
two of the fort's granaries, probably of third-century date in
their present form. They are buttressed, as usual, and both have
loading-platforms outside (on the right). The granary nearer the
path is the smaller of the two and its floor was supported by the
large blocks visible in the middle. That beyond is divided into
two parts by a middle wall. Under the flower-bed further away

83   Blackstone Edge, Roman road

is the site of the north gate. The rest of the fort still lies buried, or rather the part spared by the river Ribble, which has removed the whole of the SE corner and the south and east gates. The earliest fort of turf and timber was presumably founded by Agricola c. AD 78, and this was rebuilt in stone under Trajan in the early second century, and at least twice repaired. Occupation continued to the end of the fourth century. The first garrison, recorded on an altar in the museum, was a cavalry regiment of Asturians from Spain. The third-century garrison of Sarmatians has already been mentioned.

The two other visible relics of BREMETENNACVM are hardly worth seeing. Leave the museum and turn right along the river bank. On the right is a long holly bush, and adjoining this at the far end, almost hidden by shrubbery, is a Roman well *in situ*. This was in the courtyard of the CO's house. If you want to see the overgrown remains of the bath-house situated outside the fort, turn right at 'The White Bull' along Water Street and then right along Greenside. Ask for permission at the house on the right behind white metal gates, as the bath lies in its back garden.

The Roman trunk-road to the north from York is still largely followed by the A1, which passes by or through the Roman towns at Aldborough (see below) and Catterick (App. I). At Scotch Corner, then as now, the road splits. The left fork heads over the Stainmore Pass and is described below, while the right-hand fork made for Corbridge and Hadrian's Wall via forts at Piercebridge, Binchester, Lanchester and Ebchester, all in County Durham. At each of these forts stone remains are visible today.

Piercebridge (NZ 2115) lies on B6275 7m north of Scotch Corner. Turn off in the village just north of the church along a short track, and then walk through a farmyard on the left between two barns. The NE corner of the fort, excavated in 1934, has been left exposed in the field beyond. The fort-wall can be seen turning the corner. Note in particular its thickness and the superbly-cut plinth and facing-blocks. The circular structure built into the rampart on the east side is a medieval kiln. More impressive is the very well-preserved sewer, one side of which stands over seven feet high. The building erected over it, of which foundations and a doorway are visible, was clearly the fort's latrine. Pottery found here and elsewhere in the village indicates that this fort was a totally new foundation of c. AD 300 and formed part of the reorganization of the British defences by the emperor

84 *Binchester, hypocaust flue-tiles*

Constantius. Its exceptionally large size (nearly 11 acres)
indicates the importance of the position, and it is inconceivable
that such a site was not defended in earlier centuries. The
preceding fort, presumably Agricolan and/or Hadrianic,
probably lay in the field to the east, straddling the Roman road
which bypassed the visible fort. This road crossed the Tees by a
timber bridge carried on stone piers, and some of the piers, the
south abutment and the paved river-bed, were found and
excavated in 1972. The remains are in a good state of preservation,
buried in silt left by the river which has now shifted course. The
site will be preserved as an Ancient Monument, but it is not
expected to be accessible to the public before 1975 or 6. It lies on
the south bank of the river, close to the point where B6275 makes
a right-angled bend to join the Roman alignment.

The next fort to the north is **Binchester** (NZ 2131). This was
the Roman VINOVIA, meaning 'the pleasant spot'. From the
centre of Bishop Auckland, take the Durham road (A689) and
then turn immediately left by 'The Sportsman' along a minor
road signposted 'Newfield 3'. Follow this for about one mile,
and stop at the top of the hill. Opposite the farm, on the left of
the road, is a bungalow, where you should ask permission to
visit, for the key and for directions. The east and north ramparts
are very prominent as earth mounds in the field north of the farm
(through the red iron gate); and behind the farm is a modern shed
covering a superb hypocaust, one of the best-preserved and most
instructive examples in Britain. The concrete floor of one room
is still in position, and the wall-flues for the escaping heat can be
seen round the edges (fig 84). Underneath this floor, in perfect
condition, are 88 *pilae* of Roman tiles partially blackened by the
heat. Some of the larger tiles supporting the floor are stamped
N CON, for *N*(*umerus*) *Con*(*cangiensium*), the name of the unit
which made them. Three fine arches, two perfectly preserved,
allowed the heat to circulate in the adjoining room (fig 85). The
centre arch and the floor of this adjoining room appear still
intact in a drawing made when the building was first found in the
early nineteenth century. The destruction was reputedly caused
by later explorers who expected to find buried treasure underneath and ripped down the centre arch in their desire for quicker
access. Further digging was done in 1878–80 and 1964, and the
hut was put up in 1969. The hypocaust lies within the area of the
fort, and may be part of the baths in the commanding officer's

house. Binchester was a cavalry fort, founded by Agricola,
evacuated in the early second century and reoccupied about 160.
To the south lay an extensive civil settlement.

The next fort, **Lanchester** (NZ 1546), was built under Lollius
Urbicus c. AD 140 at a period when both Ebchester to the north
and Binchester to the south were empty. It was designed to hold a
nominal garrison of 1,000 men. Towards the end of the second
century this was a Spanish cohort of Vardulli, who had the
exceptional honour of being Roman citizens. Evacuated from
about 196, it was reoccupied under Gordian (emperor 238–44),
as two fine building-inscriptions now in the Durham Cathedral
collection attest. Its garrison at this time was a cohort of Lingones
500 strong, reinforced by a unit of Suebians, who dedicated an
altar to their Germanic goddess Garmangabis. This now stands
in the south porch of Lanchester church. To reach the site of the
fort, which lies 8m NW of Durham, leave the A691 in Lanchester
and take the B6296 for Wolsingham. At the top of the hill, bordering the left-hand side of the road, you will see a long stretch of
stone core belonging to the north wall of LONGOVICIVM. No
facing-stones survive, but the stone core of the walls is visible

85   *Binchester, hypocaust arches and* pilae

round nearly the entire circuit. In places it still stands six feet high. Inside the fort the only feature is a nettle-filled hollow showing some pieces of stonework, possibly part of the commandant's house. Virtually no trace remains of the two aqueduct-channels which brought water from the north-west. As so often with Roman forts, the superb position, commanding land in all directions, cannot fail to be noticed.

Between here and Corbridge there was a small fort on the Derwent at **Ebchester** (NZ 1055), the Roman VINDOMORA and now a village on the A694 12m SW of Newcastle. A clay-and-timber fort of Agricolan date (c. AD 80) was rebuilt in stone in the early second century, abandoned in 140, and then reoccupied from about 163 to the close of the fourth century, with at least one major rebuilding, c. 300. The only visible relic at the site is a hypocaust in an apse-shaped room; it was probably part of the bath-suite in the commandant's house. The stone *pilae* and walls of this are still three feet high. We owe their preservation to the generous action of Mr Dodds of Mains Farm, who found the remains in 1962 when digging near his barn. Subsequent excavation showed that the hypocaust went out of use and was filled with debris at the end of the third century. Mr Dodds also maintains a little museum in a shed nearby. To reach the spot, turn off the main road by the bus-shelter near the church. Mains Farm is the first house on the left after the corner bungalow. There are a few Roman stones in the church porch.

The Roman road which swung west at Scotch Corner headed over the Stainmore Pass for the Eden Valley. Closely followed by the A66, it still forms one of the major east-west highways in North Britain. The route is littered with Roman earthworks, and I will describe them in the order in which they occur when approached from the east, and not in strict chronological sequence. For the first eleven miles the A66 is dead straight and follows the Roman alignment. The first change in direction occurs at **Greta Bridge** (NZ 0813), where a fort was situated. Turn off the A66 at the Morritt Arms Hotel, which sits on its north defences, along the road to Brignal. The conspicuous remains of the earth rampart-mound and double ditches which formed the southern defences of MAGLONA are visible in the first field on the left. Virtually no excavation has been done here, and the length of occupation is unknown.

Only $5\frac{1}{2}$ miles further west is the fort at **Bowes** (NY 9913), the

Roman LAVATRAE. This guarded the eastern end of the Stainmore Pass, as did the Norman Castle which obliterates the NW angle of the fort. The churchyard occupies the NE corner, and a cemetery the eastern half, but the rampart-mound of its south and west sides (in the field south of the castle) are still well preserved. Note in particular the drop in the cemetery wall where it crosses the south rampart. Excavations here in 1966–7 revealed that the original rampart raised by Agricola c. AD 78 consisted of huge river-boulders set in clay with a rear revetment of turf and a front revetment of timber. In the second century a subsequent clay rampart was cut back to receive a stone wall, later replaced by a second wall nearly eight feet thick which was crudely repaired in the fourth century. Near the cemetery wall, outside the fort, a large hollow showing odd pieces of stonework marks the site of the bath-house, plundered in the nineteenth century. An inscription now at Cambridge records that this building, *vi ignis exustum*, 'burnt by the violence of fire', was restored in the governorship of Virius Lupus (AD 197–202), when a cavalry squadron of Spanish Vettones was the garrison at Bowes. By 208 this had been replaced by the first cohort of Thracians from Bulgaria, who erected a dedication-slab to the emperor Severus and his sons Caracalla and Geta. This can be seen, poorly lit and nearly illegible, in the north transept of Bowes church. The name of Geta, as usual, had been scrubbed out after his murder. Some traces of the aqueduct-channel which brought water to the fort from the NW can be located with the help of a detailed map (see article cited in the Bibliography).

One of the few spare-time pursuits open to an officer serving in such a distant outpost of the Empire must have been hunting, and it was no doubt to appease the local moorland god that two rustic shrines were built in a wild and desolate spot, a couple of miles south of the fort, on the west bank of the East Black Sike near its confluence with the Eller Beck. One was rectangular and the other, 25 yards to the south, was circular. In them were found altars dedicated to the god Vinotonus, equated with the Roman god of hunting and woodland, Silvanus. The best-preserved, erected by the commander of the First Thracian Cohort, Caesius Frontinus, who came from Parma in North Italy, is now displayed behind the ticket-counter in the Bowes Museum at Barnard Castle (10–4, 5 or 5.30; Sun. 2–4 or 5). Very little can be

seen at the site today, and I have therefore listed it in Appendix I;
but the walk across Scargill Moor to find it is a splendid one, and
a feeling of the past will not be difficult to capture on this high
and windy moor where little has changed since Roman times.

The next fort west of Bowes was at Brough, 13 miles away on
the other side of the Stainmore Pass. In between was a series of
signal-towers designed to transmit messages by semaphore. They
may be part of a larger system, perhaps from the headquarters of
Hadrian's Wall near Carlisle to the military capital at York, but
only in moorland such as here do earthworks escape from the
cultivation which has obliterated them elsewhere. The most
accessible of these signal-posts is on **Bowes Moor** (NY 9212), 4m
west of Bowes and a short distance east of Bowes Moor Hotel.
Look out for a P-sign and the most easterly of three circular
litter-bins on the south side of the A66: the signal-station is
situated on the *other* side of the road between these two markers,
25 yards north of the fence. The remains consist of a turf rampart,
10 feet thick, and a V-shaped ditch outside it. The upcast from
the latter formed a lesser mound on the outer lip of the ditch and
this is clearly visible on the north, the best-preserved side of the
signal-station. There is an entrance on the side facing the road.
Inside the enclosure there would have been a timber tower. To the
west the outlook is very fine, and you may be able to spot a slight
pimple on the skyline. This is the signal-station of Roper Castle,
very similar to that on Bowes Moor. It can be found with the
help of a 1″ OS map, after a long climb over boggy ground
(App. I). Eastwards from the Bowes Moor post the view to
LAVATRAE is blocked by a low spur, from which another signal-
station, not now visible on the ground, relayed messages to the
fort.

Nearly 2m further west is the summit of the Stainmore Pass
(1,468 feet), and the remains of the best-preserved marching
camp in Britain, at **Rey Cross** (NY 9012). Stop in the parking-
place on the left (south) of the road, where the Cross is railed off
and labelled with an AM sign. Go back to the P-sign, where there
is a gate in the fence, and then walk due south to the edge of the
ravine. In doing so you will pass through the more easterly of the
two south gates, and from here, with the help of the plan (fig 86),
you will be able to trace the entire outline of this magnificent
earthwork. Limestone quarrying has removed the southern half
of the western defences, and this accounts for the confusing

unevenness of the terrain here, while part of the northern
rampart has slipped into the bog. Elsewhere it is traceable by the
lighter colour of the grass and the boldness of the rampart, 20
feet wide and often over six feet high. No less than nine *titula*
survive, each defending a gate. Two more have probably been
obliterated by the road. Rock lying just beneath the surface made
it impractical to dig a ditch, which only appears near the NE
angle. Rey Cross is big enough to hold a legion, and since the
course of the road, which itself must have been built in the first
century, bends slightly in order to pass through two gates of the
camp, the earthwork belongs to the earliest Roman campaigns
in the area. It probably held the tents of the Ninth Legion under
Petillius Cerialis during his campaigns against the Brigantes in
AD 72 and 73.

One mile west of Rey Cross the A66 leaves the Roman alignment and soon afterwards a minor road goes off to Kaber. Just
after the other loop of this road joins the A66, the latter makes a
dangerous double bend and rejoins the Roman road. At this
point (be careful about parking), near some road direction-
arrows, a track leads off to a field-gate on the right. Walk along
this for ten minutes and you will see an AM sign marking the
Roman fortlet of **Maiden Castle** (NY 8713). This small post,
probably only holding about 50 men, was a link in the signalling
system between Brough and Bowes and also a convenient

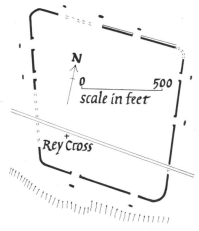

86   *Plan of Rey Cross*

stopping-place for convoys after the long haul up from Brough.
It commands a magnificent view over the Eden Valley, with
Brough Castle visible in the middle distance. Westwards its view
is blocked by the Stainmore Pass, but it is in sight of the Roper
Castle signal-station (see above) and thence messages could be
relayed to Bowes. It is unlikely to be earlier than the middle of
the second century, which in itself dates the other signal-stations
on the Stainmore route. The remains now consist of four stony
banks about six feet high, representing the original stone
defences. There are two gates. A single ditch appears on the
north, marked by the inner set of reeds. The outer row of reeds
indicates the line of a cart-track which probably follows a Roman
road by-passing the fortlet.

The fort at **Brough** (NY 7914) lies $\frac{1}{2}$m south of the A66, under
the Castle. The latter [AM ; S] has obliterated its northern half
and it is not clear how much of the impressive rampart and ditch
of its southern half is the work of Roman soldiers or Norman
castle-builders. A dedication-slab of AD 197, now virtually
illegible, is in the church porch. The Roman name was VERTERAE.

Westwards from Brough the land becomes cultivable again and
the Roman earthworks are consequently more damaged. The
next fort of which anything is visible is **Brougham** (NY 5328), and
once again, significantly of course, Romans and Normans agreed
in their choice of a strategic position. Brougham Castle [AM ; S]
lies 2m SE of Penrith, just off the A66. It has removed the
northern quarter of BROCAVVM, but the rest of the Roman fort
can be traced as a slight bank and ditch in the field south of the
castle, especially near the crossroads with the B6262. A first-
century date is unproven, as all the finds date from the second
century to the close of the fourth. More interesting than the
remains of the fort itself are the inscriptions preserved at the
Castle. Of those in the Outer Gatehouse, one is a well-carved
tombstone of Crescentinus, who died aged 18 (fig 88). It was set
up by his father Vidaris, possibly a Germanic name. Note the
pine cone in the pediment, a common funerary symbol. Next to it
is the relief of a boy in a cloak with the inscription : 'Annamoris,
his father, and Ressona, his mother, had this put up.' In the
Inner Gatehouse are three stones found during excavation in the
fort's cemetery in 1966–7, when over 200 burials, mostly
cremations, were uncovered. A fragment of another tombstone
is built into the ceiling of a short passage in the second floor of the

Keep. The deceased in this case is Tittius . . ., who lived 32 years 'more or less'. This form of words is sometimes used on Christian tombstones.

Between Brougham and Brough there was an intermediate fort at Kirkby Thore, but nothing is visible on the ground today. An unusual Roman relic does, however, exist nearby, $\frac{1}{2}$m SE of **Temple Sowerby** (NY 6226). Apart from the better example at Chesterholm, this is the only undoubted Roman milestone in Britain which occupies its original position. It stands about $4\frac{1}{2}$ feet high, looking a little sorry for itself in its iron cage. It is situated on the verge of a lay-by on the north side of the A66.

From Kirkby Thore a Roman road, known as the Maiden Way, ran straight to Hadrian's Wall near Greenhead, and en route is the fort of **Whitley Castle*** (NY 6948). There is no stonework visible here today, but the remarkable system of ditches protecting the fort on the SW, where the command of ground is weakest, makes it an outstanding site comparable only with Ardoch in Scotland. From Alston take the Brampton road (A689) for two miles until it descends to cross a narrow bridge over a stream. Immediately after this there is a track on the left

87   Whitley Castle, aerial view

which leads sharply back to Whitlow Farm. Ask here for
permission to visit the fort, which lies five minutes' walk north
of the farm, beyond the furthermost outbuilding. The magnificent
SW side displays a conspicuous rampart-mound and as many as
seven ditches (fig 87). Parts of the NW and SE sides are also very
impressive. One of the highest forts in Britain (1,050 feet), it
departs from the normal playing-card shape, forming a rhomboid
to take full advantage of the hillock on which it lies. The site of
the HQ is marked by uneven ground adjoining the field-wall in
the centre of the fort. Of Whitley Castle's history little is known.
It was built in the second century, and all the spectacular ditches
seem to have been part of the original scheme. A couple of
dedication-slabs indicate building activity in the period 213–9,
perhaps after the fort had been destroyed. The stone wall may
have been added to the rampart at this time. One of the
inscriptions tells us its garrison, the Second Cohort of Nervii
from the lower Rhine, but the Roman name of Whitley Castle is
unknown. One of its functions was probably to control nearby
lead-mines.

Brougham lay on the major western artery to Carlisle and
Scotland. The platform of the next fort to the north, VOREDA, is
clearly visible beside the A6 (Old Penrith, App. I). From Carlisle
a road ran direct to the Cumberland coast at Moresby near
Whitehaven (App. I), and all three of the forts which line this
route have left traces on the ground (Old Carlisle, Caermote and
Papcastle, all App. I). Other coastal forts apart from Moresby
were at Burrow Walls near Workington, Maryport and Beckfoot.
These were designed to protect the western approaches to
Hadrian's Wall, and the system of milefortlets and towers
continues along the coast from Bowness, where the Wall ends,
to beyond Beckfoot. Of all these fortifications, however, only
that at **Maryport** (NY 0337), the Roman ALAVNA, has left any
visible trace, and even here there is nothing to see except the
prominent fort-platform and faint traces of the ditches on the
west and south. An Agricolan fort is highly probable but no sign
of it was found during excavation in 1967, which revealed four
building-periods in stone beginning with the emperor Trajan in
the early second century. Occupation continued to the end of the
fourth century. In 1870, a remarkable find was made of 17 altars
buried in pits 350 yards NE of the fort. They are unweathered and
clearly have been ceremonially buried soon after erection: the

reason for this was the regular renewal of vows for the emperor's safety on January 3rd or on the anniversary of the emperor's accession, when new altars were erected. The one illustrated (fig 89) is dedicated to the personification of the emperor's Victory by Titus Attius Tutor, commander of the first cohort of Baetasians from the Rhine who had the honour of Roman citizenship (as indicated by the letters C.R. in the inscription). This garrison was at Maryport in the later second century before being transferred to Reculver in Kent. Other stones inform us of earlier garrisons – the first cohort of Spaniards under Hadrian and the first cohort of Dalmatians from Yugoslavia under Antoninus Pius. The position of the pits indicates that the parade-ground, on which the altars were erected, first lay NE of the fort. This area was later developed as a civilian suburb, and the parade-ground was then moved to a plot 100 yards south of the fort, where its *tribunal* was later known as Pudding Pie Hill. A new inscription, found in 1966, refers to a third cohort, possibly of Nervii, and these were probably at Maryport in the fourth century. All these fine inscriptions, together with many other finds from the fort and its neighbourhood, are in the Senhouse collection at Netherhall Lodge. This, the largest private collection of Roman inscriptions in Britain, is unfortunately not open to the

88 Brougham, tombstone

89 Maryport, altar

public at present; and it is greatly to be hoped that local efforts to
build a new museum for this collection, to purchase the site of the
fort and to expose some of its buildings will soon be rewarded
with success.

Further south in the Lake District is the fort of **Ravenglass**
(SD 0895), the Roman GLANNAVENTA. Turn off the A595 17m
south of Whitehaven for the village of Ravenglass, and when the
road bends sharply to the right, take the lane on the left through
some white gates. This passes through the site of the 4-acre fort,
now bisected by the railway and covered by a dense plantation.
Finds indicate occupation from the time of Hadrian to the end
of the fourth century. After ½m you will come to 'Walls Castle',
the Roman bath-house which lay outside the fort. Parts of this
building, which has never been excavated, still stand to a miracu-
lous height of 12½ feet, making it the best-preserved Roman
structure in the north of England (fig 90). The first room, possibly
for undressing, has a niche in one wall and three doorways. These
have shallow relieving-arches, but the lintels beneath have
disappeared; they may have been of wood. Go through the
doorway on the left into another room, where the lower part of a
splayed window and a long stretch of pink cement-rendering are
excellently preserved. Traces of windows can also be seen in
some of the other rooms.

Nine miles NE of Ravenglass, and half-way down the west side
of the notorious Hardknott Pass, is the Roman fort of
MEDIOBOGDVM, 'the fort in the middle of the bend' in the river
Esk. This is **Hardknott Castle*** (NY 2101) [AM; A], one of the
outstanding sites of Roman Britain. The fact that this is the best-
preserved Roman fort in Britain outside Hadrian's Wall matters
less than its spectacular position: it is a veritable British Mycenae,
with magnificent views of Eskdale to the west, the Pass to the
east, and the Scafell range to the north. The visitor approaching
from the east cannot miss the fort, so commanding is its position,
but from the west it can be passed unnoticed as there is no signpost: it lies a short distance left (north) of the road. From the
time of Camden, who visited it in 1607, it has made a strong
impression on its many visitors. It has been called 'an enchanting
fortress in the air', and it needs little imagination to visualize the
fort in its heyday. Excavation was carried out between 1890 and
1894, and again as part of DOE consolidation during the 1960's.
In 1964 a fragmentary inscription, now displayed in Carlisle

museum, revealed that the fort was built in the reign of Hadrian and garrisoned by the fourth cohort of Dalmatians from Yugoslavia. It does not seem to have been occupied beyond the end of the second century, except for a possible caretaker force.

The track up to the fort passes the shell of the external bath-house, its rooms neatly labelled. Hypocausts and the stoke-hole found here in the nineteenth century have now disappeared. A circular hot-room is detached from the main building. You then arrive at the south gate, which has twin passageways but no guardrooms. The other gates are similar, but that on the north

90   Ravenglass, the bath-house

has only a single portal. The entire circuit of the fort-wall stands
to a superb height of 8–10 feet (fig 91). Note how the DOE has
departed from its usual practice and partly rebuilt the walls with
fallen stones: a slate course separates original masonry from
rebuilt work. In the centre of the fort is the headquarters
building (fig 92). It contains L-shaped store-rooms flanking the
courtyard, the cross-hall with a *tribunal* at one end, and three
administrative rooms at the back. The middle one would have
been the chapel of the standards. To the west (left) of the HQ is
the commandant's house, but only an L-shaped block was
completed. To the east is a pair of buttressed granaries, originally
a single building, but later given a dividing wall. Remains of
loading-platforms can be seen at the south end. The rest of the
fort would have been filled up with wooden barrack-blocks, and
it may be that the superstructure of the central range was also of
timber. Finally, you should round off your visit to the site by
walking up to the parade-ground, an artificially levelled area 200
yards east of the east gate. It is the finest example in Britain.

After Hardknott, the fort at **Ambleside** (NY 3703) is a grave
disappointment. It was excavated in 1913–5 and 1920, after
which two gates, some angle towers and the central range of
buildings of the stone fort were fenced off and kept open. The
stonework was rarely well-preserved, and as the tops of the walls
have been turfed and not consolidated one gets the impression
that the site is very overgrown. The National Trust, who own it,
ought to be able to do better. A plan displayed on the site, however, does make it possible to identify the various buildings. The
visible stone fort was built in the second century and continued
in use well into the fourth. Preceding it, on a slightly different
site, was a clay-and-timber fort, now invisible. Its excavator
claimed an Agricolan date for it, but no pottery is earlier than
AD 90. These remains of GALAVA lie in Borrans Field (NT sign),
on the south side of the short A-road which links the A593 and the
A591, by-passing Ambleside. The finds are kept in the National
Park Centre at Brockhole, which is 2m south on the A591.

The next fort to the east, Low Borrow Bridge near Tebay
(App. I), lay on the main western trunk-road from Carlisle to
Manchester. On this road is a Roman milestone at **Middleton**
(SD 624859). It now stands near the top of a slope in the second
field south of Middleton Church, which is situated midway
between Sedbergh and Kirkby Lonsdale on the west side of the

A683. The Roman inscription on it (fig 93) reads simply MP LIII, 53 miles (from Carlisle), but its discoverer re-erected it 200 yards from its find-spot and carved another inscription lower down on the stone. This records that the milestone was dug out of the ground and set up again by William Moore in the year 1836.

91   *Hardknott, the fort-wall*

92   *Hardknott, the HQ building*

The long catalogue of forts in the Pennines and the Lakes has now come to an end, and we can turn aside from the military to consider the civilian aspects of life in northern Britain under Roman rule. Nearly all the forts had villages (*vici*) clustered around them, but none are visible today. On the larger scale, the *colonia* at York has been mentioned, and there were three other towns in Yorkshire, at Aldborough, Catterick (App. I) and Brough-on-Humber (nothing visible). **Aldborough** (SE 4066) [AM; S], a village near Boroughbridge off the A1167, was ISVRIVM, the tribal capital of the Brigantes. A small town grew up here at the end of the first century, probably on the site of a fort. 55 acres were enclosed by an earth bank and ditch in the second half of the second century, and this defence was given a stone wall in the middle of the third century. One hundred years later bastions were added but none are now visible. Very little remains of the town-wall in the section kept by the DOE, which was excavated in the early nineteenth century. First a portion of the back of the wall is visible, originally obscured by an earth rampart-bank. Then comes an internal tower. Further on is a second stretch of wall, and part of another tower, which have

93   Middleton, inscribed milestone

been largely rebuilt. The position of the wall elsewhere is marked
by a pair of concrete strips, and at the end of the path these
should turn a corner and not keep straight on. Fragments of an
angle tower are visible here. To the left, under the trees, is a
quarry worked by the Romans.

Of the interior of ISVRIVM little is known in detail, but the large
number of polychrome mosaics recorded from the eighteenth
century onwards reveal its wealth during the fourth century.
Two of these are still visible and are reached by a footpath from
the town-wall. They are the most northerly mosaics at present
visible in Britain (but see Beadlam, below). One, found in 1848,
is in perfect condition: it is entirely geometric and features an
eight-pointed star in the centre. The other, which is badly
damaged, was discovered in 1832. Its main panel depicted a lion
under a tree, but only the tree, a paw and part of the mane survive.
Both mosaics belonged to the same house. A cruder pavement
illustrating the myth of Romulus and Remus being suckled by the
she-wolf is now in Leeds City Museum (weekdays 10–6.30).
Another, depicting the Muses, has been reburied. Some of the
smaller finds from Aldborough are displayed in the site-museum.
Otherwise, a figure of Mercury in the church, and an earthwork
called Studforth Hill, which may or may not be the amphitheatre,
are all that can be seen of ISVRIVM outside the DOE enclosure.

The mosaics at Aldborough suggest a considerable degree of
romanization, and this is apparent also in the large number of
villa-sites now known in the east riding of Yorkshire. At the
height of their prosperity, in the fourth century, many seem to
have been fitted with mosaics, painted plaster and hypocausts.
The most remarkable mosaics of all come from a villa at Rudston
near Bridlington, and are now displayed in the **Hull** Museum of
Transport and Archaeology (10–5, Sun. 2.30–4.30). One of these,
a single geometric mosaic, is competent enough: it shows what a
local craftsman could achieve when he kept to conventional
patterns. The second, much damaged, portrays a lively aquatic
scene. The fish are not brilliantly drawn, but the artist has
achieved a moderate degree of success. But when he tried his hand
at a more ambitious subject (identical borders prove that the
same craftsman was working on both mosaics), the result was
ludicrously bad. This third pavement has a central roundel
depicting Venus, the goddess of love and beauty, but there is
nothing beautiful about this wild creature (fig 94). Her face is

hard, her body lacks any sense of proportion, her stance is ungainly. Wearing nothing but armlets, her hair streaming behind her, she has dropped her mirror while a merman holds up what looks like a primitive back-scratcher (probably a torch). The surrounding panels are equally childish: three shaggy huntsmen and four crude animals, two of them labelled in misspelt Latin, surround the central figure. You can view the piece as amusing or just downright bad, but it remains a fascinating illustration of the level to which a local craftsman could sink in his attempt to copy ambitious classical subjects beyond his technical ability.

In 1972 two further pavements were lifted from Rudston and neither of them is yet on display. One of them portrays a charioteer in a four-horse chariot. This floor, which has busts of the four seasons in the corners, is of more competent workmanship than the Venus pavement. Also in Hull Museum, and also not yet on public display, are some fine mosaics from Brantingham, near Brough-on-Humber, which were discovered in 1962. The central circle contains the bust of a crowned goddess while water-nymphs recline in the surrounding lunettes.

94   *Hull Museum,* Venus mosaic

At present (1972) there is no villa-site open to the public in the north of England. But this situation is soon to be remedied when **Beadlam** (SE 634842) is excavated and conserved as an Ancient Monument. The field containing the villa, which adjoins the south side of the A170 1½m east of Helmsley, had long been known to contain 'old buildings', but only excavation in 1966 revealed their Roman date. In 1969 the site was more thoroughly explored, when two wings of the villa were excavated down to the latest fourth-century levels. The north building was in fine condition, with walls standing several courses high. One room contained a geometric mosaic, which had partially collapsed into the hypocaust below. The west block, which was more badly robbed, contained a small bath-suite at one end. A third building lies to the east, but it has only been trial-trenched. These excavations have been back-filled, but the site has been bought for the nation, and in a few years' time, it is hoped, Beadlam Roman Villa will be excavated and opened to the public.

Most of the Yorkshire villas are concentrated in the East Riding around the Vale of York, but isolated examples have been found away to the north, near Piercebridge and Durham, and also to the west at Gargrave near Skipton. Elsewhere, agricultural communities continued to live in native farmsteads and villages, and numerous examples of these can be seen. Just two will be included here. They are quite well preserved, but consist of nothing more than a series of grass ridges, and so they are unlikely to prove of any great interest. At **Grassington** (SE 0065) the settlement itself has not been securely located, but there is a large area of ancient fields to be seen. Each cultivation-strip measures about 375 feet by 75 feet, and is defined by well-preserved banks. Pottery makes it certain that the fields were farmed in the Roman period. Grassington lies about 7m north of Skipton on the B6265. Turn off this road along Main Street and fork left along Chapel Street. After 200 yards a track goes off to the right near a telegraph-pole and two houses called Oak Bank and Wood View. Follow this until a gate bars the way. The first gate in the wall on the right of the track beyond this point leads into the field where the ancient banks lie.

The other native site is at **Ewe Close** (NY 6113) in Westmorland. It is near the village of Crosby Ravensworth, which is signposted from the B6260 (Appleby to Tebay). Turn right by the telephone-booth in Crosby and first left by the post office. Bear left when the track forks and then follow this for 1½m, through one farm, until it peters out at another. Go through the farmyard, keeping the hay-loft to your right, and pass through the gate on your left. Cross the stream and make for the gate straight ahead, avoiding the path wheeling up to the right. Now follow the field-wall on your right to the top of the hill. Ewe Close lies in the field beyond, where the wall makes a 90° turn to the left. A lot of ridges and a few hut-circles are all that can be made out of these confusing and complicated earthworks. There are probably several farmsteads grouped together here, lining the Roman north-south trunk-road which passes 20 yards west of the complex.

In the closing years of the Roman occupation, when the province of Britain was being threatened both by barbarian incursions from the north and by Saxon pirates from across the North Sea, a series of signal-towers was built along the Yorkshire coast. They were solid stone structures, perhaps 100 feet high, each set in a courtyard surrounded by a wall and an outer ditch. Five of them are known, from Huntcliff (near Saltburn) in the north to Filey in the south, and more undoubtedly existed. They were designed to give early warning of impending naval raids, and the news was then transferred by beacon-fire and messenger to military units stationed at Malton and beyond, which then tried to co-ordinate resistance to the attack. Today, only at the **Scarborough** example (TA 0589) [AM; SSM] can the plan of one of these signal-towers be made out. It lies on the edge of the cliff east of the castle, but the site was later occupied by a series of medieval chapels and no Roman masonry is now exposed. The outline of the signal-station has, however, been marked out in concrete, and the surrounding ditch has been dug out on the south and partly on the west. The east side of the remains has slipped into the sea. This chain of signal-stations represents the last desperate attempt to maintain peace and security in Roman Britain. Excavation has shown that they had a short life of only 20 or 30 years after their erection c. AD 370. Then came the end, at some of them dramatically. At Goldsborough (App. I) the skeleton of a short man lay face down across a hearth fire. His hand was twisted behind him, perhaps because he had been stabbed in the back. Another man lay at his feet, sprawled on top of the skeleton of a powerful dog. The days of Roman rule in Britain were numbered.

Chapter 8

Hadrian's Wall

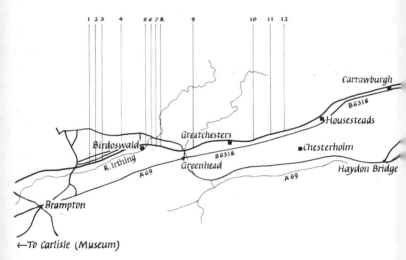

Unlike some of the sites in this book, Hadrian's Wall cannot fail
to stir the imagination. It has fascinated countless people,
scholars and ordinary visitors alike, from the time of Bede (AD
731) to the present day. The remains are, in parts, strikingly well
preserved, and they are situated amid some of the most
spectacular scenery in the British Isles. But the deepest impression
on a visitor to the Wall is made by the sheer magnitude of the
undertaking, which expresses so well the essential flavour of
Roman civilization: here was a regime that not only had the
confidence to make the bold decision of building a wall from sea
to sea, but also had the vast resources of manpower and money,
as well as the tremendous organizational ability, that were

1 Denton Hall
2 Heddon
3 Planetrees
4 Brunton
5 Chesters Bridge Abutment
6 Black Carts
7 Limestone Corner
8 Peel Crag
9 Winshields
10 Cawfields
11 Walltown

12 Poltross Burn
13 Gilsland
14 Willowford
15 Harrow's Scar
16 High House
17 Piper Sike
18 Leahill
19 Banks East
Visible *forts* are marked on the map
with a square; also some roads, rivers
and modern towns.

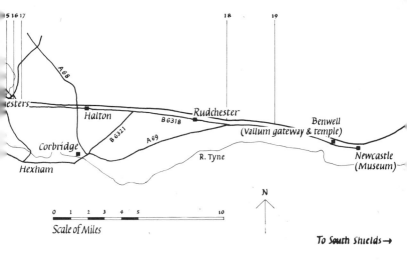

required to build it and manage it for close on 300 years. From
the engineering point of view especially, the achievement is
staggering: over a million cubic yards of stone needed to be
quarried, carried to the spot and set in place. All the right
ingredients are there: the great Wall of Hadrian is not just the
most exciting relic of the Roman occupation of Britain, but perhaps the largest and most remarkable building-programme ever
undertaken in these islands at any time.

Hadrian's barrier, however, is much more than a single wall
running across the Tyne-Solway isthmus: it is an immensely
complicated group of works, and the problem of their precise
relation, function and date has only been finally resolved, through

careful excavation, in the last 50 years. Many, perhaps most, of
the people who wander among the ruins of the Wall each year go
away without really understanding either its complexity or
purpose. Some background information is essential to a proper
understanding and enjoyment of its remains.

About AD 105, Agricola's conquests in Scotland were finally
given up and a frontier was fixed along the Stanegate. This is the
name by which the Roman road from Carlisle to Corbridge is
known. It was built by Agricola c. AD 80 and some of the forts
on its route were his foundations. More were then built, and the
road was probably extended westwards and eastwards, though
less is known about these parts than about its central sector. In
118, soon after Hadrian became emperor on the death of Trajan,
there was a rebellion in Britain and the 'Britons could no longer be
held under control.' We have no details beyond these words of
Hadrian's biographer, but it is a safe guess that the tribes involved
were the Brigantes of northern England and the Selgovae and
Novantae of southern Scotland. In 122, after order had been
restored, the emperor came to Britain to assess the situation for
himself. As a consequence of this famous visit, Hadrian's Wall
was constructed: in the absence of any suitable natural frontier
(once the decision had been taken not to overrun the whole
island), an artificial one had to be created.

The original plan was relatively uncomplicated. The existing
Stanegate forts were to hold the main fighting garrison, but the
actual frontier was to be marked by a ditch and a wall on the
commanding ground a few miles to the north. The **Ditch**, on
average about 27 feet wide and 9 feet deep, accompanies the wall
on its north side, except where cliffs make it unnecessary. The
Wall was to run from Newcastle to Bowness on the Solway.
From Newcastle to the river Irthing, over half its length, it was
to be built of stone, 10 feet thick and perhaps 20 feet high,
including the parapet. West of the river Irthing, where limestone
was difficult to obtain, the Wall was to be of turf, 20 feet wide at
base and probably only 15 feet high, including a timber breastwork. At intervals of one Roman mile (1,620 yards) fortlets,
known as **milecastles**, were constructed, each having two gateways (one through the Wall) and barrack accommodation for
about 30 men. These milecastles were built of timber west of the
Irthing, of stone elsewhere. Between each were two **turrets**,
everywhere built of stone and about 14 feet square internally.

The ground floor often contained hearths and was no doubt used
as a resting-place for soldiers off-duty. A timber ladder to the
upper floor rested on a low stone foundation. The top, as recent
excavation has proved, was not an open platform with
crenellations, but was covered by a sloping roof. Each turret,
perhaps 30 feet high, was to be used primarily for watching
enemy movements north of the Wall, and signalling back to the
Stanegate if the trouble was more than the local milecastles could
cope with. (Milecastles are numbered from the east, and the
same number, followed by *a* or *b*, is given to the two turrets on the
west side of each milecastle).

The Wall and its associated turrets and milecastles were
built by detachments from all three of the British legions.
Differing construction styles, especially in the gateways of milecastles, together with the evidence of inscriptions, make it
possible to assign individual structures to individual legions (as is
sometimes indicated below). The construction parties were
divided up into various groups, some working on the foundation
of the Wall, some on the turrets and milecastles, others on the
Wall-superstructure, and others, perhaps not legionaries, on
digging the Ditch.

Sometime after work had started, probably in AD 124, an
important alteration was made to the original scheme. This was
the decision to move the main fighting force forward from the
Stanegate onto the Wall itself, where it was housed in a number
of **forts**, originally 12 in number (including an already existing
fort at Newcastle), but eventually 16. At the same time, or shortly
afterwards, other decisions were taken: to narrow the Wall from
10 feet to 8 feet in width, to extend the Wall from Newcastle
eastwards to Wallsend, and to replace the Turf Wall in stone for a
stretch of five miles west of the Irthing (as far as the natural fault,
after which limestone is absent). Up to this time, many of the
turrets and milecastles had been completed, and on either side
short wing-walls had been built to the broad gauge, in
expectation that the forthcoming curtain-wall would be of the
same width. But the building of the actual curtain-wall was
lagging far behind: it was nearly finished as far as the North
Tyne, and work was also in hand in the sector east of the river
Irthing in Cumberland. All this results in a complicated sequence:
(i) from Wallsend to Newcastle, the Wall is narrow (eight feet)
on a narrow foundation; (ii) from Newcastle to the North Tyne

(Chesters), the Wall is broad (10 feet) on a broad foundation, though the final portion had not been given the finishing touches; (iii) from the North Tyne to the Irthing the Wall is narrow on a foundation sometimes narrow, sometimes broad; (iv) for five miles west of the Irthing the Wall is narrow on a narrow foundation; (v) for the rest of its course the Turf Wall was not rebuilt in stone until about AD 160, when it was given an intermediate width of nine feet.

Very soon after the forts had been built, or as soon as they had been planned, an earthwork known as the **Vallum** was constructed a short distance south of the Wall. It consisted of a flat-bottomed ditch, about 20 feet wide at the top and 8 feet wide at the bottom, and some 10 feet deep; on either side was a berm of 30 feet flanked by two turf mounds 20 feet wide and originally 6 feet high. The whole Vallum was thus about 120 feet across. This earthwork in some ways is the most remarkable of all the components of Hadrian's frontier. It is a formidable obstacle, evidently designed not to be crossed, but its form shows that it is not a proper military defence. Its purpose was to delineate the area under strict military control, above all to prevent civilians or other unauthorized persons from wandering too close to the military zone: this they were allowed to enter only through the large Vallum gateways opposite every fort.

These two additions of forts and Vallum to the original scheme give us some indication of the hostility with which the whole idea of a frontier-wall was received by the local peoples. Hadrian's biographer says that the Wall divided the Romans from the barbarians, but it would be more exact to say that its purpose was to separate the Brigantes of north England from the tribes of south Scotland, to prevent collusion between them, and so, it was hoped, to lessen the scale of any future uprising. The placing of the striking force on the Wall-line shows that pressure from the north needed to be dealt with more speedily and effectively than was possible when the main body of troops was on the Stanegate; and the building of the Vallum shows that the tribesmen behind the Wall were sufficiently restless to warrant an additional deterrent to their contacting friends in the north.

The main purpose of the Wall, then, was to provide a fixed frontier to the Roman province of Britain, and to separate two sets of potential trouble-makers. This was its political role. In military terms, it acted as a superb cover for movements against an enemy unable to predict from which fort or milecastle troops might sally out. It is important to remember that the Wall itself was never meant to be employed as a fighting-platform.

Another commonly-held fallacy must also be cleared away. Legionaries did *not* 'tramp the Wall'. They built it, as we have seen, but they did not normally garrison it. That was the job, as usual, of the auxiliary units of the Roman army. The total garrison, assuming all 16 forts and all the milecastles were fully manned, was probably in the region of 11–12,000 men.

A few words must now be said about the history of Hadrian's Wall. It was begun in 122 (120 according to an alternative suggestion) under the supervision of the governor Aulus Platorius Nepos, then a close friend of Hadrian. Most of it was finished by about 128. In 139–40, when the Antonine Wall was built, Hadrian's Wall was evacuated. The mounds of the Vallum were breached in places and its ditch filled in. Milecastle gates were removed. The forts were given caretaker garrisons, possibly skeleton detachments of legionaries. In 155 the Brigantes revolted and the Antonine Wall was evacuated, and a year or two later Hadrian's Wall was fully recommissioned: the milecastle gates were rehung and the Vallum was restored in most places to its former state. By 159–60 the Antonine Wall was reoccupied and caretaker garrisons were on Hadrian's frontier. By about 163, however, as recently shown by B R Hartley's detailed study of the samian pottery, Hadrian's Wall had again been fully regarrisoned. It was probably at this time, or perhaps in 156–7, that the rest of the Turf Wall was rebuilt in stone. More controversial is the date of the first destruction of Hadrian's frontier. It is usually believed to have happened in 196–7, when Clodius Albinus stripped Britain of troops in an attempt to become emperor. Virius Lupus, sent by Severus to recover the province, had to buy off the Maeatae of south Scotland, and this is usually taken to mean that they had already destroyed the Wall and its works. If so, it is very odd that the Wall lay in ruins for 10 years or more, for it was not until the governorship of Alfenus Senecio (205–8) that restoration was begun. Some scholars, however, now believe that the Wall was not destroyed in the troubles of 196–7 but in another calamity in 203–4; only future work will be able to resolve the point. In this reconstruction (Severan), some of the turrets were demolished, the gateways of the milecastles were narrowed, and the Vallum was not restored:

a few of the forts' civilian suburbs were allowed to grow over its filled-in course.

The expeditions of Severus to Scotland in 209–11 gave peace to the Hadrianic frontier until 296, when it was again destroyed by barbarians. Its garrison was supporting another pretender to the imperial throne, Allectus, and the Wall was reconstructed by the man who defeated him, Constantius. The third destruction was in the barbarian conspiracy of 367, and the repair was carried out by Theodosius in 369–70. Obviously the amount of reconstruction necessary in each case (Severan, Constantian, Theodosian) must have varied, but the Wall of Hadrian was certainly rebuilt in places from its foundations, as reused 'centurial stones' show. Destruction in 383, when another pretender, Magnus Maximus, tried for the throne, is less certain; at any rate, some forts were occupied after this date, and by now the soldiers had their families with them inside the protection of the walls: the undefended *vici* outside were abandoned. By 400 the final garrison had gone, and the work of the Wall was finished. The slow process of decay and destruction began, only to be halted in the present century.

Very substantial remains of Hadrian's great frontier still survive, and I can hope to do no more than indicate here which are the best-preserved or most instructive portions. For those who wish for more, the first two works listed in the bibliography for this chapter are indispensable; in particular, the OS Map of Hadrian's Wall will be found most useful even for the briefest of visits. A taste of the Wall can be had in a day (Corbridge, Chesters and Housesteads should be seen), and a fair sample can be taken in two days (visit all sites with an asterisk). All the places mentioned below can be visited, with the aid of a car, in 3–4 days. The best way to see the Wall is to walk its full length, which can be done in a fortnight. The standard direction is from east to west, and that has been adopted in the description below.

Hadrian's Wall itself ran from Wallsend to Bowness, a distance of 75 miles. But its flanks needed protection. On the west, the system of milefortlets and towers (none now visible) continued for another 40 miles down the Cumberland coast, the sea here providing a sufficient barrier. On the east the extension of the Wall to Wallsend was made to prevent an enemy slipping across the river, and there may have been one or more posts on the south

bank between Wallsend and the Tyne mouth. The latter was
guarded by a fort at **South Shields** (NZ 3667), and part of it,
found in the late nineteenth century, has been excavated and
preserved (May–Sept., 10–7.30, Sun. 11–7.30; Oct.–Apr.,
Mon.–Fri. 10–4, Sat. 10–12). The remains are lovingly tended
and carefully labelled, though the dating on some of the notices
needs to be revised in the light of recent work. This was carried
out after housing-demolition to the north of the exposed portion,
and in 1972 there was some talk of opening up this area for
permanent show. It is important to remember that the foundations at present visible are not typical of a Roman fort. The first
fort, built under Hadrian, was indeed regular, but in the early
third century virtually the whole area inside the walls was
converted into a store-base for Severus' campaigns in Scotland.
No less than 22 granaries are now known, and parts of 10 are
visible.

Follow the riverside road in South Shields (B1802, B1344)
until you reach a sign to the Roman Fort. Then turn left along
Fort Street and left again along Baring Street. The site lies on the
right. A wooden platform crosses the scanty remains of the fort-
wall, now known to be of Hadrianic date. At the far left of it is
one of the guardrooms defending the single passageway of the
west gate. Now look at the buildings on your left as you walk
towards the far end. The first is a double granary, belonging to
the original Hadrianic fort. Later, probably in the fourth century,
the floor of one of them was removed and two tile-kilns were
inserted. One of them is covered with earth, the other has been
marked out in modern materials. The stumps in front of the
granary represent the bases of a portico. The next building is also
a granary, now known to be Severan, not Antonine as labelled.
Now make for the re-erected column at the far end of the site,
and turn and face the hedge on your left. You are standing in the
courtyard of the third-century headquarters building: the column
belongs to the colonnade that once flanked it, and part of its
gutter can also be seen. But this building replaced earlier HQ's
which faced in the opposite direction: their courtyards lay partly
under the hedge, and their administrative rooms were demolished
and buried under the courtyard you are now standing in. The
plan of these earlier rooms has been partly marked out – white for
the Hadrianic period, and red for the Antonine. Beyond these
lies the cross-hall, which remained in the same position through-

out the history of the building. The *tribunal* of such halls, however, always lies on the right of anyone entering from the courtyard, and so when the HQ was turned round a new *tribunal* had to be built: that on your right is Severan, on your left Antonine. Beyond lies the massive strong-room of the Severan period, kept dry by a sump now covered by a wooden board. The administrative rooms on either side of it were given hypocausts in the fourth century; some traces of these can be seen. Beyond the back of the third-century building, but in the courtyards of earlier HQ's, is a well: it remained in use even after the building had been switched round.

Now turn to the other side of the site. Here are five granaries (and part of a sixth near the hedge) which belong to the early third-century fort. Below them the plans of earlier barracks have been marked out. The granaries did not retain their original function for very long, and in some cases they were divided up into living quarters by internal partition-walls, particularly well seen in granaries VI and VII. The alteration probably belongs to the third century, but usually it is believed to be fourth-century. At that time the garrison of ARBEIA is recorded as being a *numerus barcariorum Tigrisiensium*, a detachment of boatmen from the area of the river Tigris in Mesopotamia. This was clearly a specialist unit, capable of dealing with the dangerous shoals of an undredged Tyne, and of accompanying supplies up the river to the Wall. The last two granaries, VIII and IX, are good examples of their type: the outer buttressed wall, occasionally broken by ventilation-gaps, and the low sleeper walls which supported the floor, are clearly visible, uncomplicated by later divisions.

Before leaving the site you should visit the excellent little museum. The main exhibits are the three stones displayed on the end wall of the right-hand room. The middle one gives the name of the fort's third-century garrison, the Fifth Cohort of Gauls, who dedicated an aqueduct in AD 222. To the same period belong the magnificent tombstones which flank it. On the right is that of a freedwoman (former slave) called Regina, who came from Hertfordshire (CATVALLAVNA). She was eventually married to her master, Barates, who came from Palmyra in Syria, and the Latin inscription has been translated into Palmyrene at the bottom. The wicker chair in which she sits and the wool-basket on her left give us a rare glimpse of the furniture of Roman

Britain. Even better preserved is the beautiful tombstone of the freedman Victor, who came from Mauretania (NW Africa) (fig 95). He is shown reclining on a couch at the (pagan) heavenly banquet, while a tiny slave holds up a wine jar filled from the large bowl on the floor. The stylized tree cut on the wall behind Victor is a symbol of paradise. Once again the details of the furniture will be noted. Both tombstones are probably the work of the same sculptor, and stylistic comparisons suggest that he may have come from Palmyra himself.

A visit to Hadrian's Wall is best preceded by a study of the exhibits in the Museum of Antiquities in the University of **Newcastle** (weekdays 10–5). This is one of the outstanding Roman collections in the country. The many inscriptions displayed here form the basis of our knowledge of the Wall's history. The one illustrated (fig 96) comes from a milecastle and simply records the emperor (Hadrian, lines 1–2), the governor (A. Platorius Nepos, line 4), and the builders (men from the Second Augustan Legion, line 3). Some of the stones from forts north of the wall are mentioned in Chapter 9 (figs 119–20), and various other exhibits are noted, in passing, below. Especially important are the scale-models of the Wall and its structures as they may once have appeared (fig 2), and with these in mind the

95   South Shields, tombstone of Victor

visitor to the Wall can better appreciate the original appearance
of the ruins before him. There is also an impressive full-scale
reconstruction of the Carrawburgh Mithraeum.

The first Roman remains on the line of the Wall are in **Benwell**
(NZ 2164), 2m west of Newcastle. Nothing can be seen of the
fort of CONDERCVM, but two structures which lay outside its walls
have been preserved. One is the tiny temple of a native god,
Anociticus or Antenociticus [AM; A], on the left-hand side of
Broomridge Avenue (signposted from the A69). Of three altars
known from the temple, two use the latter form of the god's
name, one the former. All are now in the museum at Newcastle,
but two have been replaced by casts (now nearly illegible) at the
site. Also in Newcastle is the head of the god himself. It is a
powerful rendering, and well displays, like other pieces of
Romano–British art (cf. especially the Bath pediment, and the
Gloucester head), the strong influence of Celtic traditions, here
represented by the large baggy eyes and the deeply-grooved,
snake-like hair.

Return from the temple to the A69, turn left and then first
left (Denhill Park). At the bottom of this road is the sole visible
example of one of the Vallum gateways which existed opposite
every Wall-fort [AM; A]. The ditch of the Vallum was not dug
in the centre, and the sides of the resulting causeway have been
revetted in stone with an opening left for drainage. The roadway
over it was closed by a large doorway, of which one pier and a
pivot-hole survive. These gateways ensured a strict control over

96   Newcastle Museum, milecastle inscription

movements into and out of the military zone.

One mile further west along the A69, immediately after the roundabout (B-road to Blaydon), the first extant fragment of Hadrian's Wall may be seen behind railings on the left of the road. About 300 yards further on, also on the left, is the much longer stretch at **Denton Hall** (NZ 1965) [AM; A]. This is a good example of the broad Wall, and bonded into it is turret 7b, the work of Legion XX. The pivot-hole of the door and the base for the stairway will be noted. Excavation in 1929 revealed that the turret was still in use in the fourth century. Another fragment of Wall-foundation can be seen on the left of the road at West Denton [AM; A], another 300 yards further west.

Very little is visible of the Wall or its attendant works for nearly two miles, until you approach Heddon, where the Vallum is well preserved on your left. Just before the village of **Heddon** (NZ 1366), 110 yards of the broad Wall have been consolidated [AM; A] (turn left along The Towne Gate if you wish to stop). The structure built into the west end of this stretch is a post-Roman kiln.

At Heddon, turn right off the A69 along the B6318. This is the Military Way, built by General Wade in 1751. For many miles the Wall is invisible, as it was ripped down at that date to provide a foundation for the road. $1\frac{1}{2}$m beyond Heddon is a crossroads (Horseley and Wylam, left; Standfordham and Ponteland, right), and immediately west of it the fort of VINDOVALA, **Rudchester** (NZ 1167), straddles the B-road. The earth mound which covers its stone defences is not impressive; it is best viewed at the SE corner (turn left at the crossroads and look over the first field-gate on your right). 4m west of Rudchester, $1\frac{1}{2}$m past the reservoirs, both Vallum on the left and Wall-Ditch on the right become conspicuous. Take the unsignposted road on the left immediately before the notice announcing the Corbridge road (B6321), and stop at the gap in the hedge on the left. The Vallum is not very impressive here, but the gaps in the flanking mounds and the causeways across its ditch are clearly visible. This is one of the few places along the course of the Vallum where the breaches made about AD 140 were not later repaired. It is worth walking back to the B-road to look at the picturesque, tree-grown stretch of Wall-Ditch, which is in good condition at this point. 2m further west is the fort of ONNVM, **Halton** (NY 9968): turn left over the cattle-grid before the bend-sign, just after Halton Red House. The road passes through the southern part of the fort, but only the mounds of its ramparts and uneven ground marking the sites of interior buildings can be seen today.

After another ½m comes a roundabout where the A68 crosses the B6318. There was a gateway through the Wall at this point (Portgate), taking Dere Street into Scotland: its route is described on p. 277 ff. Here it is convenient to make the 2-m detour to **Corbridge*** (NY 9864), and visit the remains of CORSTOPITVM [AM; SSM], ½m west of the modern town. Most of the structures in the exposed portion belong to the third and fourth centuries, when Corbridge was a flourishing town and a military supply-depot for the Wall. Below them lies a succession of earlier forts: the one built by Agricola c. AD 79/80 was burnt and rebuilt c. 105 and abandoned c. 124, when forts were moved to the line of the Wall. Its garrison was probably a cavalry regiment, the *Ala Petriana*, then 500 strong but later doubled in size. To it belonged a certain Flavinus, whose tombstone, depicting him riding down his barbarian foe, is now in the south transept of Hexham church (other stones are displayed at the north end). The fort was rebuilt in stone c. 139 with the Antonine advance into Scotland, and it probably remained in use until the early third century.

The present site, which represents only a small part of the final settlement, is bisected by the Stanegate. The first portion of this road, still lined by its side gutters, represents the final fourth-century level, which is many feet higher than the original first-century surface. On the left, immediately below the road and half-buried by it, are the lower parts of some columns. These supported a porch in front of the two large buildings you see beyond, which are the best-preserved granaries in Roman Britain (fig 97). For once, substantial portions of the floor remain in position. The ventilation-openings between the buttresses are also clear, and one in the right-hand wall of the second granary is still in perfect condition. Immediately next to it is an elaborate fountain consisting of three elements: an aqueduct-channel, originally covered with stone slabs; a fountain-house, of which only a few blocks remain; and a basin into which water was discharged. Its sides became so worn down by the sharpening of knives that the fountain can hardly have worked properly later on. The third structure on this side of the Stanegate is a vast building, perhaps a storehouse, consisting of four wings enclosing a courtyard. The fine quality of the massive masonry blocks will be noted. The building was never finished except on the side facing the Stanegate. Why is not known. It is usually dated to the early third century. Fragments of two buildings are visible within the courtyard. That nearer the granaries was originally the *sacellum* of the HQ building of the second-century stone fort; this part alone had not been demolished during the erection of the grand storehouse, and it was then converted to other uses, probably domestic. Little is known at present about the other building exposed within the courtyard.

At the far end, you should mount the steps and survey the jumble of fragmentary remains on the south side of the Stanegate. Subsidence has contributed to the crazy effect. It is well to have a good look at Alan Sorrell's reconstruction-drawing which is displayed here. From this you will see that the area consisted of two military compounds, surrounded by enclosure-walls. These take an irregular course to avoid temples and other buildings fronting the Stanegate. The compound-walls can be recognized by their more massive construction (five feet wide), and the projecting plinth at their bottom. At the beginning of the fourth century the compounds were united by building a wall, broken

97 *Corbridge, the granaries*

by an entrance, along the Stanegate. The buildings inside these compounds do not merit detailed inspection. They consisted of officers' houses, stores, workshops and clubs. A small administrative building in the west compound, adjoining the path near the museum, has an underground strong-room approached by steps.

The little museum is a humble building, but the collection inside is well arranged. There is a good selection of military equipment, some important inscriptions, one partly recoloured to give an idea of its original polychrome effect, and some interesting sculptures. One is a rugged, unrealistic portrayal of a lion devouring a stag (the Corbridge Lion), another is part of a frieze from a temple (fig 98). It represents the crowned Sun-god riding on a winged horse towards a pedimented building, in which stands Castor or Pollux. The temple it came from was probably dedicated to Dolichenus, an eastern deity equated with Jupiter, and he is named on an altar also in the museum. Other fragmentary sculptures testify to the remarkable diversity and elaboration of the buildings that must once have graced this distant settlement of the Roman Empire.

Return now to the B6318. For three miles west of Portgate the Ditch on the north of the road and the Vallum on the south are in an outstanding state of preservation. The Wall itself is buried beneath the road, but when eventually the two part company, after descending a 1:8 hill one mile before Chollerford, a piece of Wall is signposted on the left at **Planetrees** (NY 9269) [AM; A]. This interesting stretch preserves the junction between the broad wall and a portion only six feet thick, standing on broad foundation. It probably marks a total reconstruction from ground-level in the third or fourth centuries. A drainage-culvert is also visible here.

You are now approaching the North Tyne and the central sector of Hadrian's Wall, where the scenery becomes more beautiful and the Roman remains better preserved. A long stretch of the Wall, seven feet high and incorporating a well-preserved turret (26b), is only a short distance from Planetrees. Turn left along the A6079 at the bottom of the hill and you will see **Brunton** turret (NY 9269) [AM; A] signposted on the left. It is the mostly westerly section of broad Wall on a broad foundation, for it was when the curtain-builders had got this far that the order came to change the width from 10 to 8 feet. The turret, built by men from Legion XX, preserves its door-sill and pivot-hole, and an uninscribed altar and the lower part of a corn-mill can be seen inside.

Return to the crossroads and turn left for Chollerford. Most visitors now go on to Chesters, but if you have half an hour to spare you will not regret parking immediately before the river-bridge and taking the path on the left which leads to **Chesters bridge abutment** (NY 9169) [AM; A]. The Wall ends in a tower which sits on the massive masonry apron forming the abutment (fig 99). This is now high and dry as the river has moved some yards to the west. There was a corresponding abutment on the other side, now in the water, and three stone piers in between. They supported a superstructure of timber, though the first (Hadrianic) bridge on the site may have had stone arches. The visible remains probably belong to the third century. Two other features should be noted: one is a phallus carved for good luck on the northward face of the abutment; the other is a channel running underneath the tower, and originally covered by the huge slabs that lie shattered amid the ruins on the south side. Water racing through this channel would have turned a mill-wheel in the tower, and part of the apparatus, found in the ruins, is now in Chesters Museum.

Turning left in Chollerford, you will soon see the signpost to the Roman fort of **Chesters*** (NY 9170) [AM; Mar.–Apr. 9–5, Sun. 2–4.30; May–Sept. 9–5.30, Sun. 2–5; Oct.–Feb. 9.30–4, Sun. 2–4]. This is a charming spot, set in a lush estate beside the North Tyne. The remains of CILVRNVM, mainly excavated in the nineteenth century, are well preserved, though the isolation of the

98   Corbridge, a temple frieze

individual structures in wire cages makes it less easy to understand the original layout of the fort than at Housesteads. The
path first leads to the north gate: of its two portals, the west has
been cleared down to the original Hadrianic level, the other
preserves a sill of a later date. In the next enclosure is part of a
double barrack-building, alongside a street with a gutter; as
usual there are more spacious quarters for officers at the far end.
As you make your way to the east gate, in the same enclosure,
you will pass a partially-exposed stable (on the right): Chesters
was a cavalry fort, and its third-century garrison was the Second
Ala of Asturians from Spain. The east gate, entirely Hadrianic in
form as all later masonry was removed in 1867, is very well
preserved: the cap from which the rear arch sprang is still in
position on the south side. Now leave the fort and walk down to
the river, passing a fragment of the Wall on your way. You will
soon reach the bath-house, one side of which still stands to a
height of 10 feet. A porch, added later, gives access to the large
changing-room (fig 100). The seven niches probably held wooden
lockers for clothes, and no doubt there was once a second row
above. On the river side is a heavily-buttressed latrine. From the

99   *Chesters, the bridge abutment*

changing-room the bather would cross the worn threshold, and
turn left into the cold-room with its cold plunge-bath. Then he
had a choice of hot rooms, though not all belong to the original
building. Returning to the lobby he could either keep straight
ahead for the hot-dry suite, or turn left for the long room of moist
heat. This was originally divided into two parts, the *tepidarium*
and the *caldarium*. Its floor and hypocaust have completely
disappeared, but the stoke-hole survives at the far end, and, on the
right, the imposing wall of the hot plunge-bath still has the lower
part of a window (fig 101). Another set of warm rooms runs
parallel on the river side.

From the bath-house you may like to wander down to the
river. If the water is low a bridge abutment and two piers may be
visible; the eastern abutment can be seen on the far side (see
above). Returning to the fort, you first reach the hypocaust of the
commandant's private bath-suite. Its floor is supported by a
mixture of brick and stone pillars: the irregularity is due to
partial reconstruction, probably in the fourth century. The
hypocausts in the living-rooms are also additions to the
original building. In the centre of the fort is the headquarters

100   Chesters, bath-house, undressing-room

building, the clearest example visible in Britain. The entrance led
to a courtyard surrounded by a covered colonnade on three sides.
The gutters and part of the courtyard paving are visible, and on
one of the flags near the well a phallus has been carved for good
luck. The courtyard led to the covered cross-hall, with a *tribunal*
on the right from which the officer could address his assembled
troops. Beyond are five administrative buildings, the central one
of which contained the statue of the emperor and the regimental
standards (fig 102). In the third century, a strong-room, still
covered by its roof, was inserted below the floor (fig 103): it now
appears to stick up above ground, but the floor-level elsewhere
was much higher at this period than it is now, as the excavators
removed the later floors to expose the Hadrianic masonry.
Finally, you should visit the rest of the defences: a single-
portalled gate on the east side (near the commandant's house),
an angle tower, two interval-towers, and the south and west gates
all remain exposed. Of the south gate, one portal was blocked up
soon after being built, but its blocking-wall has been removed to
reveal the Hadrianic masonry; the other remained in use,
resulting in a build-up of road-levels and the raising of the east
portal. Its rear threshold, much worn, is built of re-used gutter-
stones. The west gate was entirely blocked up, but once again the
blocking-walls have now been removed. A water-tank can be
seen in one guardroom, and beyond it some ovens. A portion of

101   Chesters bath-house, apse of hot bath

Hadrian's Wall is also visible, adjoining the south guardroom: the fort lay astride the Wall, and three of its gateways, therefore, opened into enemy territory. A tour of the Chesters Museum, crammed full of sculptured and inscribed stones, will complete your visit to the site.

Now continue westwards along the B8316. After climbing the hill you will see a fine, newly-conserved piece of Wall and a turret at **Black Carts** (NY 8871) [AM; A]; they deserve closer inspection. Turn off, therefore, along the next lane on the right. The back wall of the turret is still seven feet high, but the front has been reduced to ground-level. The adjacent Wall is built to the narrow width, and so this is the first visible turret with wing-walls of the broad gauge. Two 'centurial stones', recording the erection of stretches of Wall by working-parties of legionary *centuriae*, are also visible here. One is on the bottom course of the south face, 12 blocks west of the end of the turret's wing-wall. The other, on the bottom course of the north face mid-way between the turret and the wooden gate, reads COH I . . . ('the first cohort of . . .'). As these stones were always placed on the south side when the Wall was originally raised, it looks as though this portion was

102   Chesters, inside the HQ

103   Chesters, the headquarters building

104   Limestone Corner, the unfinished Ditch

105   Carrawburgh, the Vallum

entirely rebuilt in a later reconstruction, and the centurial stone
was incorporated into the outer face as if it were a normal
building-stone.

After Black Carts, the road climbs again and more of the Wall
is visible. On the downward slope there is a lay-by on the right
near an iron gate. This leads at once to the stretch of Ditch on
Limestone Corner (NY 8771), here unfinished because of the
hardness of the rock (fig 104). It is an imposing sight, and a
sobering reminder of what Roman engineers were capable of
achieving without the use of explosives. A mile further on, after
passing a superb stretch of the Vallum (fig 105), you will come to
the car-park adjoining the fort of BROCOLITIA, **Carrawburgh**
(NY 8571), of which only a lofty earth rampart-mound is at
present visible. It was added later than the main series of forts,
about AD 130–3. Outside is the fine little temple of Mithras,
excavated in 1950 [AM; A]. Founded soon after AD 205, twice
refurbished before its destruction in 297, it was rebuilt again, and
then finally desecrated in the early fourth century, presumably by
Christians. The visible remains represent the building in its final
form (fig 106). An ante-chapel containing the statuette of a
mother-goddess is separated from the nave by a screen (some
concrete posts, representing wooden uprights, remain). Low
benches, revetted with a wooden interlace, flank the nave, where
stand smashed representations of the torch-bearers and four tiny
altars. The stone walls visible half-way along the benches mark
the limits of the first Mithraeum, which was only half the size of
the present building. At the end are three magnificent altars, and
in the shelf behind them would have stood the bull-slaying
relief. A few words about Mithraism and a reconstruction-drawing of a ceremony in progress will be found on p. 314. The originals of the inscriptions and sculptures are now in the Newcastle
museum, together with a full-scale reconstruction of the building.
The shrine of Coventina, a nymph to whom numerous offerings of
all kinds were thrown, is now represented by the marshy well a few
yards to the north, adjoining the field-wall and surrounded by
wooden rails.

Now press on for another 4m and visit the most famous and
popular of all the Wall-forts, **Housesteads***** (NY 7968) [AM;
SSM]: if it is high summer and you want to visit the site in
comparative peace, be sure to arrive early. Its Roman name was
VERCOVICIVM, meaning 'hilly place', but it is widely known by the

incorrect form Borcovicus. The third-century garrison was an
infantry cohort of Tungrians (from Belgium), 1,000 strong. The
fame of Housesteads is mainly due to its dramatic setting, on the
edge of a craggy precipice in a lonely part of Northumberland.
The little museum has a few items, notably a relief of three hooded
deities, and an uninscribed slab flanked by cupids. A few buildings of the large civil settlement are exposed near the south gate,
by which the fort is entered. Now walk up the slope, along the
line of the *via principalis*. The first building on the left, recently
excavated and soon to be opened to the public, is the commandant's house. In its visible, third-century form it consists of four
wings around a courtyard, but only the north and west wings are
of Hadrianic origin. Two rooms of the west wing contain latrines.
Next comes the headquarters building, which also dates mainly
from the third century. It contains the usual courtyard, cross-hall
(with *tribunal*) and five administrative rooms, but it is not well
preserved. Behind it is the hospital, at present under excavation:
it is the only visible example in Britain. Next to the headquarters
is a pair of granaries. One has been marred by the insertion of a
post-medieval kiln, but elsewhere the pillars that supported the

106   Carrawburgh, Temple of Mithras

now-vanished floor may be seen. After the granaries you reach
the north wall of the fort. Built up against the back of this is a long
store-building and, immediately in front of it and partly buried
under it, are the footings of a small square structure with hearth-
bases. This is turret 36b, demolished about AD 124 when the order
came to place forts on the Wall itself. It will be seen from the
position of the turret that Hadrian's Wall was originally designed
to run a little behind its present course. Now turn right to the
north gate. Originally a roadway sloped up to it from outside,
but this was removed in 1853 to expose the massive foundations.
A water-tank rests against one of the well-preserved guardrooms.
Now walk clockwise round the fort-wall. The earth rampart
originally backing this has been removed to expose the stonework. Interval-towers will be noted en route. From the NW
corner the Wall can be seen running down to the Knag Burn,
where a customs-gateway, flanked by a pair of guardrooms, was
inserted in the fourth century. Before reaching the east gate, you
will see two long buildings on the right, both fourth-century in
their visible form. The first is a barrack-block with seven separate
rooms and a workshop, but its plan is very different from the

107   Housesteads, the latrine

standard blocks of earlier periods. The second is a long store-building with a bath-suite inserted at one end. At the east gate, note the deeply-rutted threshold of the north portal; that on the south was blocked up in the third century and became a guard-chamber, while the original guardroom became a coal-store. At the SE corner is the most fascinating building at Housesteads, the best-preserved latrine in Roman Britain (fig 107). The soldiers would have sat on wooden seats erected over the deep sewers on either side, and washed their sponges – the Roman equivalent of toilet-paper – in the water running along the gutter in front of them. Two basins were provided for rinsing their hands. It is a remarkable monument to Roman hygiene, the level of which was not equalled until the present century. After passing the south gate and rounding the SW angle (an oven is visible in one building here), you reach the west gate, still standing to a spectacular height.

The walk along Hadrian's Wall westwards from here is always a popular one, though other stretches equally fine but less well known exist elsewhere (especially on Peel Crag and at Walltown). This stretch is owned by the National Trust, whose policy is to leave a turf capping on the Wall for the convenience of visitors. The tremendous views over a vast tract of the Northumbrian fells make the walk particularly memorable, but structurally there is not a great deal to note. After emerging from a

108   Housesteads, milecastle 37 (north gate)

picturesque coppice, you will notice a few offsets on the inside
face of the Wall, marking the junction between different portions
of slightly differing widths. Presumably each building-gang had a
different idea about what was meant to be the exact width of the
Wall, and discrepancies had to be rectified in this manner.
Milecastle 37 is soon reached, the work of the Second Legion.
The visible stone barrack was matched by another of timber.
The north gateway is very fine (fig 108). The massive masonry of
the gate-piers, together with the two springers *in situ* and more
voussoirs of the arch lying on the ground, are of Hadrianic date.
In the destruction at the end of the second century, the enemy
attempted to lever over these jambs, so that they are now out of
the perpendicular. In position, too, is the Severan stonework
which reduced the gateway to a narrow postern. Thereafter, the
Wall can be followed over Cuddy's Crag with its famous view to
the east, and on over Hotbank Crags (1,074 feet), where Crag
Lough comes into view, before it drops down to Milking Gap
and milecastle 38 (whence the stone in fig 96 came). No turrets are
visible on this stretch. Visitors with cars, of course, will have to
retrace their steps to Housesteads.

After Housesteads, it is convenient to visit one of the Stanegate
forts, where an ambitious programme of excavation is now under
way. The fort is **Chesterholm*** (NY 7764), usually known by its
Roman name of VINDOLANDA [Apr. 9.30–5, May–Sept. 9.30–
6.30; Oct.–Mar. 10.30–3.30 for the new excavations; fort AM;
A]. It is signposted from the B8316 ½m west of Housesteads
car-park. The track up to the site follows the line of the Stanegate,
and on the right, opposite the farm, a Roman milestone survives
in situ, now without an inscription [AM; A]. The excavations in
progress are designed to uncover the whole of the *vicus*, or civil
settlement, which accompanies the third- and fourth-century
fort further east. Much more of the *vicus* will, of course, be
visible by the time this book is printed. In 1972 only a 15-room
mansio (inn) and a small corridor-house, both lining a paved
street, had been fully excavated and consolidated; the military
bath-house, more compact than Chesters' but also well-preserved
(seven feet high in parts), was awaiting restoration. Short
sections of turf and stone Wall will also have been built to give
visitors an idea of their original appearance. Beyond the *vicus*
lies the fort, an entirely new foundation of c. AD 205, but at least
two earlier forts, one Agricolan and the other Antonine, are

known to exist further west, buried beneath the visible *vicus*. The
north and west gates were excavated and conserved in the 1930's,
together with the headquarters building. The latter is excellently
preserved, and has many interesting features not visible in the
Chesters example. A few foundations of the third-century
principia, which faced in the opposite direction, can be seen here
and there, but the visible layout belongs entirely to the fourth
century. Several rooms round a small courtyard in the front half
of the building were turned into store-rooms in the Theodosian
reorganization (c. 370): parts of their ventilated floors remain,
built of stone flags resting on sleeper walls (fig 109). Beyond is the
usual cross-hall with its *tribunal* on the right; the latter still
preserves its moulded edge, and the steps leading up to it. Of the
administrative rooms at the back, two features are outstanding:
the unusual ⊓ -shaped pit for storing pay-chests and other
valuables; and the ornamental stone screens flanking rooms on
either side (fig. 109, right of pole). A full-size replica of this
principia will be erected to the west of the *vicus* to serve as the
site-museum, and it is also hoped to uncover all the rest of the
buildings of the fort. In 1972, work was in progress on a latrine

109   Chesterholm, the headquarters building

at the NE corner. If sufficient money is forthcoming, and excavation is not too hurried, we should learn an enormous amount about both military and civilian life on the frontier in the closing years of the Roman occupation, and the consolidated remains will form the most extensive single site visible in Roman Britain.

Instead of returning immediately to the B6318, you may like to continue along the Stanegate (untarred) for one mile, until you reach a minor road. 200 yards before it, on the right, the base of another Roman milestone is visible. Turn right at the road, and as you descend to the stream, you will see the outlines of two temporary camps in the field on your left (perhaps better viewed from the other side of the stream). Several examples are known in the Wall region: some were used in training, but these two would have sheltered troops engaged on building or reconstructing the Wall. Go straight across at the B-road to Steel Rigg car-park. You then have the choice of going west or east. Westwards, a 15-minute walk takes you up to **Winshields** (NY 7467), the highest point on the Wall (trig-point, 1,230 feet), with spectacular views as far as the Solway on a clear day. No Wall is visible until a long stretch just past the summit [AM ; A], but at the start the Ditch is rarely better preserved. Eastwards, on **Peel Crag** (NY 7567), there is much more of the Wall to see: it is just as spectacular, and the scenery as fine, as the more famous Housesteads sector. Three offsets will be noted on the inner face of the Wall on the superb level stretch (see p. 263 for an explanation). After 25 minutes you drop down to Castle Nick milecastle (no. 39), the work of the Twentieth Legion. Its gateways are made of small stones, as the usual massive blocks were probably too awkward to transport to this remote spot. In the Severan period the gateways were reduced in width, and this later stonework remains in position at the south gate.

From Steel Rigg, turn right onto the B-road and then second right (signposted Whiteside). On the left, between road and stream, the rampart-mounds of the fortlet of Haltwhistle Burn are visible, built under Hadrian but only briefly occupied. On its north side, at the point where the road swings to the left, is a small temporary camp. Park here, and walk along the track leading straight on. On the right, the low defences of another tiny camp can be made out. Both are too small to have served other than as training-exercises in camp-building. Next you cross the Vallum, which is most striking as it stretches away to the right in a near-perfect state of preservation. Then the Military Way is clearly visible, laid in the later second century to link forts and milecastles. Finally you reach the Wall at **Cawfields** (NY 7166) [AM; A]. Here is milecastle 42, built by the Second Legion (fig 110). The massive masonry of its south gate stands six feet high, thus preserving the bolt-hole. It is worth walking to the end of the consolidated stretch of Wall to the east, in order to see a magnificent fragment, still nine feet high, attacking Thorny Doors (fig 111). So steep is the slope here that the foundation of the Wall must be stepped, for the courses are laid nearly at right-angles to the lie of the ground. In places such as this, you can fully appreciate just how tremendous an engineering achievement Hadrian's Wall is.

Return once more to the B-road, turn right and first right (unsignposted). Keep straight on at the fork, and after the third gate across the road you come to the south gate of AESICA, **Greatchesters** (NY 7066). A good deal is visible here – most of the south and west ramparts and their gates, some barracks and the arch of the underground strong-room in the *principia* – but the ruins are in a sorry state, overgrown and neglected. The place is

110 Cawfields milecastle

perhaps worth a visit to show how exposed masonry deteriorates when it is not treated, and to enable us to admire even more the consolidation work of the men from the DOE. Greatchesters would look very different with a little help from them. The fort was a later addition to the Wall than most, as it was not built before AD 128. The main item of interest is its west gate, which alone of all the gates visible on the Wall still has blocking-walls across both portals. Excavators at other forts removed such masonry to expose the thresholds beneath. A six-mile leet brought water to the fort from the north : parts of it can be traced

111   Hadrian's Wall at Thorny Doors

with the help of the OS Map of Hadrian's Wall.

   Follow the B8316 for another three miles until a signpost to **Walltown*** (NY 6766) [AM ; A] appears on the right, ½m east of Greenhead. Follow the DOE signs. The path leads to a hollow between the trees, but it is better to climb up the slope on your right, until you reach turret 45a. This was built as an independent signalling-tower, probably under Trajan, and was later incorporated into the Wall. From here westwards for some 400 yards the Wall is at its very best. First comes a magnificent dive

112   Hadrian's Wall on Walltown Crags, looking west

into one of the Nine Nicks of Thirlwall, and the effortless climb up the far side (figs 112 and 113). Six yards west of the DOE notice, a 'centurial stone' reading COH III can be seen built upside down into the north face of the Wall (for the implication, see above, p. 257). Then, still standing to a stately height of 7–8 feet, the Wall weaves a sinuous course round whinstone outcrops (fig 114). At one point where it has to change direction suddenly on a steep slope, the inner face is 'stepped' slightly to ensure stability. Finally, this exciting sector is abruptly ended on the edge of a quarry, which has sadly removed the Wall for $\frac{1}{4}$ mile. If you have time you may like to follow the Wall eastwards from turret 45a. Most of it is visible, unconsolidated, all the way to Greatchesters, but it lacks the grandeur of the DOE stretch. Turret 44b, above Walltown Farm, still stands nine courses high.

After Walltown, the dramatic parts of Hadrian's Wall are past, and you leave the crags for the gentler slopes of Cumberland. Turn right in Greenhead onto the A69 and then immediately right along the B6318. Just before the railway-bridge at the beginning of Gilsland, turn left and visit milecastle 48 at **Poltross Burn** (NY 6366) [AM; A], the most instructive on the Wall.

113   *The same stretch as it may have appeared, looking east*

Both gates were narrowed in the Severan reconstruction, and
the blocking-wall is clearly visible at the north gate. There is an
oven at the NW corner and, in the NE, a staircase to the rampart-
walk. The outlines of the two stone barracks survive. The milecastle was built by the Sixth Legion with broad gauge wing-walls
on either side; one of these can be seen, together with a fragment
of narrow Wall on broad foundation. The latter feature continues
as far as the Irthing.

Go under the railway-bridge, turn left at the junction and stop
on the brow of the hill. On your left a DOE board advertises the
sector of Wall in the former vicarage garden of **Gilsland** (NY
6366) [AM; A]. Here it only stands 3–4 feet high, but there is no
better place to study the narrow Wall on a broad foundation.
The newly-uncovered stretch near the railway has some superb
drainage-culverts, because of the proximity of a stream, and here
it can be seen most clearly that the narrow Wall does not merely
rest on broad foundation, but on three courses of broad Wall. It
seems that construction of the curtain-wall was actually in
progress here when the order came, in 124 or 5, to reduce the
width of the Wall, and rather than demolish what was already
constructed, the builders merely carried the Wall on upwards at
its new width.

On the other side of the road, the Wall is impressively visible
on its broad foundation all the way to **Willowford*** (NY 6266)

114   Another view of the Wall on Walltown Crags

[AM; A] and the bridge over the Irthing. First comes an excellent example of a turret (48a) with wing-walls built to the broad gauge (fig 115). Nearer the farm a cart-track runs in the Ditch, and turret 48b is visible. Then comes the final slope down to the Irthing. The bridge-abutment here is a very complicated structure displaying work of three periods. It is less impressive than the example at Chesters. Starting from the wicket-gate on the north side of the Wall, you will first see a large masonry embankment which protected the ground here from erosion by the river. The latter has now shifted far away. Then come two culverts which belong to phase II and were probably connected with a water-mill. Rounding a bridge-pier and a paved section of river-bed, you come to the massive abutment of period III, which blocks up one of the culverts. This work incorporates the earliest abutment, the edge of which is marked by the diagonal line running across the ruins here. The small tower which sat on this first abutment was entirely demolished in phase II, but its NE corner is marked by the slight recess visible on the Wall-face here – the Wall was extended across the site of the tower. The tower was then replaced by a much larger one to the east, built, as can be seen, with re-used

115　*Willowford, turret 48a*

masonry blocks. The dates of the changes at Willowford are not known.

Walkers should be able to cross the Irthing and climb up the bank opposite, now much steeper than in Roman times. Motorists must return to Gilsland, turn left and follow the B6318 for about 1¼m until Birdoswald is signposted on the left. From the car-park ½m later you can walk along a fine stretch of the Wall to the poorly-preserved **Harrow's Scar** milecastle (NY 6266) [AM; A]. Parts of its walls and one blocked gate are visible, but most of the stonework inside belongs to a post-Roman farmstead. The Wall here is narrow on a narrow foundation, for it was not built in stone until late in Hadrian's reign. The earlier Turf Wall, which for two miles west of the Irthing takes a slightly different course to that of the Stone Wall, is not now visible except for a short sector mentioned below.

Nearly opposite the car-park is the farm-drive leading to the fort of **Birdoswald*** (NY 6166) [AM; A]. Its defences are more interesting and better preserved than those of any other Wall-fort. On the left of the drive is the NW corner, still standing over six feet high. Clamber up the bank to have a look at the angle tower. Its doorway has been blocked, probably in the fourth century. Some second-century ovens, often rebuilt, are visible within. After a short break comes an interval-tower with a flagged floor of Severan date. The main west gate still lies buried. Beyond is part of the wall of a Roman granary, now serving as a retaining-wall at the south end of the garden. Continuing along the west rampart you pass the lesser west-gate (single portal) and reach the SW angle. Here is visible some vivid evidence of the reconstruction necessary on Hadrian's Wall after the barbarian incursions: the bottom two courses are probably Hadrianic, the next three (set back a little, giving a step-like appearance) are Severan, and the top two are Constantian (or possibly post-Roman). Next comes the south gate. Both thresholds of the Hadrianic gate, together with pivot-holes, are visible; the later blocking-walls have been removed. The irregular masonry of the wall on the left belongs to a fourth-century rebuilding. Both the flanking guardrooms have kilns and ovens. Next, it is worth walking to the edge of the promontory for the view over the Irthing. The name of the fort, CAMBOGLANNA, which means 'the crooked bend', refers to the winding course that the river takes here. Now follow the fort-wall round the SE angle. Just after the gap are more signs of Roman rebuilding: a 20-foot stretch, 4½ feet high (beneath a thin stone bonding-course), is not quite flush with the rest of the masonry and is built of larger stones. The east gate is excellently preserved (fig 116). In both portals remains of two successive pivot-holes can be seen, probably Hadrianic and (above) Severan. The massive jamb of the right-hand (north) portal still stands to its full height and the springer of the arch is in position. In the fourth century, this portal became a guardroom, and part of its back wall is still visible. The door of the original, adjacent guard-chamber was then blocked up and a new door opened in its south wall, giving access to the portal now used as a guardroom. At the same time masonry was inserted between the back and front central piers. Two rounded window-stones lie on the grass near the south guardroom, which lies over the site of Hadrian's Turf Wall. Until the Stone Wall was built on a new alignment, then, Birdoswald fort projected north of the barrier. Finally, a stile at the north end of the east rampart, near a post-Roman kiln, gives access to an interval-tower.

Westwards from Birdoswald you will get your last view of a substantial length of Hadrian's Wall. Turret 49b is also exposed

116 Birdoswald, the east gate

here. Then, $\frac{1}{2}$m later, look out for the first track on the left (white gate), which leads to **High House** (NY 6085). Just after passing through a fence on this track you will see a low broad mound stretching for a short distance on the left. This is the only visible fragment of the Turf Wall. Do not confuse it with the high mounds and ditch of the Vallum which lie immediately beyond and are a striking sight in both directions. $\frac{3}{4}$m west of here, on the minor road, the lines of the Turf and Stone Walls coincide, and remain so, with one short exception, all the way to Bowness. Neither Wall is visible at the point of intersection, but the Ditches of both are boldly preserved. Soon afterwards, three Turf-Wall turrets will be passed. These were built of stone from the beginning and the Turf Wall came right up to either side; when the latter was replaced in stone, it too stood up against the existing turrets, and its masonry is never bonded with that of the turrets. First comes turret 51a, **Piper Sike** (NY 5865) [AM; A], excavated in 1970 and the least well preserved. A cooking-hearth and a flagged platform, of uncertain purpose (?ladder-platform), can be seen inside. Turret 51b, **Leahill** (NY 5865) [AM; A], like Piper Sike, seems not to have been used after the second century. Finally, 100 yards west of Pike Hill (where there was an earlier stone signal-tower, cf. p. 268; it is soon to be exposed and consolidated by the DOE) comes the imposing turret of **Banks East** (NY 5764 [AM; A]. Unlike the other two this was occupied until 296. Here the plinth that was a characteristic of Turf-Wall turrets is perfectly preserved on the north, and the stone Wall of Hadrian abuts on each side. A hearth and a ladder-platform can be seen within the turret, and a fallen piece of superstructure lies nearby. The view to the south is very fine.

Further west, all the way to Bowness, Hadrian's Wall has little of interest for the visitor. Short stretches of Ditch or Vallum appear here and there, but the Wall itself has disappeared completely except for the smallest fragments. Even the remaining five forts have left little visible trace. That at Stanwix, now a northern suburb of Carlisle, was the largest fort on the Wall. Here was stationed the commander-in-chief of the Wall garrison and a cavalry regiment 1,000 strong, the *Ala Petriana*. The position of this headquarters so near the western end may seem surprising, but when the 40 miles of Solway posts, which were an integral part of the Hadrianic frontier, are included, Stanwix is near the centre of the system. It is also in this part that the Wall's

command of ground to the north is weakest. Across the river, at
Carlisle (NY 3955), lay the flourishing town of LVG VVALLIVM. All
that can be seen of it now is the single building exposed in the
garden of the Tullie House Museum. The latter [weekdays
Apr.–Sept. 9–8, Oct.–Mar. 9–5; Sun., Jun.–Aug. only, 2.30–5]
contains another impressive display of sculptured and inscribed
stones and of small objects, though it lacks the modern surroundings of the Newcastle museum. A recorded commentary on the
exhibits is available for hire.

Note: this map does *not* mark all the sites between Risingham and Chew Green (described pp. 278–285) or on the Antonine Wall (heavy black line between Forth and Clyde, described pp. 292–300).

Ross and Cromarty

Nairn-shire

Morayshire

Banffshire

Invernessshire

Aberdeenshire

Glenmailen

Normandykes

Raedykes

Kincardineshire

Angus

Perthshire

Cleaven Dyke

Inchtuthill

Gask Ridge

Kaims Castle

Ardoch

Kirkbuddo

Argyllshire

Fife

Kinross

Dunbarton-shire

Stirlingshire

Watling Lodge

New Kilpatrick

Duntocher

Renfrew-shire

Rough Castle

Croy Hill

Cramond

East Lothian

Mid Lothian

Castle Greg

Lyne

Peeblesshire

Berwickshire

Lanarkshire

Ayrshire

Selkirkshire

Pennymuir & Woden Law

Roxburghshire

Chew Green

High Rochester

Risingham

Swine Hill

Northumberlan

Dumfriesshire

Burnswark

Birrens

Kirkcudbrightshire

Chapter 9

Scotland

and England beyond Hadrian's Wall

1: Between the walls

Driving into Scotland along Dere Street (A68) is an exhilarating experience. For many miles the modern road sticks resolutely to the Roman alignment, rising and falling dramatically over the hilly terrain. Agricola came this way on his first campaign into Scotland, in AD 80, and Dere Street was constructed in the wake of his advance, probably in 81. Thereafter the route was used by many Roman armies marching into Scotland, and numerous earthworks which they constructed can still be traced today. Apart from the permanent posts, the remains of no less than 14 Roman marching camps are visible on an 18-mile stretch south of the Scottish border, and there is no better place anywhere in the Roman Empire to study this particular class of military antiquity. Unfortunately their dates are less well known than those of the camps further north in Scotland. Some of them are no doubt Agricolan, though only two are proved as such.

For the first seven miles from Corbridge, the A68 does not swerve from the Roman alignment. Then they part company for one mile, taking different routes to cross a stream, before joining forces again for another four-mile stretch. $\frac{1}{2}$m beyond a cross-roads signposted 'Bellingham 5' and 'Knowesgate 6', the A68 bends sharply to the right and a track marked 'Vickers Ltd. Private Property' leaves it on the left. A gate in the field-wall on the left here leads to the temporary camp of **Swine Hill** (NY 9082), which lies immediately in front of you on the other side of a rivulet. Its prominent NE corner is marked by a concrete post, as are all the other corners and the three gateways with their internal *claviculae*: it is therefore easy to trace the outline of this small and well-preserved camp. The west rampart is confused by modern ridges and the south side is rather low, but the north gate is in excellent condition. The camp would have been large enough for about three cohorts, roughly 1,500 men.

Continue along the A68 for another 3m as far as West Woodburn. As you descend the hill to cross the Rede, you will see a lane on the right signposted 'E. Woodburn 1, Monkridge 4½'. Take the farm-track opposite it, on the left of the A68, and after ½m you will have a good view of the prominent grass mounds which cover the stone ramparts of HABITANCVM, **Risingham** (NY 8986). Odd pieces of stonework are still visible, mostly at the NE angle, and there are faint traces of multiple ditches on the south and west. If you wish to inspect the site more closely, ask for permission at the farm. Risingham was a permanent fort, founded not by Agricola but by Lollius Urbicus in the mid-second century. Little is known of this earliest structure, when a mounted cohort of Gauls was its garrison. The visible fort, which served as an outpost for Hadrian's Wall, dates from the early third century. At this time the original fort was entirely rebuilt with massive defences, including polygonal projecting towers flanking the south gate. Two fine building-inscriptions, now in Newcastle, record this work. One of them is enormously long and fills the whole of the back wall of the museum. It is dated to AD 213 and records the new garrison as the First Cohort of Vangiones, brigaded with 'Raetian Spearmen and the Scouts of Habitancum'. Further alterations and repairs occurred in the fourth century.

After crossing the Rede, the modern road joins the line of Dere Street again and follows it, with the occasional deviation, as far as the next Roman earthwork. This is a temporary camp called **The Dargues** (NY 8693). One mile after the A68 is crossed by the B6320, a minor road is signposted 'High Green 4'. Carry on down the slope and over the burn and you will see two houses facing each other across the road. That on the left is 'The Dargues', as marked on the gate. Walk northwards along the A68 to the next field-gate, and from it you will see the east rampart of the Roman camp clearly visible 20 yards away. Bigger than Swine Hill, this camp is nearly large enough to hold a legion, but it is in much worse condition. The east rampart survives only in short stretches. That on the north is clear but much eroded, though its ditch, marked by dark rushes, is easily visible near the NW corner. The west side is well preserved to begin with, and the *clavicula* of a gate can be seen near the stone wall dividing this field from the next. Thereafter the rest of the west and the whole of the south ramparts are virtually invisible, though the ditch on the south (dark rushes) is clear. The farm has obliterated the whole of the SE corner.

½m after Dargues the A68 again leaves Dere Street, swinging away sharply to the right. There is a parking-place on the left of the road at the bend. Cross the road opposite the café and look over the stone wall. You are now at the NW corner of the Roman fort of **Blakehope** (NY 8594), but very little of it is visible. Excavation in 1955 showed that its turf rampart had been burnt down before the reign of Hadrian and never rebuilt. It may therefore be an Agricolan fort, one of the *praesidia* (fortifications) that Tacitus says were built in AD 81 as part of the consolidation of southern Scotland. The dark reeds clearly mark the position of its single ditch for the whole of the west and north ramparts, and the causeway leading to the north gate is marked by a break in the line of reeds. The turf rampart accompanying this ditch now only survives as a low broad mound. Do not, incidentally, be confused by the higher 'ramparts' visible to the left near the telegraph-poles; these are modern banks connected with drainage ditches.

½m later the Newcastle road (A696) joins the A68. Turn left and go on for another mile. Shortly after the turning to Otterburn camp, a driveway on the left is closed by a gate labelled 'Bagraw'. Continue on round the bend and pull onto the grass verge at the first field-gate on the left. Walk back 10 paces and look towards the gap in the stone wall on the far side of the field. You are now looking along part of the west rampart of the temporary camp of **Bagraw** (NY 8496), here visible as a prominent ridge. Most of the rest of its circuit has been obliterated. The Bagraw camp is rectangular, but elongated to make it fit onto a narrow shelf of ground. It was originally big enough to accommodate a full legion, but at some later stage it was divided into two.

There is not much to see at Bagraw and it is best to press on soon for another 1½m and visit the fort of **High Rochester*** (NY 8398). This was BREMENIVM or 'the place of the roaring stream'. There are stone remains visible here, more substantial than at any other site in Britain north of Hadrian's Wall; and after the final withdrawal from Scotland, this little post bore the distinction, if such it was, of being the most northerly occupied fort of the Roman Empire. It was founded by Agricola, rebuilt in stone by Lollius Urbicus c. 139, and rebuilt again at the beginning of the

third and the fourth centuries after enemy destruction. It was
finally abandoned in 343 after another uprising.

Just after you have passed the sign announcing the village of
Rochester, turn off to the right by the war-memorial. The house
opposite it has two catapult-balls and several Roman gutter-
stones built into its porch. The road leads up to the hamlet of
High Rochester and the site of the fort. This is entered by the
south gate, of which two blocks are visible in the right-hand
verge. The rampart-mound is prominent along the whole of this
side, but the stone wall crowning it is modern. A little to the left
of the road, however, the huge stone blocks of an interval-tower,
still six feet high, are clearly visible. The front side, where the
fort-wall originally stood, has been robbed. The tower dates from
the last, fourth-century, rebuilding. Park inside the fort and go
through a gate on the left: the track cuts through the Roman
rampart. Turn right and you come almost immediately to the
fine west gate (fig 117). The flanking towers of massive masonry,
flush with the fort-wall, make an impressive sight, and the
moulded cap of one of the gate-jambs as well as a springer of the
arch survive. The visible masonry belongs to the fourth century.

117   High Rochester, the west gate

Continue walking to the NW angle of the fort, where more
Roman work is visible. Excavation here in 1937 revealed the
foundations of three superimposed fort-walls, dating to AD 139,
205–8, and 297, and two different sizes of stonework are still
distinguishable. Also found behind the west rampart and the
north were the large *ballistaria* mentioned on a third-century
inscription, and these supported the catapults that hurled the
stone balls which you saw built into the porch by the main road.
Now return to the hamlet-green, pass to the left of the two houses
on its north side, and go through another gate. The stone blocks
visible on the right belong to one of the jambs of the Roman
north gateway. You can admire the command of terrain from
here, and you should also be able to pick out the entire outline of
the Roman temporary camp of Birdhope (see below). It lies on
rough ground to your left, on the other side of the stream but
before the modern army-huts. In front of you traces of the
multiple ditch-system are still visible and these can be followed
right round to the causeway leading to the site of the east gate,
from which the hamlet-green is again reached.

Dere Street, the Roman road you have been following from
Corbridge, skirted BREMENIVM to the east, and lining it 750 yards
south of the fort were some monumental tombs. One of them,
known locally as the Roman Well, is still visible. It is circular and
now consists of two courses of large blocks on a rubble base
(fig 118). Originally it must have been an impressive structure

118   High Rochester, Roman tomb

some 15 feet high, probably the resting-place of an important
officer. One of the stones of the lower course is decorated with
the head of an animal, perhaps a fox and a reminder of the hunting pastimes of the deceased. Two adjacent tombs are now
entirely robbed of their masonry. To find the spot (which is not
easy) go down the road from the hamlet until you reach the third
field-gate on your left (metal). Make first for the house on the
skyline and then continue straight on for another farm set in front
of some trees. About half-way between these buildings you will
reach Dere Street, which is clearly visible as a broad low *agger*
forming a lighter strip in the moorland. Then strike right towards
a long, low outcrop of rock. Before you reach it, on the west
side of Dere Street, you will see the Roman tomb.

High Rochester, like Risingham, has produced a wealth of
Roman inscriptions. Most of them are in Newcastle, but there
are some in the Durham Cathedral collection, and another is in
Cambridge. One of them, found about 1744, is a well-preserved
and well-executed example of a dedication-stone (fig 119).
Similar inscriptions would have appeared on every major
building, civilian and military, in Roman Britain, and a full

119   High Rochester, an inscription (in Newcastle)

translation of it will not be out of place: 'For the emperor Caesar
Marcus Aurelius Severus Antoninus Pius Felix Augustus, Most
Great Conqueror of Parthia, Most Great Conqueror of Britain,
Most Great Conqueror of Germany, high priest, in the nineteenth
year of his tribunician power, twice acclaimed Imperator, four
times consul, proconsul, father of his country, the loyal first
cohort of Vardulli, Roman citizens (C R), part-mounted (EQ),
one thousand strong (∞), styled Antoniniana, built this under
the charge of . . ., the emperor's propraetorian legate.' The
building it adorned is unknown. The date of the stone is AD 216,
as we know the year of the magistracies held by the emperor,
who is here given his full official titles. He is better known as
Caracalla. The inscription also gives the name of the garrison,
and another stone from the site, also in Newcastle, tells us that
they were brigaded with a unit of scouts (*exploratores*): the
Spanish Vardulli cannot have been at anything near their full
strength, for 1,000 + is far too many men to fit into such a small
fort. Yet another inscription, also in Newcastle, came from the
east gate and declares that a *vexillatio* of the Twentieth Legion
(from Chester) built it. Crude figures of Mars and Hercules
flank the inscribed panel. Finally, a poorly-executed but ambi-
tiously-conceived stone may be mentioned. It represents Venus
and two water-nymphs disporting themselves in their bath; they

120   High Rochester, Venus and nymphs (in Newcastle)

seem a little offended by our presence (fig 120).

On regaining the A68 from BREMENIVM, turn right. If you want to see a Roman altar (itself well-preserved but the inscription is illegible), take the first track on the right: the altar is built into the wall near the front door of the last house on the left of this track. Return once more to the main road and continue to the end of the village, where you should take another track, involving a sharp right turn off the A68. Continue straight along this, avoiding the modern camp, and park at the metal gate. Keep walking until you see a white-star marker-post on your left. This is at the SE corner of **Birdhope** (NY 8298) temporary camp. The camp is in a fine state of preservation, its entire circuit being easily traceable by the lighter colour of the grass growing on the ramparts and by the white posts which mark its corners. There were three gates (one on each side except the north) defended by *titula*, but the latter have nearly disappeared into the bog. The substantial rampart suggests that the troops encamped here were staying for some time. The camp lies within a much larger, earlier enclosure, of which few traces now survive.

The rest of the Roman earthworks along the Northumberland sector of Dere Street lie within the Redesdale army camp, and as the area is used as a firing-range, permission to proceed must be sought from the duty officer on arrival (or phone Otterburn 658 to check in advance). The entrance lies ¾m beyond the turning to Birdhope. Two roads lead north from the centre of the camp (look at the map in the officer's hut if you have no 1″ map of your own). The more westerly passes through the Roman marching camp of Bellshiel (App. I); but it is better to take the eastern road, which winds a little on leaving Redesdale Camp and then joins Dere Street. This it follows, dead straight, for nearly three miles. Soon after joining the alignment, when you are level with the half-way point of the pinewoods on the hill away to the right, you will see four star-markers, at present silver-grey, which stand at the corners of **Sill Burn South** camp (NY 826996). It is small, rectangular and unusually narrow. There are *claviculae* at the north and south gates. Also on Dere Street, a few yards further on (about level with the end of the pinewoods just mentioned), another marker indicates the corner of **Sill Burn North** camp (NY 826999). Like its neighbour it is in good condition, though ploughing has removed the east rampart.

Shortly after this a road goes off to the right to Silloans farm-

house. The point of intersection marks the position of the south
gate of **Silloans** camp (NT 823005), but it is the least conspicuous
of all the earthworks on this route. As Dere Street passes straight
through the north and south gates of the camp and destroys the
titula which once defended them, and as Dere Street was constructed c. AD 81, Silloans must be one of Agricola's marching
camps in his Scottish campaign of AD 80.

Two miles further on the road bends near a farmhouse. Turn
left at the fork just after this. At the next junction, ¾m later, a
road goes off on the right to Ridleeshope. A few yards along this
is the west rampart of **Featherwood East** camp (NT 8205), the
SW corner of which is marked by a rusty star-post to the right of
the road. This earthwork measures about 1320 by 1350 feet, and
has a gate and *titulum* in each side, but it is now less conspicuous
than the Sill Burn camps. Return to Dere Street. After a further
½m, this time on the left of the road, is **Featherwood West** camp
(NT 8105). Now difficult to locate, it was slightly larger and less
regular than its neighbour, and had five gates.

Soon after the road turns sharply to the left, there is another
junction. Turn right here and keep climbing for about 1¼m.
When you come over the pass (1,674 feet) you will have a dramatic
view of the **Chew Green*** (NT 7808) earthworks on the other side
of the valley. They are perhaps more impressive from afar than
from closer quarters, for they are extremely complex (see plan,

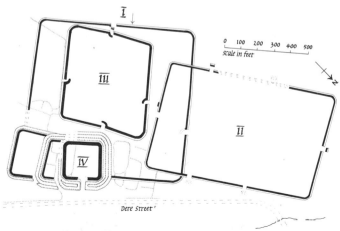

121   *Plan of the earthworks on Chew Green*

fig 121). As their excavator Sir Ian Richmond wrote, the group
'rewards the connoisseur in such sites rather than someone
visiting Roman earthworks for the first time, striking though the
first impression can hardly fail to be'. Further complications are
added by the much slighter enclosure-banks of post-Roman date:
they have not been indicated on fig 121. The sequence of earthworks, established by Richmond in 1936, is as follows. Camp I
occupies the best ground and is the earliest construction here. It
is an Agricolan marching camp of c. AD 80, big enough for a full
legion. A few years later a small permanent convoy-post was
built on the site occupied by the later fortlet (IV), but it is not now
visible. The second main phase of activity belongs to the mid-
second century. The troops on arrival at the site first built a
temporary camp (II) to the north of the main earthworks. They
then constructed III, a strong semi-permanent labour-camp.
The nature of its occupation is suggested by the more substantial
size of its ramparts, still over three feet high, and by the pits and
metalled streets which were found inside. The men living in III
were engaged on erecting IV, a small permanent fortlet
surrounded by triple ditches except on the south. These form the
most conspicuous remains at Chew Green. On its south side are
two annexes used as waggon-parks, with entrances on Dere
Street. This route must have seen heavy traffic during the occupation of Scotland, and the fortlet was clearly designed to house a
small force assisting and protecting convoys over the remote
moorland.

From Chew Green walkers will be able to follow Dere Street
into Scotland to the next site, Woden Law, about three miles to
the north. On the way they will pass a Roman signal-station on
the summit of Brownhart Law (App. I). The motorist, however,
has to make nearly a complete circle to reach Woden Law.
Return the way you have come as far as the junction, turn right,
and you will eventually reach the A68. Follow this over the
Scottish border and ignore the A6088 on the left. You need the
first turning on the right three miles further on, signposted
Edgerston Tofts and Hownam. At the crossroads four miles
later, take the road labelled Hownam and Hindhope. After
another mile comes the junction at the bottom-left corner of the
sketch-map (fig 122). Here is another group of Roman temporary
camps, the best preserved in Scotland: **Pennymuir** (NT 7514).
The largest, camp A, encloses 42 acres and could have

accommodated two legions. Its rampart is in an excellent state, 15 feet wide and up to four feet high. The east half of the north side, near the road, is outstanding, and the whole of the west side, with two *titula*, is impressively visible as a light strip of grass contrasting with the dark colour of the surrounding moorland. Most of the south and east sides have been destroyed. Camp B is smaller and later than A. Its west rampart is also well preserved. The defences of C were on a less massive scale and the surviving portion is no more than one foot high. Camp D has been almost obliterated.

At Pennymuir you can rejoin Dere Street and motor along it, through the ford of the Kale Water, to the road-junction on the other side. From here a 20-minute walk takes you to the native fort and Roman siege-lines of **Woden Law*** (NT 768125). Go past a mountain-hut until you are level with the trees away to the left; a steep climb up the hill to your right will then bring you to the site. The summit of the Law is crowned with a pre-Roman hill-fort. Its defences were first built in the early first century AD and were strengthened before Agricola's invasion (P on inset in fig 122). Surrounding this fort on all sides except the west is a

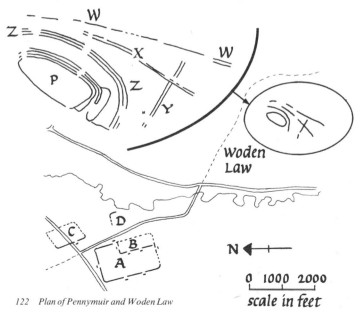

122   Plan of Pennymuir and Woden Law

remarkable, well-preserved earthwork consisting of two banks and three ditches (Z). It is a uniform distance of 70 feet away from the native ramparts, and excavation has shown that the outer bank of Z was flat-topped and built on a stone ballast: it was clearly intended to support the heavy Roman catapult-machines. Thus in theory the besiegers would be out of the range of a hand-thrown missile from the native fort, but could themselves bombard the natives. Elsewhere on the hillside are three independent siege-lines, W, X and Y. All have been erected in short stretches only, by separate working-parties, and are clearly unfinished. The banks of Z too are not entirely even. Their unfinished nature, the insignificance of the hill-fort and the tactical uselessness of W, X and Y point to an inescapable conclusion: Roman troops, bivouacked at Pennymuir, erected these earthworks at various periods as part of their peacetime training. The siege-lines were never used in real warfare, and indeed, the native fort would easily have been stormed without them.

We have followed Dere Street into Scotland and seen the many forts and camps that line its route. Its destination was Inveresk on the Forth (App. I), but apart from another marching-camp (Channelkirk, App. I) no further visible remains lie beside it north of Pennymuir. The reason, quite simply, is that Scotland becomes more cultivable, and Roman earthworks have suffered as a result. Brief mention must be made, however, of the site at Newstead on the Tweed. The succession of large and very strongly-defended forts discovered here make it clear that TRIMONTIVM was a major stronghold, the king-pin of the occupation network of southern Scotland. Founded by Agricola c. AD 81, it was finally abandoned about 100 years later. Excavations have yielded a remarkable haul of metal tools and weapons, which now fill several cases in the National Museum of Antiquities in Edinburgh. One is a fine late-first-century cavalry parade-helmet (fig 123). There is nothing whatever to see at Newstead today, except for a commemorative stone erected in 1928 beside the B6381, 1¾m east of Melrose. But the beautiful back-drop of the triple Eildon Hills which gave the fort its Roman name makes a visit to the site worth-while. The most northerly hill (1,327 feet) is crowned by a native hill-fort, in the centre of which is a Roman signal-station (App. I).

In the eastern half of southern Scotland I will mention just two

more sites, Lyne and Castle Greg. The fort at **Lyne** (NT 1840),
near the upper reaches of the Tweed, lay on an east-west road
linking Newstead with the western trunk route. 5m west of
Peebles on the Glasgow road (A72) is the junction with the
B712 to Drumelzier; ½m beyond it is a turning on the right to
Lyne village; you want the next track on the right, to Lyne
church. Park before entering the churchyard. The fort lies in the
field on the left, 200 yards west of the trees. There is not a great
deal to see here. The rampart has been nearly levelled by
agriculture, but survives as a bold mound at the NE, NW and
SW corners and as a ridge along the west side. Of the ditch-
system only the outer ditch on the east and south sides is visible
today. This was originally V-shaped but is now flat-bottomed.
Its edges are lined by two surprisingly well-preserved mounds,
formed by piling up the earth excavated from the ditch. The

123   Newstead, a parade-helmet (in Edinburgh)

causeway leading to the site of the east gate is also notable. The
central buildings of this fort were of stone, but the rampart was
of turf only. Excavations in 1901 and 1959–63 revealed that it was
built c. AD 158 and occupied for only a few years. It is, however,
only one of a series of Roman works in the vicinity. There was a
tiny fortlet 160 yards to the north, a temporary camp enclosing
Lyne village, and an Agricolan fort of c. AD 81 on a bold eminence
at Easter Happrew, ½m east-south-east on the other side of Lyne
Water. All these are normally invisible from the ground, but a
crop-mark of the north rampart of the Agricolan fort could be
seen from the second-century site in the summer of 1972.

   Castle Greg (NT 0459) in Midlothian deserves a brief mention
as it is among the best-preserved examples of a Roman fortlet in
Britain. It probably dates from the mid-second century. Measur-
ing just 150 feet by 180 feet, the single earth rampart and double
ditches of this convoy-post are in perfect condition. The only
entrance is in the east side. It lies 3m SE of West Calder, on the
east side of the B7008, ⅝m north of its junction with the A70.

   Roman earthworks in the western part of southern Scotland
fall into two distinct categories. The most accessible sites, such
as the camps at Cleghorn and Little Clyde and the fort at
Castledykes, are so poorly preserved that they do not warrant
detailed description, and are therefore listed in Appendix I. On
the other hand, three earthworks in superb condition lie in
very remote areas, and 1″ OS maps and a deal of patience are
needed to track them down. These are at Redshaw Burn in
Lanarkshire, and Durisdeer and Raeburnfoot in Dumfriesshire
(all in App. I). The first two are Antonine fortlets like Castle
Greg, their single gates defended by *titula*. Raeburnfoot consists
of a fortlet inside a larger enclosure, both apparently Antonine.
NE of here, on high moor between Eskdale and Borthwick
Water, a remarkable stretch of Roman road can be followed for
about 6½m. In places the Roman engineers cut through the peat
to the natural rock and used that as the road-surface. On Craik
Cross Hill it passes the site of a signal-station (App. I).

   Two sites near Hadrian's Wall can conveniently close this
section on southern Scotland. Just as the eastern half of the Wall
had outlying forts at Risingham and High Rochester (though a
later addition to the original Hadrianic scheme), the western
end was also protected by a series of advance-posts of which
Bewcastle in Cumberland (App. I) was one and **Birrens** (NY

2175) in Dumfriesshire another. The latter, BLATOBVLGIVM, was founded by Agricola and also occupied under Hadrian. The visible fort was first constructed about 142, when the garrison was the first cohort of Nervii from the Rhine, but it was burnt down and rebuilt in 157/8. This we know from an inscription, now in Edinburgh's Museum of Antiquities, which also records a different Rhenish regiment, the second cohort of Tungrians, as its garrison. There is not much to see at Birrens today, but the rampart survives as a bold mound on all sides except the south, where the stream has eroded it, and there are faint traces of a system of six ditches on the north. Turn northwards off the A74 immediately west of its junction with the B722, 7m NW of Gretna Green. After one mile the minor road crosses a river-bridge and the fort lies on the left just beyond it.

Much more interesting than Birrens are the nearby practice siege-camps of **Burnswark*** (NY 1878). Continue on into Middlebie, turn left and keep going for 1¼m, over the stream, until the road makes a 90° turn to the left, ½m before Ecclefechan. Turn right here (not signposted) and keep straight on for two miles. When the metalling ceases, take the right fork and park when the wood on your left ends. A field-gate here leads immediately to the SW corner of the first (south) Roman camp. This is in an excellent state of preservation. The entire, roughly rectangular, circuit can be traced with ease. The gates in the middle of the south, east and west sides are protected by normal-sized *titula*, but the three entrances on the north are shielded by enormous mounds, known locally as The Three Brethren. They were built to support the Roman catapult machines which were used in assaulting the native hill-fort on the prominent summit ahead. Excavations here at the turn of the century found 67 Roman lead sling-bolts, and it was then believed that a real attack did indeed take place. More recent work, however, in 1967–70, has shown that the native ramparts (now largely invisible) were not standing when the bullets were fired, and it is clear that the 'attack' was only a training-exercise. In the NE corner of the Roman camp is a small fortlet, of mid-second-century date, and excavation has shown that the camp was built after it. From the native fort at the top you can see the outline of another Roman camp on the north side of the hill. This is unfinished and it too must have been built for practice, as it is too far below the native fort to have served any useful purpose in its bombardment. From the top too you can admire the spectacular views in all directions, and on a clear day Hadrian's Wall is visible.

2: The Antonine Wall

While the great Wall of Hadrian is a familiar monument, especially to the many thousands who trek its course each year, it is not so well known that the Romans built another frontier-barrier in these islands, and, more importantly, that substantial stretches of it still survive. Almost immediately after the death of Hadrian in 138, the new emperor Antoninus Pius ordered a fresh advance in Britain and the building of another wall, this time entirely of turf. The literary evidence is confined to a single sentence: 'he (the emperor) conquered the Britons through Lollius Urbicus the governor and after driving back the barbarians built another wall, of turf (*muro caespiticio*).' Archaeological evidence shows that the campaign was already planned in 139 and completed by 142/3, when a coin depicting Britannia, much as she appears on our own coinage, was minted (fig 124). The reason for building another wall was apparently trouble in southern Scotland, but of the details we know nothing. At any rate Hadrian's Wall was evacuated, and the whole of southern Scotland refortified and regarrisoned.

The Antonine Wall is a much simpler structure than the Hadrianic frontier, and is the product of a single plan without later modification. It ran for 37 miles from Bridgeness on the Forth to Old Kilpatrick on the Clyde. The Wall had a stone foundation 14 feet wide, on which rows of cut turves were laid to a height of nine feet. The sides of the turf Wall sloped inwards, so that it was only about six feet wide at the top, on which was built a timber patrol-walk about five feet high. On the north the Wall was accompanied by a massive ditch 40 feet wide and at

124   Britannia on a coin of AD *142/3*

least 12 feet deep. On the south ran a military service-road.

The frontier was manned, like Hadrian's Wall, by men from the auxiliary cohorts of the Roman army, though small numbers of legionaries also seem to have been stationed on it. The garrison was housed in 18 or 19 forts attached to the south side of the Wall at roughly two-mile intervals. These were defended by turf ramparts, except for two examples which had stone walls. Barracks were of timber, but the central range of buildings usually had stone foundations. The close spacing of these forts makes it unlikely that there was a complete system of milecastles and turrets as on Hadrian's Wall, but three fortlets are known where distances between forts are greater than usual, and six signalling-platforms ('beacon-stances') about 18 feet square also survive.

The Wall itself, and some at least of the forts, were built by detachments from all three of the British legions. Their work is attested by 18 stone tablets or 'distance-slabs'. Each construction party would have set up one of these at the beginning and the

125   Antonine Wall, a distance-slab (in Glasgow)

end of its allotted stretch. A particularly fine example was
ploughed up in 1969 (fig 125). The inscription, spread out over
different portions of the stone, reads: 'For the emperor Caesar
Titus Aelius Hadrianus Antoninus Augustus Pius, father of his
country, a detachment of the Twentieth Legion Valeria Victrix
built 3,000 feet.' In the centre is a Roman standard-bearer
bowing in respect to the personification of the province of
Britain, who is putting what may be a victory-wreath into the
beak of the eagle on the standard. On either side is a grotesque
portrayal of an ancient Briton, as seen through Roman eyes.
Each kneels in captivity, his hands tied behind his back. Below
is the running boar, the symbol of the legion. This splendid stone
is now in the Hunterian Museum of the University of Glasgow,
along with many other finds from the Wall and all but two of the
distance-slabs (Mon.–Fri. 9–5, Sat. 9–12). The Bridgeness
stone, which marked the eastern end of the Wall, is housed in the
National Museum of Antiquities in Edinburgh, where the
Newstead collection (see above), a Roman silver hoard from
Taprain Law, and many other important finds from Roman
Scotland are also displayed (Mon.–Sat. 10–5, Sun. 2–5).

   A few words must be said about the fortunes of the new
frontier. It has long been known that there were certainly two
separate occupations of the Antonine Wall, but the precise
dating of these has been a subject of constant dispute. The length
of the first occupation was about 13 years, for a serious crisis in
north Britain in 155 caused the frontier to be temporarily
abandoned, and its forts were dismantled before withdrawal. By
about 159 the situation was calm enough to allow reoccupation,
but about 163 the Antonine Wall was again abandoned, probably
after enemy destruction, and Hadrian's Wall was fully
recommissioned. If this dating, based on a recent study of samian
pottery, is accepted, it means that Antoninus' massive engineering work had an active life of less than 20 years. Hitherto the end
of the second occupation has usually been dated to c. 185, but in
either case the Antonine Wall and the attendant reoccupation of
Scotland must be regarded as a failure. There are traces at a few
of the Wall-forts of a mysterious third occupation, and it may
have been the intention of the emperor Severus, who campaigned
in north Scotland in 208/9, to reoccupy the Antonine Wall; if so,
the plan came to nothing.

   Though the more northerly frontier was less than half the

length of Hadrian's Wall, it was flanked by deep estuaries which
had to be guarded. Little is known at present about posts at the
western end, but on the east there were forts at Carriden, very
close to Bridgeness, and at Cramond and Inveresk (App. I).
Cramond (NT 1977) is now a delightful village about 6m west
of the centre of Edinburgh and 1½m north of the A90. The fort
built here about 142 shows the same history of an evacuation and
a later destruction as the Antonine Wall. This is not surprising,
for its harbour provided a good anchorage for transport-ships
and Cramond no doubt became a supply-depot for the Wall,
much as South Shields served Hadrian's Wall. Unlike forts on
the barrier, it was thoroughly repaired and reorganized at the
beginning of the third century, when it was a base for Severus'
Scottish campaigns. Even after his withdrawal, the fort and
civilian settlement were still inhabited. One stretch of wall,
which belongs to a workshop built under Severus, is still visible,
and the outlines of many other buildings within the fort have been
marked out and labelled. The site, excavated in 1958–63, lies near
the church, on the right of the road before it descends steeply to
the harbour. There a pedestrian-ferry and a 10-minute walk

126   Antonine Wall-Ditch at Watling Lodge

along the sea-shore on the other side will bring you to Eagle
Rock [AM; A], which juts out onto the beach. On its east face,
now protected by a grille, a figure standing in a niche has been
cut out of the natural rock. It is now very worn, and all details
have been obliterated. When first discovered the carving was
thought to represent an eagle, but it is more likely to be a figure
of Mercury, protector of travellers. It was probably cut by
Roman soldiers to bring good luck to ships entering and leaving
Cramond harbour.

Whereas the Antonine Wall itself has suffered badly over the
centuries from cultivation and now only remains in a very few
places, the great Ditch is a more formidable obstacle to the
plough and it often survives impressively in places where the
Wall has completely disappeared. A substantial portion of the
Ditch near the eastern end of its length is visible in **Callendar
Park** (NS 8979), beyond the greensward on the south side of the
A9, $\frac{1}{2}$m east of Falkirk. It is about six feet deep and can be traced
here for $\frac{1}{3}$m. Far more impressive is the stretch at **Watling
Lodge*** (NS 8679) [AM; A], one of the outstanding remains of the
Antonine frontier (fig 126). Here the Ditch survives in something
like its original dimensions, some 40 feet wide and 15 feet deep,
and gives a magnificent impression of the formidable nature of
this man-made obstacle. To reach it, turn off the A8 in Camelon,
1m west of Falkirk, along the B816 to High Bonnybridge (Union
Road). Go left over the canal, then right at the T-junction and
first right along Lime Road. The Ditch lies behind trees on the
left of this road (blue DOE notice).

Now continue along the B-road, which twists to the left and so
crosses the line of the Wall. Turn right at the next crossroads.
On your left, by a sign reading 'Ancient Monumet (*sic*): No
Dumping of Rubbish', there begins the picturesque stretch
running through **Tentfield Plantation** (NS 8579). Here both Wall
and Ditch survive in fine condition and they can easily be
followed, though much overgrown with bracken and trees, as
far as the railway-line one mile away. Two beacon-stances
survive in this portion, but they are difficult to spot. They consist
of slightly raised mounds projecting from the back of the Wall.
One lies opposite the third telegraph-pole west of the crossroads,
the other 50 yards east of the railway. Beyond, the Roman frontier
can be traced all the way to Rough Castle, but it is more
convenient to approach the latter from the west. Continue,

therefore, along the B816 to High Bonnybridge, and turn right
towards Bonnybridge. Immediately before crossing the Forth-
Clyde canal, where the road kinks to avoid an iron-foundry, you
should take a lane on the right. (There is a DOE signpost, but it
is only visible if you are coming from the north: in that case,
leave the A803 in Bonnybridge, cross the canal and turn first
left.) Soon after crossing the railway, the road, now untarred,
bends to the left. Stop at the green mesh-work gate on the left
and walk back 18 paces. The large mound which you will see
projecting from the back of the Antonine Wall almost as far as
the stone wall is a beacon-stance.

From here onwards both Wall and Ditch survive in superb
condition all the way to Rough Castle. Just before the track
turns left to the DOE car-park, opposite the third iron gate on the
right (counting from the last stop), is the most conspicuous of all
the beacon-stances on the Antonine frontier. Excavation revealed
its stone foundation, 18 feet square, and heavy burning indicated
the use of beacon-fires for long-distance signalling. All four
stances near Rough Castle have good command of the only
known Roman road running beyond the Wall to outpost forts
in the far north, and they probably received and transmitted
messages from and to this road.

127   Antonine Wall and Ditch near Rough Castle

At the car-park there is a spectacular view of the Ditch and the Wall, which is here five feet high and nowhere in a better state of preservation (fig 127). Then a short walk, down to the stream and up the other side, leads to the fort of **Rough Castle*** (NS 8479) [AM ; A]. It is a very tiny post, occupying only about one acre, but the earth rampart and ditches are very well preserved on all three sides, and so are the Antonine Wall and Ditch which form its north front. A few traces of the stone buildings excavated in 1902–3 can be seen in the middle of the fort ; they include a small office-building and a granary. The post was garrisoned by men from the sixth cohort of Nervii (from the Lower Rhine) under the command, unusually, of a centurion from the Twentieth Legion, one Flavius Betto. To the east was an annexe, also defended by rampart and ditches, and one of the buildings here was the fort bath-house. North of the fort, 20 yards beyond the Ditch, a remarkable find was made of ten rows of small defensive pits. These, described as *lilia*, or lilies, by Roman military writers, were given pointed stakes and then covered with brushwood and leaves. The idea was to deceive an approaching enemy into think- ing the ground was solid, and to capitalize on the resulting confusion. A few of these pits, unique in Britain, have been left open.

Return now to Bonnybridge and turn left along the south side of the Forth-Clyde canal (B816). After $\frac{1}{3}$m, when the houses stop, a blue board announces the **Seabegs Wood** stretch (NS 8179) [AM ; A]. Both Wall and Ditch are well preserved here, though somewhat overgrown. Another $1\frac{1}{2}$m will bring you to the complicated road-junction at Castlecary. A fort stood here, now in the care of the DOE, but it is hardly visible (App. I). Avoid the dual-carriageway of the A80 and continue along the B816 for another $\frac{1}{2}$m. Then turn right (signposted Wardpark North) and stop when the road bends. Here it crosses the line of the Antonine frontier at **Tollpark** (NS 7777) [AM ; A], as announced by two DOE boards. The Wall is not visible here, but the Ditch survives on both sides of the road. Westwards it is in very good condition and can be followed for two miles to Westerwood fort (App. I) and beyond, until it is interrupted by the railway-line. Further west, on both sides of Croy Hill, the Ditch again becomes visible, but this portion is best approached from the west.

From Tollpark cross the canal and turn left along the A803. In Kilsyth take the B802 for Airdrie. After crossing the canal

again and climbing the hill, turn left to Croy village (not signposted). Take the second road on the left, and then go right, and
left along Cuilmuir View. Park at the end of this, and you will see,
behind a fence on the right, a blue DOE notice. This marks the
beginning of the Ditch on **Croy Hill** (NS 7276) [AM ; A], and it
continues to remain impressively visible for nearly 1½m. Here too
is a particularly good position from which to admire the fine
command of the Wall over ground to the north, since the view,
for once, is not obstructed by trees, electricity pylons or factory
chimneys. The line chosen was on the northern slope of an almost
continuous range of hills. This enabled the Wall to dominate
completely the broad depression now drained by the Forth-
Clyde canal, and still to be at a safe distance from the loftier
hills on the horizon. 150 yards from the start of this stretch are
two closely-spaced signalling-platforms. They are covered with
bracken in summer and are not easy to spot. Then the Ditch,
here hewn resolutely from the solid rock, climbs to the summit of
Croy Hill, 470 feet above sea-level, and one of the highest points
of its course (cf. Winshields on Hadrian's Wall, 1,230 feet). Just
past the top a fort was situated, but nothing can be seen of it now.
Almost opposite its site the Ditch-diggers gave up in despair at
the hardness of the rock, and for 80 feet it has been left undug.
Thereafter the Ditch is excellently preserved, 40 feet wide and 8
feet deep, as far as Dullatur station.

Another long portion of Ditch, together with a second undug
stretch and another fort (App. I), can be seen between Croy and
Twechar on Bar Hill, but it is much obscured with undergrowth
and trees. Further west Wall and Ditch have left no substantial
remains for the rest of their course, except for four short sections
of the stone Wall-base which have been preserved near its western
end. The two longest can be seen in **New Kilpatrick Cemetery**
(NS 5572), which lies on the north side of the B8049 (Boclair
Road), ½m east of its junction with the A81 in Bearsden (fig 128).
Each has a drainage-culvert running across it, and one has a
'step' in it to ensure stability for the turf superstructure. Another
small piece of stone base, and a fragment of the accompanying
Ditch, were exposed and preserved in 1964 in **West Bearsden**
(NS 5372). From New Kilpatrick Cemetery, go straight across
the A81 at the traffic-lights, then turn left at a junction and go on
to a second set of lights. Turn right here, and soon afterwards
fork left along the A810 for Dumbarton. Then go first left

(Whitehurst), second right, first left and first right (Iain Road). The steps leading up to the Wall-base are near the end of this road, on the left. Finally, the tiny fragment exposed on the western slope of Golden Hill, **Duntocher** (NS 4972), may be mentioned, as it is the most westerly piece of the Antonine frontier still visible. Turn south off the A810 along Roman Road, in the eastern outskirts of Duntocher, and stop by the church. A railed-off portion of the Wall-base, including a culvert, is visible in the park on the left. Excavations on top of the hill in 1948–51 found that an Antonine fortlet, and the tiny fort which later replaced it, had both preceded the actual Wall, and it may be presumed that the latter was built from east to west. The same conclusion was reached when the terminal fort at Old Kilpatrick, now built over, was excavated in 1923–4 and 1931 (see also p. 360).

3: Romans in the far north

Though Scotland north of the Antonine Wall never strictly became part of the Roman Empire, military campaigns were carried out here on a number of occasions, and these have left their traces in the form of marching-camps, forts, fortlets and signal-towers. Our knowledge of Roman operations in the area has been vastly increased since the last war by excavation and by the aerial discoveries of Dr Kenneth St Joseph of Cambridge University. The majority of the earthworks seem to be the work of either Agricola (AD 83–5) or the emperor Severus (AD 208–11). Other generals campaigned north of the Forth-Clyde isthmus, including Lollius Urbicus in 142/3 and Constantius Chlorus in 306 (and possibly Ulpius Marcellus c. 186), but their camps have not been located. It is not, however, the shadowy records of these invasions, or even Severus' punitive expeditions, which capture our imagination, but the great campaigns of Julius Agricola in AD 83 and 84. Here is a man who still lives for us in the pages of Tacitus, and at last archaeology is starting to clothe with specific forts and camps the bare narrative handed down to us. As a result we can begin to understand Agricolan strategy a little better. He had no intention of entering the Highland mass; the valleys leading from this were carefully blocked by forts at Lake Menteith, Bochastle (pass of Leny), Dealgin Ross (Strathearn), Fendoch (Sma Glen) and Inchtuthil (Dunkeld Gorge). The idea was to prevent the Highland tribes from breaking into Strathmore and using that as the base for inevitable attacks further south.

Strathmore and Strathearn were themselves carefully protected by a line of forts, no doubt linked with harbour installations on the east coast which still await discovery. But this grand plan was never allowed to be brought to fruition. Agricola was recalled in 84/5 and the emperor Domitian soon ordered withdrawal, though this was only partial at first. Tacitus bitterly comments that 'Britain was thoroughly subdued and then immediately let slip' (*perdomita Britannia et statim missa*).

Unfortunately, with the exception of Inchtuthil, virtually nothing can be seen of Agricola's camps and forts on the ground today, and most of the sites mentioned below are later in date. One of them, the fort at **Ardoch*** (NN 8309), was founded by

128   Antonine Wall, stone base at New Kilpatrick

Agricola, but the visible remains date from 142/3 when it became
an outpost fort for the Antonine Wall. And what remains there
are! Ardoch is one of the most spectacular sights of Roman
Britain, but not in the way that Chedworth or Pevensey are.
There is not a scrap of stonework to be seen at Ardoch today:
instead it is the system of multiple ditches, surviving on the north
and east sides of the fort, which bears vivid witness to the presence
of Romans in the far north, and shows above all the steps they
were prepared to take in order to provide a defensible position
in an area known to be hostile.

To reach Ardoch, turn off the A9 11m north of Stirling, along
the A822 for Crieff. After 1½m you reach the village of Braco,
where the road bends to cross the river Knaik. Park on the right
150 yards after the bridge, and clamber over the stone wall and
up the bank beyond. From here you can see the whole of the
north rampart of the fort and the five ditches defending it. Not
all of these are of the same date, as the fort was originally
slightly longer on this north side and its rampart was protected
by just three ditches, now the outermost. When the fort was
reduced in size, two further ditches were dug in the deserted end
of the larger enclosure. The date of this alteration is not certain,
but all the ditches probably belong to the Antonine period.
Nothing can be seen of the Agricolan fort which lies below, but
pottery belonging to it was found in the excavations of 1896–7. A
tombstone now in Glasgow (Hunterian Museum) informs us that
at some stage the First Cohort of Spaniards was the garrison
here.

A wire fence across the northern ditches makes it difficult to
visit the east side of the fort from the NW corner, and it is better
to walk back to the bridge and take the track leaving the A-road
there. Go left when it forks and you will come to the SE corner of
Ardoch. From here you can visit the ditches on the east side,
which are even more staggeringly well-preserved than those on
the north (fig 129). The fort rampart is high and bold, and the
causeway striding magnificently up to the east gate is the only
break in the superb quintuple ditches. Here it is the outermost
two which have been added later.

Ardoch provided an admirable camping-ground, and it is not
surprising that five different temporary camps are known
immediately north of the fort. A 13-acre camp and a subsequent
enlargement to one of 30 acres were the work of Agricola. Both

were overlapped by a 63-acre camp, to which a small annexe
was added. Then a camp of 120 acres was constructed, overlap-
ping all the other works on the site. The 63- and 120-acre earthworks are probably Severan (AD 208/9). The only substantial
visible fragment of all these encampments belongs to the west
side of the 120-acre enclosure. Continue northwards along the
A822 for ½m and take the B827 to Comrie. After 220 yards the
road cuts through the camp, and 300 yards of rampart, with a
gate and *titulum* at the far end, can be seen running away to the
right. Parts of the east side of this camp, where it overlies an
earlier signal-station, can be traced with the help of a large-scale
map (see Bibliography).

Six miles NE of Ardoch lay another fort, Strageath, which was
also an Agricolan foundation reused as an outpost fort of the
Antonine Wall (not visible). Between the two lies a smaller post,
the fortlet known as **Kaims Castle** (NN 8612). The A822 is
straight for 1m north of Ardoch. 1¼m after it swings to the right,
and just before a minor road leaves it on the left, you will notice
a flagpole 50 yards from the left of the road. It stands in the
middle of an enclosure about 80 feet square, surrounded by a
circular ditch. A single entrance faces the road. Excavation in
1900 produced no evidence of date, but the fortlet probably
belongs to the Antonine period.

The fort at Strageath guarded the western end of a remarkable

129   Ardoch, fort-ditches on the east side

group of Roman signal-stations on the **Gask Ridge** (NN 9118 to 0220). No less than 10 are known on an 8-mile stretch of Roman road, and seven of them are still traceable, though some are obscured by undergrowth. The series is best approached from the eastern end, where a minor road runs on top of the Roman one. It leaves the A9 5m west of Perth, but you will need a 1" OS map (sheet 55) if you wish to trace the earthworks. Each consisted of a circular platform between 35 and 50 feet across, surrounded by a circular ditch and an outer bank of upcast material. There was a single entrance on the side facing the road. In the centre of the platform was a timber tower about 10 feet square and presumably two storeys high. In three examples, nos. 1, 7 and 9 (counting from the west), the tower is surrounded by a rampart as well as the usual ditch and upcast mound. The close spacing of these signal stations, and the late-first-century pottery which they have yielded, make it likely that the Gask Ridge formed a temporary frontier-line or communications-link under Agricola, for the absence of finds later than c. 90 in the forts of northern Scotland rules out a post-Agricolan date.

Both the chief Roman operators in northern Scotland needed bases. Severus built a 24-acre fort on the south bank of the Tay at Carpow, a few miles east of Perth (nothing visible), and Agricola's legionary fortress lay on the same river much further upstream, at **Inchtuthil*** (NO 1239). From Perth follow the Blairgowrie road (A93) for 12 miles until the A984 crosses it near Meiklour. Turn left here and continue for three miles until the B947 to Blairgowrie goes off to the right. At this point, take the track leaving the left-hand side of the A984 and keep straight along it wherever possible. One mile later, after bending to the right at the edge of the Tay, it peters out close to the south side of the Redoubt (5, fig 130).

The surviving earthworks at Inchtuthil are not striking, but this is one of the very few places in Britain where one can look at remains and associate them with the great governor of Britain made famous by the biography of Tacitus – Gnaeus Julius Agricola. This was the spot he chose to be the hub of his proposed operations to secure a stranglehold on the Scottish tribes, and the base fortress of the legion he had commanded earlier in his career, the Twentieth Valeria Victrix. Of the fortress today (1 on fig 130), the ditch appears as a conspicuous hollow on the east side, and the massive rampart is quite impressive on the south.

In the 50 acres enclosed by these defences nothing is now visible. But excavation between 1952 and 1965 by Sir Ian Richmond and Dr St Joseph has revealed the complete plan of the timber buildings erected there. Construction was started c. AD 83 and was still in full swing when the order to abandon the site came about four years later, after Agricola had left Britain. 64 barracks, four houses for junior officers, six granaries, a large hospital, a drill-hall, a workshop and a headquarters building had all been finished, but no commandant's house had been erected. There were four timber gateways and a single ditch, and the original turf rampart had already been modified by the addition of a stone facing-wall – the first fort in Britain to be so defended. Then came withdrawal: not a mere abandonment, but a thorough destruction in order to let nothing of value fall into enemy hands. Foundation trenches were filled with nails bent by extraction from timber posts. The hospital drain was jammed with gravel. Unused pottery and glassware were deliberately pounded into tiny fragments in a gutter of the main street. The stone from the circuit-wall was systematically dismantled. The unfired stone bath-house outside the walls was stripped and demolished. Most

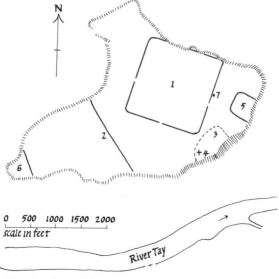

130   *Plan of Inchtuthil*

dramatic of all was the discovery of a hoard of one million unused nails of all sizes which had been buried in a pit in the workshop. They have now been distributed round the world. Agricola was of course not there to watch: he was left to an embittered retirement in Rome.

Excavation also revealed the purpose of the earthworks outside the fortress. To the SW a labour camp held the tents of soldiers during construction work; when barracks were ready inside the fortress, the area was reduced by building the 'Western Vallum' (2). To the SE a compound (3) (dotted on the plan as it is not now visible) contained offices, stores, a barrack-block and a spacious residential building. The latter was clearly designed for the officers supervising the construction of the fortress. The garrison bath-house was also sited here (4). The rampart and ditch defending the so-called Redoubt (5) are visible: this may have been a stores-compound. The native fort (6) and burial-mound (7) are post-Roman.

A short distance NE of Inchtuthil the Romans built a boundary-line called the **Cleaven Dyke** (NO 1640). Its purpose and original length are not certain, but as the earthwork is not defensive or long enough to mark a frontier, it was probably meant to delineate part of the area near the fortress under strict military control. It is now about 30 feet wide and 5 feet high, and was originally flanked by ditches 16 feet wide and 2 feet deep. The whole earthwork measured 150 feet overall. The surviving stretch, about one mile long, lies in the middle of a plantation and is not easily accessible. From Inchtuthil return via the A984 to the A93, and turn left. The road crosses the line of the earthwork after $\frac{1}{2}$m. Its southern end was guarded by a signal-station on Black Hill (App. I).

I have not visited Roman sites in Scotland north of Inchtuthil, but a few remains of Severus' marching-camps can be seen. You will need the relevant 1″ map if you wish to find them. These camps also represent roughly the line of Agricola's advance to the far north in AD 84, but none of his camps are now visible.

Hadrian's Wall had been restored in 205–8 after barbarian destruction, but the necessary counter-expedition to restore prestige and punish the raiders had not been carried out. In 207 the governor of Britain, Alfenus Senecio, wrote to his emperor, and Severus came to Britain with his sons to conduct the campaigns himself. The expeditions of 208 and 209 are very probably marked by two different series of camps, of 63 acres and 120 acres. The size of the bigger series, which extends further north, implies an enormous army, equivalent to three legions and many auxiliaries. The expedition of 210, conducted by his son Caracalla as Severus was too ill, was probably confined to southern Scotland. In 211, Severus died in York, and any ideas he may have had of reoccupying Scotland were not followed up by his son. Withdrawal was not immediate, however, and there may have been another campaign to the north in 211 or 212. As a result of these expeditions, peace reigned on Hadrian's Wall for nearly a century.

The only 63-acre camp even partly visible is **Kirkbuddo** (NO 4944, map 50) in Angus. Take the B961 from Dundee for 3m, then go left along the B978 for 7m and left again for 1m along the B9127. At the point where the road enters a wood, part of the SE and SW rampart, including the south corner, is visible on the left. A little more of the SW rampart can be seen on the right of the road. Three gates protected by *titula* also survive. The camp has been known from at least the seventeenth century, when it was in perfect condition, but the portion outside the wood has now been totally ploughed away. The top of the surviving bank is about six feet above ditch-bottom.

The other three camps are all of the vast 120-acre type. **Raedykes** (NO 8490, map 43) is reached by taking a minor road to the north off the A957, 3½m NW of Stonehaven. Its plan is irregular to suit the terrain, but it is basically rectangular with a change of direction in the middle of the north rampart. There are six gates with *titula*, two in each of the long sides and one in each short side. Excavation in 1914 showed that parts of the north and east defences, where the ground is less steep, were more substantially built than the rest of the circuit. Of **Normandykes** (NO 8399, map 40), ½m SW of Peterculter near Aberdeen, much less is visible. Only the east part of the north rampart and the NE corner survive today, forming the boundary-bank of a wood. The rest has been ploughed away. Finally, on a remote upland, there are a few remains of the camp at **Glenmailen** (NJ 6538, map 30) near Ythan Wells, north of the A96 and about 5m SSW of Turriff on the A947. Only the NE corner is well preserved, but the western half of the south side is also traceable. These fragments belong to the Severan marching-camp and are the most northerly Roman remains visible in Britain. Agricola chose the site first, however, as a 26-acre camp with distinctive gateways attributable to him was observed from the air in 1968. Another Agricolan camp is known at Achenhove in Banffshire, 15m NW of Glenmailen, and it is now clear that Agricola, like Severus a century and a quarter later, reached the mouth of the Spey. In this area, then, must be placed the great battle of Mons Graupius in AD 84, when Agricola defeated the Caledonian tribes under the leadership of Calgacus. 10,000 barbarians were killed, with only 360 losses on the Roman side. Then indeed, as Tacitus made Calgacus say in his speech before the battle, the end of Britain lay revealed (*nunc terminus Britanniae patet*).

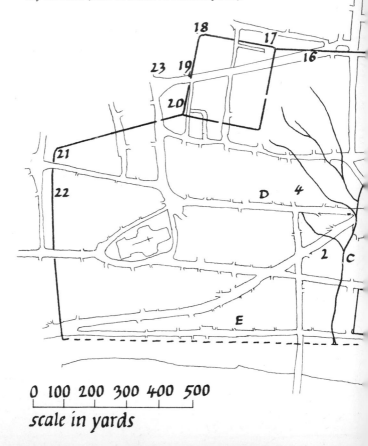

0   100   200   300   400   500

scale in yards

Chapter 10

London

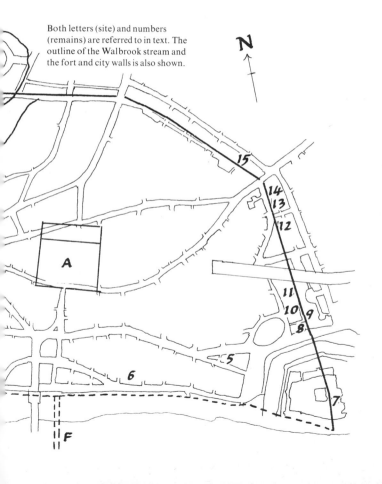

Both letters (site) and numbers (remains) are referred to in text. The outline of the Walbrook stream and the fort and city walls is also shown.

N

The vast urban conglomeration known today as London owes its origin to the Romans. There is no evidence to suggest that in pre-Roman times there was any permanent settlement in the area now occupied by the City of London. But from AD 43, when the first buildings were planted here, the city has expanded and flourished, and the almost continuous succession of occupation-layers from that day to this has resulted in a steady rise in the level of the ground. Yet, between 10 and 20 feet below the modern pavement, some traces of Roman London still remain, and it is not perhaps commonly realized just how much has been preserved of this earliest phase in the city's history.

A bridge across the Thames was essential to the Romans from the earliest stages of their occupation, and the first London Bridge, 60 yards downstream from its present successor, was no doubt constructed in the year of the invasion (AD 43). Its position (F on the map on pp. 308–9) was dictated by what was then the tidal limit of the Thames, and also by the solid gravel banks on either side of the river at this point. The bridge would undoubtedly have been accompanied by a military post, probably on Cornhill, but no trace of it has been found. But it was the trading, not the military, potential of the site that was fully realized from the beginning, and the early fort soon gave way to the first city. Streets were laid out and substantial timber buildings, some with wall-plaster and roofing-tiles, were constructed. Docks were built, and the very large amount of Claudian material found in the City suggests London's immediate importance, no doubt as the principal supply-base for the armies campaigning further north. Rapid communication with these was ensured by the great trunk-roads, which fanned out from London from the earliest years of the occupation. Though Claudius had intended Colchester to be the capital of the new province, close to the site of the most important pre-Roman settlement, it is likely that London soon usurped this position, probably after AD 60–1. Even before that, the financial headquarters may already have been in London, and, as at St Albans, earth defences may have been erected.

In AD 60 or 61, the first city came to an end, destroyed by Boudicca and her followers. The historian Tacitus, who gives us the first literary reference to LONDINIVM, says that it was already packed with traders and a hive of commerce, though not graced with the title of *colonia*. (Later it was probably given this status as a mark of honour, but we have no record of it.) London soon rose from the ashes, and it is extremely likely that at this time, and certainly before the end of the first century, the city became the official capital of the province. The first forum, a vast building about 360 feet by 200 feet, was built immediately after the revolt, 20 years or so before other known British examples; and by about AD 85, a large residence identified as the Governor's Palace had already been erected. The state cult of emperor-worship was also transferred to London from Colchester before the end of the first century, possibly in AD 61. Finally, at the beginning of the second century, a fort was established, smaller than a legionary fortress but, at 11 acres, three times the size of most normal forts. Its garrison, which included men from all three of the regular British legions, would have fulfilled a variety of functions, supervising the transference of military supplies and acting as the governor's bodyguard. London had become the political, financial and commercial capital of Britain, and the Roman genius in selecting its site is attested by its continuing role today.

Another fire swept London c. 125–130, this time probably accidental. About the middle of the century serious flooding, caused by subsidence, troubled some low-lying parts of the city. But expansion was not greatly interrupted, and when walls were built at the end of the second century they enclosed an area of 330 acres, by far the largest city in Britain and the fourth largest north of the Alps. The other dates known in the history of Roman London may be briefly noted. In 197, when Britain was divided into two provinces, LONDINIVM became the capital of *Britannia Superior* (Upper Britain). About 286, the rebel emperor Carausius established the first mint in London. In 296 the city was looted by Allectus' troops after he had been defeated by Constantius. The mint closed down c. AD 326, but about the middle of the century London was given the honorary name of AVGVSTA. Of the end little is known, but recent evidence from Lower Thames Street suggests that life continued well into the fifth and possibly the sixth centuries. Then came the Dark Ages, and the only lapse in the predominance that the city has enjoyed from Roman times to the present day.

Of the buildings belonging to the Roman city not a great deal is known. Continuous occupation has allowed archaeologists little opportunity for large-scale excavation, and even when areas of a reasonable size are available, Roman levels have usually been partially or completely removed by medieval and Victorian cellars and pits. This continuous occupation has largely obliterated the topography of the Roman city: originally London fell into two distinct halves, consisting of two gravel plateaus separated by a stream known as the Walbrook. On the top of the eastern plateau stood the most important public building, the **Forum** and **Basilica** (A on map, p. 309). This vast structure lay in the area which is now bounded on the north by Cornhill and Leadenhall, on the south by Lombard Street and Fenchurch Street, and is roughly bisected by Graechurch Street. Some parts of it have been observed at various times, mostly in the nineteenth century, and we know that the basilica was at least 500 feet long, far bigger than any other example in Britain. The main complex was probably erected early in the second century, but emergency excavation in 1969 has made it certain that an earlier, smaller forum was built immediately after the Boudiccan revolt in AD 60–1. Further information about this great city-centre is expected when Leadenhall Market is pulled down and redeveloped in the mid-1970's. At the moment, nothing can be seen of either forum or basilica, for the few walls of the latter preserved beneath Banks (App. I) are inaccessible to the public at all times.

The second remarkable public building is the **Governor's Palace** (B), situated between Cannon Street and Upper Thames Street. Various massive foundations had been reported in this area, partly after the Great Fire of 1666, partly during sewer construction in Bush Lane in 1840–1, and partly during the building of Cannon Street station in 1868, which overlies the western portion of the palace. The function of the building was only recognized during recent excavation, mainly in 1964–5, in advance of office development. A large reception-hall, 82 feet by 42 feet internally, lay in the centre of the complex, and on its south side was a garden with an ornamental pool over 100 feet long. The floor of the pool lay on a massive concrete raft six feet thick. Rooms round two sides of this courtyard have been excavated; those on the east were probably offices, and the residential quarters no doubt faced the river. The official nature of this great complex is not in doubt, and the conclusion that it is indeed the headquarters of the Provincial Governor seems inescapable. It was built in the last quarter of the first century, and so is contemporary with the Fishbourne Palace, but it seems to have been abandoned c. AD 300. By then York had effectively become the political capital of Britain, because of its close contact with the crucial northern frontier.

No remains of the Palace can now be seen, though one relic nearby ought to be mentioned. This is the **London Stone** (1), a shapeless lump of Clipsham limestone now built into the wall of the Bank of China, on the north side of Cannon Street next to St Swithin's Lane. It was first recorded in 1189 and is of either Roman or Saxon date. Sir Christopher Wren saw its foundation and believed that it was part of an elaborate monument connected with a large complex further south. That complex we now know to be the Governor's Palace, and the original position of the stone, in the middle of Cannon Street a few yards from its present site, seems to be exactly on the north-south axis of the Palace. If so, its Roman origin seems very likely, and one suggestion, that it is part of a great milestone from which distances in Britain were measured, may not be far wide of the mark. It is unlikely that we shall ever know for certain.

Another important class of public buildings were the temples, but only one has securely been identified in London. This is the notorious **Temple of Mithras** (C; 2). The discovery of this shrine in September 1954 caused a sensation. Intense public interest demanded a temporary suspension of work on the modern building (Bucklersbury House) while 80,000 people flocked to see the remains. Questions were asked in the Commons about the possibility of preserving it, but to have kept it *in situ* would have cost too much money. A compromise was reached, and the building was dismantled and eventually reassembled in its present position in Temple Court, 11 Victoria Street (2). This is about 60 yards NW of its original site on the east bank of the Walbrook stream (C). The reconstruction does give a good idea of the outline of the temple, with its nave, two aisles and an apse for the main statue-group. In addition, the entrance threshold, much worn by the tread of Roman devotees, and the bases of the pillars that supported the roof, can be seen. But there are many misleading features about the 'new' temple of Mithras: the nave was originally much lower in relation to the side-aisles, and was reached from the doorway by two wooden steps; the earth floor of the nave and the wooden floor of the aisles have both been replaced by crazy paving; a wooden water-tank in one corner

has been rebuilt in stone. Also the present position of the remains
on a lofty platform is quite the opposite of the original low-lying
site. The temple, built towards the end of the second century,
was graced with a beautiful set of sculptures, described below
(p. 326). Replicas are displayed in the main entrance to Bucklersbury House. The reconstruction-drawing shows a Mithraic
ceremony in progress in the temple (fig 131). Mithraism was a
secret religion popular with soldiers, merchants and officials. It
has some affinities to freemasonry and some to Christianity: like
the former there were different grades of initiates, like the latter
it promised salvation and joy in the world to come. Another
temple of Mithras is visible on Hadrian's Wall at Carrawburgh.

Parts of Roman bath-houses have come to light in the city,
but it is not always clear whether they were for public or private
use: an example is the small building found but not preserved in
Cheapside in 1956 (D). A much larger complex on **Huggin Hill**,
Upper Thames Street, however, is certainly a public establishment (E). Excavation in 1964 and 1969 revealed that at first there
were three unheated rooms here, before two were given hypocausts and a large apsed *caldarium* was added. The whole

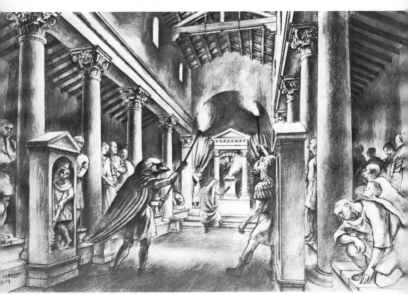

131   Walbrook Temple of Mithras, a ceremony in progress

building was demolished before the middle of the second century and some poorly-constructed private dwellings were erected on the levelled remains. Part of this bath still survives, buried beneath the courtyard east of Dominant House, 205 Upper Thames Street, but nothing can be seen of it at present except for a very overgrown stretch of Roman retaining-wall, with a double course of bonding-tiles. It lies on the north edge of the modern courtyard.

About the middle of the second century the Walbrook stream silted up, its revetting-banks collapsed, and the area was redeveloped to become one of the high-class residential districts of the city. One beautifully-preserved geometric mosaic, found in Bucklersbury in 1869, aroused as much public interest as the Temple of Mithras: 33,000 people visited it in three days. 17 feet long and of third-century date, it will be a main feature in the new Museum of London. Two much smaller geometric mosaics were found in 1933–4 during building work at the **Bank of England** (3). Both have been lifted from their original positions: one has been reset in the Bank's private museum, which contains other Roman material, and can only be visited by special appointment; the other, much restored, now lies at the foot of the main staircase and may be viewed (from a distance) during normal hours, on enquiry at the entrance-hall. A dull and dusty portion of third-century mosaic, which does remain *in situ*, exists on the premises of Messrs Peat, Marwick and Mitchell and Company, and can be visited only by prior written arrangement. The address is Selborne House, 11 **Ironmonger Lane** (4). Finally, a red tessellated floor, originally bisected by a wooden partition, can be seen *in situ* in the crypt of **All Hallows Church** (5), near the Tower of London. Another patched of red *tesserae* can be seen nearby, but this has been relaid. Several Roman finds are also displayed in the crypt, including a model of Roman London. The tombstone with a Greek inscription has almost certainly been brought to this country in recent times and is not a genuine relic of the city's past.

Much more interesting than these isolated mosaics are the remains of a Roman house and attached bath-suite in **Lower Thames Street** * (6). At present this outstanding site can only be visited by prior arrangement with what is at present the Guild-hall Museum, but by 1976 or 1977 the site will have been developed and the Roman remains preserved in a viewing-chamber. With the exception of some stretches of city-wall, the surviving fragments of Roman London are isolated relics, looking rather pathetic in their modern surroundings. Here, however, is a more substantial building, and its appeal is therefore the greater. It is also, of course, the earliest dwelling-place of a Londoner that can be seen today, and is indeed the only Roman house in London that has been extensively explored. Parts had been discovered in 1848 and 1859, and even a small portion preserved beneath the Coal Exchange. Excavation in 1969–70 has now revealed that these earlier discoveries belonged to the bath-house of a private residence. Pottery suggests that the whole building was constructed about AD 200, but more interesting is the evidence of its end. A group of 246 bronze coins points to occupation after AD 395, and an early Anglo-Saxon brooch found in the rubble of the collapsed roof implies that the house did not become ruined until c. AD 500. This is the first evidence that life went on in London well after the withdrawal of the official Roman government, and it confirms evidence from St Albans and elsewhere that Romano–British towns did *not* end in flames kindled by Saxon raiders. Of the house itself parts of two corridors serving the north and east wings, and some of the rooms of these wings, have been explored, but the main feature of the preserved remains is the fine bath-suite. A worn door-sill leads from a corridor of the house to a small undressing-room with a red tessellated floor. On either side are two heated rooms with apses. On the bather's right (west side) was the *tepidarium*, with a brick seat still visible in one of its walls; this is the part that was preserved beneath the Coal Exchange. On his left was the *caldarium*, which is in excellent shape. 29 *pilae* bases for supporting the floor can be seen, as well as the stoke-hole and flue-tiles for the hot air to escape. The walls of the room are still about three feet high. On the south side of these heated chambers was a large *frigidarium*, probably vaulted. Its floor of red *tesserae* was later covered after heavy wear with a layer of pink cement. At one end is a small plunge-bath.

The great defences of Roman London, which have left more numerous and more substantial fragments than the buildings they eventually enclosed, fall into three separate phases. Early in the second century, before the construction of the city-wall, a large fort was erected NW of the built-up area (above). This fort was the most important discovery of the post-war excavations:

though the peculiar course taken by the city-wall in the Cripplegate area had been noted before, the reason for it was only revealed in 1949.

When the city-wall was constructed, the existing north and west walls of the fort were incorporated into its circuit. This was done at the very end of the second century. At a time when most other towns in Britain were receiving only an earth bank and ditch, the capital was given a great girdle of stone walls, backed by a (contemporary) rampart of earth. The wall, some eight feet thick at base and 15–20 feet high, was made of courses of Kentish ragstone separated at intervals by tile bonding-courses. The fort-wall, however, was only four feet thick, and so fresh masonry was tacked onto its inside face (on the north and west sides) to make the defences the same width here as they were elsewhere. London's appearance at this time is suggested in fig 132: the fort is prominent in the foreground, and the forum and bridge can be seen in the background. No city-wall is shown along the river frontage (construction is conveniently depicted as still being in progress), but it seems inconceivable that such a wall did not exist even though no definite trace of it has ever been found. The

132 London c. AD 200

position of the Roman water-line, and of the probable wall, is marked by the dotted line on the map on p. 308–9.

The third phase in the fortification of Roman London came sometime in the fourth century, when projecting bastions were added to the existing wall. This seems to have been completed only on the eastern side of the city, where the bastions are solid and firmly dated to the Roman period. The western bastions, in the Cripplegate area, are all hollow and are now known to belong to the early medieval period. Curiously enough, they do not appear to have had Roman predecessors.

Remains of the Roman walls fall into two separate areas, one in the Aldersgate region, the other near the Tower. The first portion at the eastern end can be seen on the grass east of the White Tower in the grounds of the **Tower of London** (7) [AM; weekdays 10–4, 4.30 or 5.30; Sun., mid-Mar.–Oct. 2–5]. The ruins of the Wardrobe Tower sit on the site of a Roman bastion, and behind it a low portion of Roman wall, 10 feet long, survives. The rest of its line in this area, and the site of an internal turret, have been marked out in concrete. Outside the Tower, on the north side of **Tower Hill*** (8) [AM; A] is a magnificent stretch of

133   Tower Hill, the Roman city-wall

wall. It is approached through Wakefield Gardens, whence some steps lead down to what is approximately Roman ground-level. On the right only the base of the wall, and the foundations of an internal turret, are visible, but on the left the Roman work survives in splendid condition (fig 133) – 15 courses of beautifully-squared ragstone blocks, separated at intervals by four sets of bonding-bricks (the bottom two in triple rows, the upper two double). Above, the wall is medieval.

In the gardens is a nineteenth-century statue of a Roman emperor and a cast of a Roman inscription. The original of the latter is now in the British Museum, but since it is not at present on show there a mention of it may be made here (fig 134). Julius Alpinus Classicianus was the financial administrator (*procurator*) of Britain immediately after the Boudiccan revolt, when he urged policies of restraint in dealing with the offending natives. He died in London, and his tomb was set up outside the perimeter of the city. In the fourth century, it was broken up and incorporated into a bastion just north of Wakefield Gardens. The upper portion, including part of his name, was found in 1852, and it was then claimed as part of the tomb of the *procurator* mentioned by

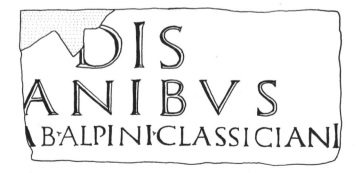

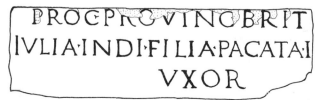

134   Classicianus' tombstone, the surviving fragments

Tacitus. This theory was later rejected until the lower part of the
inscription was found in 1935, still in position at the bottom of the
bastion. This reads PROC.PROVINC.BRIT., '*procurator* of the
province of Britain', and the identification was no longer in
doubt. It was set up by his wife Julia Pacata I(ndiana): such is the
restoration now accepted, though the cast in the gardens reads
I(nfelix), 'sorrowing'.

Now leave Wakefield Gardens and pass **Tower Hill Underground Station** (9). A fragment of Roman wall found in 1967 is
preserved in an opening high up in the tiled wall opposite platform 1 (westbound). Immediately on your right after passing the
station is the entrance to an office car-park, and set in the modern
wall at the back is another cast of the Classicianus inscription,
very close to its original find-spot (ask permission at the lodge on
the right). A few yards further north, at 40–1 Trinity Square, is
the entrance to the **Toc H Club** (10), and a stretch of the outer
face of the Roman wall is preserved in its basement. The plinth
is visible here, and a triple row of bonding-tiles. This can never
be visited in the evenings or at weekends; at other times you may
be escorted to the relic on enquiry at the entrance, but it is better
to write for permission in advance. Accessible at any time and
much more impressive is a fine stretch a little further north, in
the courtyard behind Midland House, 8–10 **Cooper's Row*** (11).
This was found in 1864 when it was incorporated in a warehouse.
The latter was knocked down in 1961, and the wall exposed. It
stands 35 feet above ground-level here, but the upper part is
medieval. The Roman portion, with considerable parts of the
inner face and rows of bonding-tiles still preserved, stands about
13 feet high (fig 135). A plaque on the right indicates clearly
what is Roman and what is not. The outer face of the wall, more
repaired but still displaying the Roman sandstone plinth, can
be seen by going through the modern breach to the other side.

Return now to Cooper's Row and go northwards, under the
railway, into **Crutched Friars** (12). In Roman Wall House (no. 1,
on the right), a substantial piece of the inner face of the wall
survives, 40 feet long and 8–9 feet high. Again this is private
property and it is best to write in advance; in 1973 the building
was in the process of being modernized. A miserable fragment is
preserved in the **Sir John Cass College** (13), 31 Jewry Street (the
porter may have time to escort you), and a larger piece exists
under '**The Three Tuns**' public house (14), 36 Jewry Street: the

135   Cooper's Row, the Roman city-wall

landlord will only show it to you if business is very slack.
Thereafter, no remains of the city-wall are visible at present
until you reach the Cripplegate area, although I understand that
a bastion in **Duke's Place** (15), off Aldgate, is to be preserved. If
so, it will be the only Roman bastion visible in London, for the
examples mentioned below are all medieval. Excavation in 1971
securely dated it to the fourth century, and found that re-used
Roman material had been employed in its construction.

For those who wish to walk, the line of the wall is followed by
Bevis Marks, Camomile Street, Wormwood Street and the road
called London Wall. There were Roman gates at Aldgate and
Bishopsgate. The next surviving portion of city-wall above
ground is that in **St Alphage Churchyard** (17), reached from Wood
Street, a turning off London Wall. The brickwork battlements are
Tudor and most of the rest of the facing is medieval, but one
interesting Roman feature is visible here. Go up the stairway on
the east side of the garden and look down at the outer face of the
wall. At the bottom, on the left, there appears to be a crack in the
masonry, but in fact there are two walls of different periods side
by side here. That on the right (outer) belongs to the Cripplegate
Roman fort, and dates to the early second century; that on the
left is the masonry added when the city-wall was built in the late
second century (as explained above, p. 317).

West of Wood Street, which passes through the site of Cripplegate, the north gate of the Roman fort, is the new Barbican
development. This impressive mass of steel, concrete and glass
is reached by pedestrian high-walks from London Wall. In the
middle, starkly contrasting with the modern architecture, is the
church of St Giles and a long stretch of city-wall. This stands on
Roman footings and incorporates Roman core, but most of the
masonry visible here is medieval, including the lower part of a
bastion. Excavation in 1966 dated the latter to the thirteenth
century, and this is presumably also the date of the spectacular
Cripplegate Bastion (18) a few yards to the west. It marks the
position of the NW corner of the Roman fort and city-wall. The
only Roman work visible in this Barbican stretch is behind the
1966 bastion, where neatly-built squared stones and slight traces
of a tile-course (not the extensive brickwork above) can be seen
in the lower part of the wall. The later bastion protected the wall
here, so making unnecessary the repair which has removed the
Roman facing elsewhere.

The **West Gate*** (19) of the Roman fort is reached by steps on the north side of London Wall (12.30–2, Mon.–Fri. only). On the left in the inspection-chamber is a good portion of the original fort-wall standing on its base-plinth, and behind, jutting up against it, is the masonry added when the city-wall was built. Then comes a fine guardroom, originally matched by another which has not been preserved. In between were two carriageways spanned by arches. Some traces of the central dividing wall remain, and one of the carriageways is still blocked with a late Roman or post-Roman wall of crude material.

From the chamber in which the gateway is preserved, access can be gained (through doors saying No Admittance) to the large underground car-park under **London Wall** (16). Officially people without cars are not admitted here, but if you ask one of the attendants you may be allowed to see a good fragment of the Roman wall, found in 1957 during clearance for the new road. This portion lies east of the Cripplegate fort and so is of one thickness and build.

At the west end of London Wall, on the corner with Aldersgate Street, the new Museum of London is at present (1972) under construction; this should be visited before proceeding further south (below, p. 324). On the other side of London Wall, opposite the entrance to the west gate, is **Noble Street** (20). Parts of the outer (fort) wall and the inner (thickening) wall are exposed here for a considerable length, including the foundations of an internal turret. At the end of this stretch comes the crucial junction between fort- and city-walls, and it was here in 1949 that the existence of the fort was first confirmed. The fort-wall can be seen curving round, with a conspicuous internal corner turret. Projecting out from it and disappearing under the modern brickwork is a tiny portion of the Roman city-wall added nearly a century later. The difference in thickness between the two will be noted. The whole of these important remains is at present very overgrown, but plans have been made to tidy up the site and lay it out as a sunken garden.

Further west, a small portion of Roman wall, together with a substantial part of one of the hollow medieval bastions, survives below the yard of the **General Post Office**, King Edward Building (21). It can be visited, Mondays to Fridays only, if prior arrangement has been made with the Postmaster, GPO, St Martin's-le-Grand. The wall turns southwards at this point, and at Newgate there was a Roman gate. It had two carriageways and large square flanking towers, and the whole structure was about 100 feet wide. Finally, a short section of the bottom of the Roman wall has been preserved under the new extension to the **Central Criminal Court** (22), north of Warwick Square. For obvious security reasons, this can only be seen by prior arrangement, and you should write to the Keeper of the Court at the Old Bailey if you wish to inspect the relic.

Outside the city limits, there is very little of Roman interest. A red tessellated pavement *in situ* is reflected in a mirror in the crypt of **St Bride's Church**, Fleet Street (off map), and the position of a Roman ditch has been marked out on the lino floor nearby. Further west there was a Roman building under Westminster Abbey, and a sarcophagus found there is now in the entrance to the Chapter House. The so-called 'Roman Bath' in the Strand is of sixteenth- or seventeenth-century date. Some of the finds from the Roman suburb in Southwark are in the Cuming Museum, Walworth Road (10–5.30 except Sun.; closes at 7 on Thurs., 5 on Sat.). A tiny fragment of red mosaic has been relaid in the south chancel-aisle of the cathedral. Slight traces of a Roman building in Greenwich Park (App. I) may also be mentioned.

Roman London has yielded a whole host of interesting finds, more than any other single site in Britain. The best are in the British Museum, but the majority are at present split between two museums, the London and the Guildhall. Both are in temporary accommodation for the moment, but their collections are soon to be amalgamated in the new **Museum of London** (23), Aldersgate Street, which will undoubtedly be one of the most important Roman displays in the country. It should be open early in 1976. There is no point, therefore, in giving a detailed guide to the existing museums, and I will merely mention a very few of the many outstanding exhibits you should look out for.

Pride of place must surely be given to the amazing haul of sculptures from the Temple of Mithras. Some pieces were found in the nineteenth century, and almost certainly come from the Mithraeum, though the building itself was not found then. The most interesting of these earlier finds is a small but complete slab depicting Mithras slaying the bull. He is accompanied by the torchbearers Cautes and Cautopates, who represent light and darkness, salvation and death. Signs of the zodiac appear in the

136   Museum of London, head of Serapis

surrounding circle. But it is the beautiful sculptures found in
1954 which deserve even closer attention. They had deliberately
been buried in the floor of the sanctuary early in the fourth
century, perhaps through fear of Christian iconoclasts, but the
building seems to have continued in use for some years after
this. One of the sculptures is a marble head of Mithras in his
Phrygian cap, and it was the discovery of this that conclusively
proved the identity of the temple. Its late-second-century date
makes it roughly contemporary with the building of the shrine,
and it is a reasonable guess that it formed part of the main bull-
slaying relief in the apse; the rest of the relief may have been of
stucco and so have perished. An enormous hand clasping the
hilt of a dagger was also found, but this cannot have belonged to a
similar group, for its scale would have been too big for the
Walbrook temple: it was probably meant to be a symbolic
object. Other sculptures found in 1954, all of marble, include a
figure of Mercury, a head of Minerva and a small damaged
group of Bacchus and his companions. But the most beautiful
discovery of all is the head of Serapis, Graeco-Egyptian god of the
underworld (fig 136). Like the head of Mithras it is an imported
work, made of Italian marble at the end of the second century
AD. On his head is a corn-measure, symbolic of the prosperity
which the god will bestow both in this life and the next. The
sensitive modelling of the face, the skill in the design and
execution of the hair, and the splendour of the burnished finish
cannot fail to be admired. The presence of so many other deities
within the temple may seem surprising, but all of them are in some
way connected with the after-life and are not therefore out of
place in a Mithraic sanctuary. Finally, an enigmatic silver box
and 'strainer' may be mentioned. Very strange scenes of combat
between men and animals, including griffins, are represented.
The precise significance of these scenes is debated, but they
presumably allude to Mithras in his role as a conqueror of death
and evil.

Space prevents more than a list of other objects to be displayed
in this museum. The fine Bucklersbury mosaic has been
mentioned, but other mosaics and wall-plaster are only tantalis-
ing fragments of the decoration that must once have adorned the
capital. A replica of the gold medallion from Arras (France)
shows a personification of the city kneeling before the emperor
Constantius, who is described as the 'restorer of eternal light'.

It commemorates the recovery of the city in 296 after the rule of
Carausius and Allectus. Behind the kneeling figure is the earliest
portrayal of the city, a schematic representation of one of the
city-gates. The medallion was minted in Trier (Germany) and
so it is unlikely that the designer had ever seen London. The
Roman name of the city can be clearly read on another famous
exhibit, a jug found in Southwark inscribed LONDINI AD FANVM
ISIDIS, 'in London next to the temple of Isis'. Another graffito, this
time scratched on tile, reads 'Austalis has been wandering off on
his own every day for the last fortnight' – usually claimed as the
first recorded example of absenteeism by a British workman.
Another British worker, this time female, is implied by the so-
called 'bikini' trunks, but whether she was employed in some
muddy job near the Walbrook (where the find was made) or as a
dancing girl in a Roman-style night-club is left open to the

137   British Museum, head of Christ on a mosaic floor

imagination. Perhaps most immediate of all the objects displayed are the simple things of everyday life, the needles and pins, the jewellery and the tools. The last in particular are remarkably close to their modern counterparts.

The most important collection of Romano–British antiquities, including some finds from London, is the property of the **British Museum** (10–5 Sun. 2.30–6), Great Russell Street. Not everything that they own can be displayed at any one time, and one of the most serious omissions at present is the Classicianus tombstone (above, p. 319). But there is plenty, of course, to enjoy here, and if you read all the labels and information-panels that are displayed with the exhibits you will leave the museum with a very thorough idea of life in Britain under Roman rule. Once again only a handful of items can be mentioned here. At the top of the main staircase is the large fourth-century mosaic from Hinton St Mary, Dorset, found in 1963. In the central roundel of the main portion of the pavement is the earliest portrait of Christ known in Britain. A Chi-Rho monogram appears behind his head, and pomegranates, symbols of immortality, are represented on either side (fig 137). The other part of the floor contains a roundel which depicts Bellerophon slaying the Chimaera. The same subject, an allegory of the triumph over death and evil, appears on a mosaic at Lullingstone, significantly close to the Christian rooms there. Next comes the main Romano–British

138   British Museum, wall-plaster from St Albans

139   British Museum, detail of the Mildenhall dish

room. The first exhibit on the right is the best of the painted panels to have come from the St Albans excavations: this one is an ambitious floral scroll on a pleasing yellow background, and two handsome peacocks and two panther heads are also visible on the surviving piece (detail, fig 138). Then come two marble portrait-busts from Lullingstone and, a little beyond them, the Mildenhall Treasure, a hoard of high-quality imported silver-ware. A photograph may give some idea of the beauty of one of the pieces (fig 139): it shows part of a great circular dish two feet in diameter, depicting the mask of Oceanus in the centre surrounded by sea-nymphs and marine beasts. The dish is the product of a Mediterranean workshop in the fourth century AD. Lullingstone again is the place of discovery of the next two exhibits, the Christian wall-plaster fragments from the room believed to have been a house-chapel. On one wall were painted figures of six Christians, their hands outstretched in the ancient attitude of prayer; on another was a Chi-Rho monogram (fig 140) (but see p. 360).

On the opposite wall is a fine bronze head of Claudius from the river Alde in Suffolk; possibly it was deposited there by followers of Boudicca in AD 60–1 after the sack of Colchester. In an ante-

140   British Museum, Chi-Rho from Lullingstone

141   British Museum, statuette of Hercules

room near the lift at the back is the best surviving figured mosaic from Roman London: found in Leadenhall Street in 1803, it depicts Bacchus riding on a tiger. At the foot of the stairs to the upper level is a Hadrianic milestone from North Wales, giving a distance of eight miles from Caerhun. Above it is the Horkstow mosaic, depicting a chariot race in a circus.

Finally, in the three showcases on the upper level are finds from more of the places described earlier in this book: in the first, military buckles and arrow-heads from Hod Hill; in the last, the handsome Ribchester helmet. The middle one contains two of the million nails from Inchtuthil, a superb gilt-bronze statuette of Hercules from Hadrian's Wall (fig 141), and a famous bronze head of the emperor Hadrian, found in the Thames. It is fitting that I should end a guidebook to Roman remains in Britain with him, for it was due to the eccentric genius of this emperor that our most famous and impressive antiquity, the great Wall of Hadrian, was ever built. But more remains of Roman Britain than a well-known frontier-barrier and objects in museum showcases: a tremendous number of monuments, differing immensely in character, can still be tracked down in these islands. Some of them may now be tucked away behind hedgerows or factory chimneys, others are lost on barren moorland, but all of them bear a living witness to nearly 400 years of Roman rule in Britain.

Gazetteer of visible remains not mentioned in the text

For explanation of the symbols, see introduction, p. 5. Places listed here do not appear in the index or on the maps at the beginning of each chapter.

Chapter One

OS Grid ref	1" map no.	Name	County	Description	Notes
TQ 1133	182 (187)	Alfoldean	Sussex	settlement(*e*)	1
TQ 0317	182 (197)	Hardham	Sussex	settlement(*e*)	1, 2
SU 8426	181 (197)	Iping	Sussex	settlement(*e*)	1
TQ 4054	171 (187)	Titsey	Surrey	villa(*s*)	3
TQ 4565	171 (177)	Orpington	Kent	villa(*s*)	4
SU 8105	181 (197)	Bosham	Sussex	building(*s*)	5
TQ 0544	170 (187)	Farley Heath	Surrey	temple(*s*)	6
TQ 8032	184 (188)	Iden Green	Kent	paved ford (*s*)	7
TR 1342	173 (189)	Stowting	Kent	barrow (*e*)	
TR 1752	173 (179)	Bishopsbourne	Kent	barrow (*e*)	
SU 810402	169 (186)	Alice Holt	Surrey	pottery kilns (*e*)	8

Notes

1 Three small road staging-posts, all displaying remains of earth ramparts.

2 Cut through by railway. Only S side and NE corner. Occupied AD 50–150.

3 Small building excavated 1864, but now largely overgrown with nettles. Parts of two rooms clearly visible, one with hypocaust. Ask permission and directions from South Lodge, on B-road.

4 Flint walls and red tessellated pavements project from bank of driveway to Borough Council Depot and Offices, off Crofton Road, immediately SW of, and adjacent to, Orpington Station.

5 W wall of nave of Bosham Church is of Roman masonry with brick bonding-course. Base for Roman arch remains *in situ* below bases of Saxon chancel arch.

6 Foundations of a typical Romano–Celtic temple, partly restored in modern concrete. Dug in nineteenth century in the usual fashion of the day, as this ditty by Martin Tupper c. 1848 amply demonstrates:

> Many a day have I whiled away
> Upon hopeful Farley Heath,

> In its antique soil digging for spoil
> Of possible treasure beneath.

7 Large Roman slabs crossing a stream which has now altered course. Unfortunately vandalized.

8 Series of irregular mounds, mostly in S end of forest, covering sites of Roman kilns.

Chapter Two

OS Grid ref	1″ map no.		Name	County	Description	Notes
ST 4401	177	(193)	Waddon Hill	Dorset	fort (e)	1, 2
ST 0827	164	(181)	Wiveliscombe	Somerset	fort (e)	1, 3
SX 0366	186	(200)	Nanstallon	Cornwall	fort (e)	1
SX 6699	175	(191)	North Tawton	Devon	fort (e)	1
SY 2390	177	(193)	Seaton	Devon	bath-house (s)	4
ST 5222	177	(183)	Ilchester	Somerset	town (e)	5
SZ 4888	180	(196)	Carisbrooke	Hants, IOW	villa (s)	6
SZ 0099	179	(195)	Wimborne Minster	Dorset	building (s)	7
SU 7763	169	(175)	Finchampstead	Berkshire	milestone (s)	8
SU 3288	158	(174)	Kingston Lisle	Berkshire	barrow (e)	9

Notes

1 See p. 61 for context.
2 Very slight.
3 Roman date not proven, but virtually certain.
4 Behind new housing-estate off Homer Lane. Excavated 1969. Badly decayed.
5 Section of rampart in fields E of village.
6 Crumbling mosaic in hut in vicarage garden; rest mostly overgrown. Permission from the vicar.
7 Tiny piece of tessellated floor is *in situ* on S side of the Minster's nave.
8 Uninscribed. In gardens of 'Banisters', a short distance from place of discovery.
9 Overgrown with nettles.

Chapter Three

OS Grid ref	1″ map no.		Name	County	Description	Notes
SO 4074	129	(137)	Leintwardine	Hereford	fort (e)	1
SO 4442	142	(161)	Kenchester	Hereford	town (e)	2
SP 0425	144	(163)	Spoonley Wood	Glos	villa (s)	3
SO 5610	142	(162)	Scowles	Glos	iron mine	4
SP 2712	144	(163)	Widford	Oxon	mosaic	5

Notes

1 Only on W side of village.
2 Almost totally ploughed out; best on NE near farm.
3 Difficult to find; walls mossy and nettle-grown; one mosaic (Victorian replica) is visible. Permission from E W Bailey, Charlton Abbots Manor.
4 Opencast rocky hollows, much overgrown with foliage.
5 Fragment *in situ* in floor of church.

Chapter Four

OS Grid ref	1″ map no.		Name	County	Description	Notes
TM 0308	162	(168)	Bradwell-on-Sea	Essex	fort (s)	1
TF 7844	125	(132)	Brancaster	Norfolk	fort (e)	2
TL 3257	134	(153)	Bourn	Cambs	barrow (e)	
TL 3954	148	(154)	Barton	Cambs	barrow (e)	
TL 4841	148	(154)	Ickleton	Cambs	barrow (e)	
TL 4534	148	(154)	Langley	Essex	barrow (e)	
TL 3507	161	(166)	Broxbourne	Herts	barrow (e)	
TL 3717	148	(166)	Standon	Herts	barrow (e)	
TL 3813	148	(166)	Easneye Wood	Herts	barrow (e)	
TL 8961	136	(155)	Eastlow Hill	Suffolk	barrow (e)	

Notes

1 Saxon Shore fort of OTHONA. One overgrown fragment of S wall 4 ft long and the same high; near cottage, to right of fine seventh-century chapel largely built of Roman materials.
2 Depression marking ditch on W side is all that remains of Saxon Shore fort of BRANODVNVM.

Chapter Five

OS Grid ref	1″ map no.		Name	County	Description	Notes
SP 0483	131	(139)	Metchley	Warwicks	fort (e)	1, 2
SK 0095	102	(110)	Melandra	Derbys	fort (e)	1, 3
SK 1882	111	(110)	Brough-on-Noe	Derbys	fort (e)	1, 4
SO 8688	130	(139)	Greensforge	Staffs	fort (e)	1
SO 6978	130	(138)	Wall Town	Salop	fort (e)	1
SK 3854	111	(119)	Pentrich Camp	Derbys	fortlet (e)	
TL 1297	134	(142)	Water Newton	Hunts	town (e)	5
SP 3459	132	(151)	Chesterton	Warwicks	town (e)	
SP 6948	146	(152)	Towcester	Northants	town (e)	6
TL 1298	134	(142)	Castor	Northants	building (s)	7
TF 3061	114	(122)	Revesby	Lincs	barrow (e)	8
SK 9876	104	(121)	Riseholme	Lincs	barrow (e)	
TL 2174	134	(142)	Great Stukeley	Hunts	barrow (e)	9

Notes

1 See p. 149.
2 NW corner of large fort, reconstructed, behind new building of
   Medical Faculty, University of Birmingham.
3 ARDOLITIA, occupied from Agricola to mid-second century.
4 NAVIO, occupied c. 75–120, 155–350.
5 Clearest on S, nearest road. Field-boundary follows N rampart.
   Ermine St very clear leading up to E gate (*agger*). Crop-marks
   showing street-plan of interior visible in summer.
6 Earth ramparts at NW corner of LACTODORVM, in field W of police
   station; reached by footpath to Greens Norton (signpost).
7 Two lumps of Roman walling project from modern wall on Stocks
   Hill, opposite church. Centre of vast Roman pottery industry.
   Relaid mosaic in dairy at Milton Hall.
8 2 barrows, excellently preserved, 8 ft high, not overgrown.
9 Low and very overgrown. Note rise and fall of fence bordering road.

Chapter Six

Chester:
The following visible fragments of the fortress, all on private property,
were not included in the text above: (i) 48 Eastgate St (guard-chamber);
(ii) 35 Watergate St (column-base); (iii) 104 Watergate St (furnace
arch); (iv) 18 St Michael's Row (mosaic panel); (v) 22 St Michael's
Row (wall); (vi) 28 Eastgate St (Browns) (column-base).

OS Grid ref	1" map no.		Name	County	Description	Notes
SS 7998	153	(170)	Blaen-cwmbach	Glamorgan	marching-camp (*e*)	
ST 0098	154	(170)	Twyn y Briddallt	Glamorgan	marching-camp (*e*)	
ST 059878	154	(170)	Pen-y-Coedcae	Glamorgan	marching-camp (*e*)	1
SO 379007	155	(171)	Usk	Monmouth	fort (*e*)	2
ST 379917	155	(171)	Coed-y-Caerau	Monmouth	fortlet (*e*)	3
SO 1621	141	(161)	Pen-y-Gaer	Brecknock	fort (*e*)	4
SS 5697	153	(159)	Loughor	Glamorgan	fort (*s*)	5
SS 6097	153	(159)	Mynydd Carn Goch	Glamorgan	2 practice camps (*e*)	
SN 8510	153	(160)	Coelbren Gaer	Glamorgan	fort (*e*)	6
SN 862102	153	(160)	Coelbren	Glamorgan	marching-camp (*e*)	7
SN 924164	141	(160)	Ystradfellte	Brecknock	marching-camp (*e*)	8
SN 8026	140	(160)	Arosfa Gareg	Carmarthen	marching-camp (*e*)	9
SN 7735	140	(146)	Llandovery	Carmarthen	fort (*e*)	
SN 919507	141	(147)	Caerau	Brecknock	marching-camp (*e*)	10
SN 647485	140	(146)	Pant-teg-Uchaf	Cardigan	practice camp (*e*)	11
SN 6456	140	(146)	Llanio	Cardigan	bath-house (*s*)	12
SO 0292	128	(136)	Caer Sws	Montgom	fort (*e*)	13
SO 2098	128	(137)	Forden Gaer	Montgom	fort (*e*)	

OS Grid ref	1" map no.	Name	County	Description	Notes
SN 8281	127 (136)	Cae Gaer	Montgom	fortlet (e)	14
SN 828067	153 (160)	Hirfynydd	Glamorgan	fortlet (e)	
SN 856935	127 (136)	Pen-y-Crogbren	Montgom	fortlet (e)	
SJ 1004	117 (136)	Llanfair Caerinion	Montgom	fortlet (e)	15
SH 7457	107 (115)	Bryn-y-Gefeiliau	Caernarvon	building (s)	16
SH 477454	115 (123)	Derwydd-bach	Caernarvon	marching-camp (e)	17
SH 860278	116 (124)	Pont Rhyd Sarn	Merioneth	practice camp (e)	
SN 927699	128 (136)	Esgairperfedd	Radnorshire	marching-camp (e)	18
SN 985717	128 (136)	St Harmon	Radnorshire	marching-camp (e)	19
SJ 4163	109 (117)	Heronbridge	Cheshire	settlement (e)	
ST 4791	155 (171)	Castle Tump	Monmouth	building (s)	20
SS 9569	155 (170)	Llantwit Major	Glamorgan	villa (e)	21

Notes

1 Only E end and angles are well preserved.
2 SE side of BVRRIVM, E of Court House.
3 Immediately NE of pre-Roman 'enclosure' marked on OS map.
4 Best preserved on N.
5 Part of fort-wall exposed in S side of castle mound (1972).
6 Whole fort visible as prominent banks, partly marked by field-boundaries.
7 Best on W side, and part of E.
8 Only a very low bank, best preserved near SE corner. Fire-breaks in the plantation are so positioned as to leave the ramparts free from trees.
9 Nearly whole circuit can be traced.
10 Most of N and W sides are traceable. $\frac{1}{4}$ m S is site of a Roman fort, partly covered by the farm (very prominent platform, but no real remains of ramparts).
11 Unfinished. N side 2 ft high. Another similar camp nearby (SN 641493) is now obscured by trees.
12 Remains of hypocausts, etc. clearly visible, but vandalized. On S side of a fort-site (invisible). Ask permission and directions from farm.
13 Best preserved on SW in lane near station.
14 See p. 189.
15 Excellent preservation; Roman date not proven.
16 Prominent mounds with some stonework exposed; in annexe on W side of a fort (invisible).
17 Reed covered, at best 1 ft high: parts of NW and SW sides. A Roman fort and fortlet, now entirely quarried away, existed $\frac{1}{3}$ m E.

18 Most of circuit traceable.
19 Only S end, including *clavicula* at S gate, is visible.
20 On Ministry of Defence property and not accessible to the public.
21 Enclosure-banks, and mounds covering walls, of Roman villa.

Chapter Seven

OS Grid ref	1″ map no.	Name	County	Description	Notes
SJ 8397	101 (109)	Manchester	Lancs	fort (s)	1
SD 9909	101 (109)	Castleshaw	Yorks	fort (e)	2
SD 9249	95 (103)	Elslack	Yorks	fort (e)	
SD 9390	90	Brough-by-Bainbridge	Yorks	fort (e)	
SE 5703	103 (111)	Doncaster	Yorks	fort (s)	3
SD 4762	89	Lancaster	Lancs	fort (s)	4
SD 6531	95 (102)	Mellor Moor	Lancs	fortlet (e)	5
NZ 0558	77	Apperley Dene	N'umberland	fortlet (e)	
NY 998104	84	Scargill Moor	Yorks	shrines (s)	6
NY 8811	84	Roper Castle	W'morland	signal-station (e)	7
SD 913655	90	Malham Moor	Yorks	marching-camp (e)	
NY 4938	83	Old Penrith	Cumb'land	fort (e)	
NX 9821	82	Moresby	Cumb'land	fort (e)	
NY 2646	82	Old Carlisle	Cumb'land	fort (e)	8
NY 2036	82	Caermote	Cumb'land	fort (e)	9
NY 1131	82	Papcastle	Cumb'land	fort (e)	10
SD 5190	89	Watercrook	W'morland	fort (e)	10
NY 3827	83	Troutbeck	Cumb'land	marching-camps (e)	11
NY 6001	89	Low Borrow Bridge	W'morland	fort (e)	
SE 2299	91	Catterick	Yorks	town (s)	12
SE 1387	91	Middleham	Yorks	building (s)	
SE 6775	92	Hovingham	Yorks	barrow (e)	13
NZ 8315	86	Goldsborough	Yorks	signal-station (e)	14

Notes

1 Fragment of E fort-wall of MAMVCIVM. Under a blocked railway-arch in a timber-yard at the end of Collier Street, off Liverpool Road.
2 2nd century fortlet built within earlier Agricolan fort.
3 Part of E wall of DANVM, N of Church St, uncovered in 1972, *may* be preserved.
4 Fragment of late-4th cent. fort, known as Wery Wall, is visible on left of Bridge Lane, off Church St (near back garden of 96 Church St).
5 Almost totally ploughed out.
6 See above, p. 221. The best approach is from Spanham farmhouse, 1⅛m to E. Circular shrine is still very conspicuous, opposite

footbridge over stream. Site of northern shrine is marked by a heap
of stones.

7   See above, p. 222.
8   Fort-ditches superbly preserved on W and W half of S sides.
    Causeway at E gate is also very clear.
9   Smaller fort inside NW corner of larger. Ramparts of both are
    grassy, rest of area full of reeds.
10 Only very faintly visible.
11 3 camps here: smallest (384274) has two gates with external
    claviculae; second (382273), crossed by road, has two gates with
    internal *claviculae*. Ramparts of both 2 ft high. Third (largest)
    camp is very difficult to trace.
12 Stretch of E wall of CATARACTONIVM, excavated and restored in
    19th cent. Overgrown. On S side of A6136, 200 yds E of A1 bridge,
    adjoining inside of racecourse track.
13 Very well-preserved, c. 10 ft high.
14 Now only a prominent mound; no stonework visible.

Chapter Eight

Numerous other Roman antiquities are visible on the Wall or in the Wall
region, apart from the selection described above. They can be found
with the help of the OS *Map of Hadrian's Wall* (HMSO 1964), although
there is very little to see at some of the sites marked on it as 'remains of'.
The inscribed Roman quarry-face called Rock of Gelt, near Brampton,
is worth mentioning here, as it does not appear on the map. It is very
difficult to find, and it is wise to look up beforehand: R G COLLINGWOOD
and R P WRIGHT, *Roman Inscriptions of Britain I* (OUP 1965), nos.
1007–16, where a large-scale map of its location can be found.

Chapter Nine

OS Grid ref	1" map no.	Name	County	Description	Notes
§ 1					
NY 8199	70	Bellshiel	N'umberland	marching-camp (e)	1
NT 7909	70	Brownhart Law	Roxburgh	signal-station (e)	
NZ 135885	78	Longshaws	N'umberland	fortlet (e)	2
NT 4224	69	Oakwood	Selkirk	fort (e)	3
NT 4754	62	Channelkirk	Berwicks	marching-camp (e)	4
NT 555328	70	North Eildon	Roxburgh	signal-station (e)	5
NT 3472	62	Inveresk	Midlothian	bath-house (s)	6
NS 213644	59	Blackhouse Moor	Ayrshire	signal-station (e)	
NS 7357	61	Bothwellhaugh	Lanarks	fort (e)	7
NS 9146	61	Cleghorn	Lanarks	marching-camp (e)	8

OS Grid ref	1" map no.	Name	County	Description	Notes
NS 9244	61	Castledykes	Lanarks	fort (e)	9
NS 944265	68	Wandel	Lanarks	marching-camp (e) and fortlet (e)	10
NS 9916	68	Little Clyde	Lanarks	marching-camp (e)	11
NT 0314	68	Redshaw Burn	Lanarks	fortlet (e)	12
NS 9004	68	Durisdeer	Dumfries	fortlet (e)	12
NY 2599	69	Raeburnfoot	Dumfries	fort/fortlet (e)	12
NT 303047	69	Craik Cross Hill	Dumfries	signal-station (e)	12
NT 0901	68	Tassiesholm	Dumfries	fort (e)	12
NY 389792	76	Gilnockie	Dumfries	marching-camp (e)	13
NY 1282	75	Torwood	Dumfries	marching-camp (e)	14
NX 9681	75	Carzield	Dumfries	fort (e)	15
NY 5674	76	Bewcastle	Cumb'land	fort (e)	16
NY 5771	76	Gillalees	Cumb'land	signal-station (e)	17

§ 2

OS Grid ref	1" map no.	Name	County	Description	Notes
NS 7978	61	Castlecary	Stirling	fort (e)	18
NS 7677	61	Westerwood	Dumbarton	fort (e)	3
NS 7075	61	Bar Hill	Dumbarton	fort (e)	19
NS 6774	60	Auchendavy	Dumbarton	fort (e)	3

(Only additional fort remains are listed here; other visible pieces of Wall and Ditch can be found with the help of the OS *Map of the Antonine Wall*, HMSO 1969.)

§ 3

OS Grid ref	1" map no.	Name	County	Description	Notes
NO 1739	49	Black Hill	Perthshire	signal-station (e)	20
NN 9028	55	Fendoch	Perthshire	signal-station (e)	21
NO 023149	55	Dunning	Perthshire	marching-camp (e)	22
NS 565998	54	Menteith	Perthshire	marching-camp (e)	23

Notes

1 Much obscured by field-banks.
2 Rampart about 4 ft high over the entire circuit.
3 Very faint.
4 Part of gigantic 165-acre camp, probably third-century.
5 See above, p. 288.
6 Four hypocaust *pilae* with a lump of concrete on top, in the private garden of Inveresk House. It is part of the bath-house outside the Antonine fort (under St Michael's Church); an Agricolan fort was on a separate site ½m away (under Lewisvale Public Park).
7 Access difficult. Outline marked by field-boundaries. SE rampart 5 ft high. Antonine.
8 Well preserved but obscured by conifers and long grass.
9 Faint except on E. Antonine, with Agricolan occupation below.

10   Rampart and ditch of fortlet are visible on NE, and S. On S side
     of fortlet, immediately adjacent, parts of the S and E rampart and
     ditch of the camp can be traced.

11   Best preserved near NW angle in field beyond farm.

12   See above, p. 290

13   Most of SE side of camp, including two *titula*, is well preserved;
     partly in a wood.

14   Single surviving side is a field-boundary.

15   Only SE angle is visible on the ground. Antonine.

16   Outpost fort of Hadrian's Wall. First Hadrianic, but totally
     rebuilt under Severus on a very unusual hexagonal plan. Of latter,
     only SW rampart survives as a bold mound; lower bank in front of
     it is post-Roman. Castle sits on NE corner and contains many
     Roman stones. Famous Bewcastle Cross, c. AD 675, in churchyard.

17   Connected Bewcastle with Birdoswald on Hadrian's Wall.

18   Bisected by railway-line; originally stone walls surrounded fort –
     odd signs of it peep through the turf. Above, p. 298.

19   See above, p. 299.

20   See above, p. 306.

21   ¾m W of site of Agricolan fort, of which the complete plan was
     recovered in 1936–8.

22   430 ft of bank and ditch, 3–4 ft high, preserved in Kincladie Wood,
     on W side of B934.

23   Parts of two sides of an Agricolan camp, up to 1 ft high, in rough
     moorland on S side of Lake Menteith.

Chapter Ten

All the visible fragments of Roman London which are still *in situ* have
been mentioned in the text (as far as I know). The only exceptions are
the following, but for security reasons none of them can ever be visited
by members of the public:

Basilica: Blurton's shop, Graechurch Street
         National Provincial Bank, Cornhill
         Bank of Australia and New Zealand, Cornhill
Wall: basement of GPO Headquarters Building, Aldersgate
         Bowyer Tower, Tower of London

In Greater London, a tiny piece of red tessellated floor belonging to a
Roman building in Greenwich Park (TQ 3977) has been preserved. It
is set in an enclosure in the N part of the Park, 100 yds from the E wall,
half-way between Vanbrugh and Maze Hill Gates.

Some museums displaying Romano-British material

This list is not complete, but it gives most of the major Romano-British collections with the exception of those in private hands and those in small site-museums (Richborough, Chedworth, Housesteads, etc.). A museum mentioned in the text is indicated by a page number in brackets; if the mention is more than a passing one, the number appears in bold type. In towns where there are several museums, the full title of the relevant one has been given to avoid confusion. Opening times can be found in *Museums and Galleries in Great Britain and Ireland*, an ABC Travel Guide published annually.

Aylesbury
Bangor, Museum of Welsh
   Antiquities
Barnard Castle (p. 221)
Basingstoke
Bath, Roman Museum (pp. 95,
   and **98**)
Bedford, Museum
Birmingham, City Museum and Art
   Gallery
Bradford, City Art Gallery and
   Museum
Brecon
Brighton, Museum and Art Gallery
Bristol, City Museum (p. 106)
Bury St Edmunds, Moyse's Hall
   Museum
Buxton
Caerleon (p. **176**)
Cambridge, University Museum of
   Archaeology and Ethnology
   (pp. 144, 221 and 282)
Canterbury, Royal Museum (p. **40**)
Cardiff, National Museum of Wales
   (pp. 187, 192 and 196)
Carlisle (pp. 228 and 275)

Carmarthen (p. 198)
Castleford
Chelmsford
Chester, Grosvenor Museum (p. 180)
Chichester (p. 43)
Cirencester (pp. **103** and 113)
Colchester, Castle Museum (p. **121**)
Dartford
Devizes
Doncaster
Dorchester, Dorset County Museum
   (pp. 65 and **67**)
Dover
Dumfries, Burgh Museum
Dundee, City Museum and Art
   Galleries
Durham, Cathedral Collection
   (pp. 219 and 282)
Edinburgh, National Museum of
   Antiquities (pp. 288, 291 and 294)
Edinburgh, Huntly House Museum
Evesham
Exeter, Rougemont House Museum
   (p. 70)
Falkirk
Folkestone

Bibliography

This bibliography is intended for the reader who wants more information about a given site than the scope of this book allows. The list is far from comprehensive, but references to other works will be found in many of the books and articles given below. A cross (+) denotes a work suitable for the non-specialist reader.

Abbreviations used

AA:	Archaeologia Aeliana (4th series)
Antiq.:	Antiquaries, Antiquarian, Antiquary
Arch.:	Archaeological, Archaeology
Arch. Camb.:	Archaeologia Cambrensis
Arch. Cant.:	Archaeologia Cantiana
Archit.:	Architectural
BBCS:	Bulletin of Board of Celtic Studies
CA:	Current Archaeology
CW:	Trans. of Cumberland and Westmorland Antiq. and Arch. Soc. (2nd series)
Hist.:	Historical
Inst.:	Institute
J:	Journal
JBAA:	Journal of the British Arch. Association
JRS:	Journal of Roman Studies
N.H.:	Natural History
Proc.:	Proceedings
PSAS:	Proc. of Soc. of Antiq. of Scotland
R.C.H.M.:	Royal Commission on Historical Monuments
Soc.:	Society
TBGAS:	Trans. Bristol and Gloucestershire Arch. Soc.
Trans.:	Transactions
Univ.:	University
V.C.H.:	Victoria County History

Introduction

Guidebooks to Roman Britain

+J HAWKES, *Guide to Prehistoric and Roman Monuments in England and Wales*, Chatto & Windus, rev. ed., 1973

+L COTTRELL, *Seeing Roman Britain*, 2nd ed., Pan 1966

+G DURANT, *Journey into Roman Britain*, Bell 1957

None of these are comprehensive and all are out of date. More recent is the list of sites given in +E S WOOD, *Collins Field Guide to Archaeology*, Collins, 3rd ed., 1972, and the notes provided in the series + *Regional Archaeologies* (Heinemann) and + *Discovering Regional Archaeologies* (Shire Books); but errors in these can lead the reader on fruitless missions. Some of the notes in the Penguin series + *Buildings of England*, ed. N PEVSNER, are useful, especially the more recent volumes; but whether the remains described are visible or not is not always clear. The + *OS Maps of Ancient Britain* (2 sheets) include some sites, but also a few inaccuracies.

General Works

S FRERE, *Britannia*, Routledge 1967

+I A RICHMOND, *Roman Britain*, Penguin, 2nd ed., 1963

+A L F RIVET, *Town and Country in Roman Britain*, Hutchinson, 2nd ed., 1964

+P HUNTER BLAIR, *Roman Britain and Early England*, Nelson 1963 (paper, Sphere 1970)

+A BIRLEY, *Life in Roman Britain*, Batsford 1964

+D DUDLEY and G WEBSTER, *The Roman Invasion of Britain*, Batsford 1965 (rev. ed. Pan 1973)

+D R WILSON, *Roman Frontiers of Britain*, Heinemann 1967

+R MOORE (ed.), *The Romans in Britain, a selection of texts*, Methuen, 2nd ed., 1963

+OS *Map of Roman Britain*, HMSO, 3rd ed., 1956

J LIVERSIDGE, *Britain in the Roman Empire*, Routledge 1968 (paper, Sphere 1973)

+G I F TINGAY, *From Caesar to the Saxons*, Longmans 1969

The Archaeology of Roman Britain

General: R G COLLINGWOOD and I RICHMOND, *The Archaeology of Roman Britain*, Methuen, 2nd ed., 1969

The Roman Army: +G WEBSTER, *The Roman Army*, Grosvenor Museum, Chester, 1956

G WEBSTER, *The Roman Imperial Army of the First and Second Centuries A D*, Black 1969

Towns: J S WACHER (ed.), *Civitas Capitals of Roman Britain*, Leicester Univ. Press 1966

Villas: A L F RIVET (ed.), *The Roman Villa in Britain*, Routledge 1969

Rural Settlement: C THOMAS (ed.), *Rural Settlement in Roman Britain*, Council for British Arch. 1966

Temples: M J P LEWIS, *Temples in Roman Britain*, Cambridge Univ. Press 1966

Roads: +I D MARGARY, *Roman Roads in Britain*, Baker, rev. ed., 1967

THE VIATORES, *Roman Roads in SE Midlands*, Gollancz 1964

Inscriptions: R G COLLINGWOOD and R P WRIGHT, *The Roman Inscriptions of Britain*, Vol. I, Oxford Univ. Press 1965

Art: +J M C TOYNBEE, *Art in Roman Britain*, Phaidon 1962

J M C TOYNBEE, *Art in Britain under the Romans*, Oxford Univ. Press 1964

Chapter One

General: +R F JESSUP, *South-East England* (People and Places), Thames & Hudson 1970

Richborough: +DOE *Guide*, HMSO (pamphlet)

B CUNLIFFE (ed.), *Richborough V*, Soc. of Antiq. 1968

Britannia i (1970), 240–8

Britannia ii (1971), 225–31

Reculver: + B PHILP, *The Roman Fort at Reculver*, Reculver Excavation Group, 5th ed., 1969 (booklet)

Lympne: +L COTTRELL, *The Roman Forts of the Saxon Shore*, HMSO 1964 (booklet)

Dover: *CA* 25 (March 1971), 52–5; *ib*. 28 (Sept. 1971) 133; *ib*. 38 (May 1973), 81–8 (forts)

The Observer Colour Supplement, 23 April 1972, 41–7 (house)

Arch.J. lxxxvi (1929), 29–46 (lighthouse)

Pevensey:	+ DOE *Guide*, HMSO 1952 (booklet)
Holtye:	+ I D MARGARY, *The London-Lewes Roman Road*, n.d., guide pamphlet obtainable from The White Horse, Holtye
Canterbury:	+ S S FRERE, *Roman Canterbury*, Canterbury Excavation Committee, 4th ed., 1965 (booklet) *Britannia* i (1970), 83–113 *JBAA* xxviii (1965), 1–15
Rochester:	*Arch.Cant.* lxxxiii (1968), 55–104
Chichester:	R A WATSON (ed.), *The Chichester Excavations* I (by Alec Down & Margaret Rule), Chichester 1971 J HOLMES, *Chichester, The Roman Town*, 1965 (Chichester Papers 50) (booklet)
Fishbourne:	+ B CUNLIFFE, *Fishbourne, a Guide to the Site*, Times Newspapers 1971 (booklet) + B CUNLIFFE, *Fishbourne, a Roman Palace and its Garden*, Thames & Hudson 1971 B CUNLIFFE, *Excavations at Fishbourne* 1961–9, 2 vols., Soc. of Antiq. 1971
Bignor:	+ S E WINBOLT and G HERBERT, *The Roman Villa at Bignor*, guidebook 1930 *JRS* lii (1962), 189
Lullingstone:	+ G W MEATES, *Lullingstone Roman Villa*, HMSO 1962 (guidebook)
Keston:	*CA* 14 (May 1969), 73–5
Stone-by-Faversham:	*Antiq.J.* xlix (1969), 273–94

Chapter Two

General:	+ L V GRINSELL, *The Archaeology of Wessex*, Methuen 1958 + P J FOWLER, *Wessex* (Regional Archaeologies), Heinemann 1967 + A FOX, *South-West England* (People and Places), Thames & Hudson 1964 (rev. ed. 1973) C THOMAS (ed.), *Rural Settlement in Roman Britain*, Council for British Arch. 1966, 43–67 and 74–98
Old Burrow, Martinhoe:	*Proc. Devon Arch. Soc.* xxiv (1966), 3–39

Hod Hill:	I A RICHMOND, *Hod Hill II*, British Museum 1968
	Arch.J. cxxiii (1966), 209–11 (summary)
Maiden Castle:	+ DOE *Guide*, HMSO (pamphlet)
Jordon Hill:	RCHM *Dorset* II, iii, HMSO 1970, 616–7
Dorchester:	*ibid.* 531–92
Exeter:	+ A FOX, *Exeter in Roman Times*, Univ. of Exeter 1971 (booklet)
Winchester:	*Arch.J.* cxxiii (1966), 182–3
	Proc. Hampshire Field Club xxii (1962), 51–81
Silchester:	+ guidebook (obtainable from Silchester and Reading Museums)
	+ G C BOON, *Roman Silchester*, Max Parrish 1957; cf. review in *Antiq.J.* xxxviii (1958), 113–4 (rev. ed. David & Charles 1974)
Rockbourne:	+ guidebook; cf. review in *Britannia* ii (1971), 321–2
Bokerley Dyke:	*Arch.J.* civ (1947), 62–78; *ib.* cxviii (1961), 65–79
Woodcuts, Rotherley:	*Arch.J.* civ (1947), 36–48
Berwick Down:	C THOMAS (ed.), *op.cit.* (see General), 46–7
Meriden Down:	RCHM *Dorset* III, ii, HMSO 1970, 298
Cerne Giant:	+ M MARPLES, *White Horses and Other Hill Figures*, Country Life 1949, ch. 8
	+ H L S DEWAR, *The Giant of Cerne Abbas*, The Toucan Press, Guernsey, 1968 (booklet)
Chysauster:	+ DOE *Guide*, HMSO (pamphlet)
Carn Euny:	+ DOE *Guide*, HMSO (pamphlet)
Cornish milestones:	R G COLLINGWOOD and R P WRIGHT, *The Roman Inscriptions of Britain* I, Oxford Univ. Press 1965, nos. 2230–4
Brading:	+ guidebook; for mosaics, J M C TOYNBEE, *Art in Britain under the Romans*, Oxford Univ. Press 1964, 254–8
Newport:	*Antiq.J.* ix (1929), 141–151 and 354–71
Combley:	*Proc. Isle of Wight N.H.& Arch. Soc.* vi, 4, (1969), 271–82
Carisbrooke:	+ DOE *Guide*, HMSO (booklet)
Portchester:	+ DOE *Guide*, HMSO (booklet)
	CA 4 (Sept. 1967), 100–4

Antiq. J. xliii (1963), 218–27; *ib.* xlvi (1966), 39–49; *ib.* xlix (1969), 62–74

Bitterne:
M A COTTON and P W GATHERCOLE, *Excavations at Clausentum* 1951–4, HMSO 1958; cf. review in *JRS* lii (1962), 271–2

Chapter Three

General:
I A RICHMOND, 'Roman Gloucestershire', *Arch. J.* cxxii (1965), 177–81
+ K S PAINTER, *The Severn Basin* (Regional Archaeologies), Heinemann 1964
+ M HEBDITCH and L GRINSELL, *Roman Sites in the Mendips, Cotswolds, Wye Valley and Bristol Region*, Bristol Arch. Research Group 1968 (booklet)

Charterhouse:
+ J CAMPBELL, D ELKINGTON, P FOWLER and L GRINSELL, *The Mendip Hills in Prehistoric and Roman Times*, Bristol Arch. Research Group 1970 (booklet)
Britannia ii (1971), 277 (plan)

Bath:
+ B CUNLIFFE, *Guide to the Roman Remains of Bath*, 1970 (booklet)
+ B CUNLIFFE, *Roman Bath Discovered*, Routledge 1971
B CUNLIFFE, *Roman Bath*, Soc. of Antiq. 1969

Gloucester:
+ J F RHODES, *Catalogue of Romano–British Sculptures in Gloucester City Museum*, 1964 (booklet)
+ L E W O FULBROOK-LEGATT, *Roman Gloucester*, 1968 (booklet)
TBGAS lxxxvi (1967), 5–15
CA 26 (May 1971), 77–83

Cirencester:
+ *Corinium Museum, a short Guide*, n.d. (booklet)
+ A THORNTON, *The Mosaic Pavements of Corinium*, n.d. (booklet)
Arch. J. cxxii (1965), 203–6
Britannia i (1970), 227–39
CA 29 (November 1971), 144–52

Keynsham & Somerdale: *Archaeologia* lxxv (1924–5), 109–38
King's Weston: + guidebook by G C Boon
                                        TBGAS lxix (1950), 5–58
Wadfield: *JBAA* i (1895), 242–50
Great Witcombe: *TBGAS* lxxiii (1954), 5–69
                                        Britannia i (1970), 294 (plan)
Chedworth: + NT guidebook (by R Goodburn)
                                        TBGAS lxxviii (1959), 5–23
Woodchester: + guidebook available at each opening
North Leigh: + M V TAYLOR, *The Roman Villa at North
                                        Leigh*, Oxford Univ. Press 1923 (booklet)
                                        R G COLLINGWOOD and I RICHMOND, *The
                                        Archaeology of Roman Britain*, Methuen
                                        1969, 143 (and plan)
Lydney: T V and R E M WHEELER, *The Prehistoric,
                                        Roman and Post-Roman Remains in Lydney
                                        Park*, Soc. of Antiq. 1932
Blackpool Bridge: + I D MARGARY, *Roman Roads in Britain*,
                                        Baker 1967, 332–3
                                        + A W TROTTER, *The Dean Road*, Bellows,
                                        Gloucester, 1936

Chapter Four
General: I A RICHMOND, 'Roman Essex', in VCH
                                        Essex iii (1963), 1–23
                                        + R R CLARKE, *East Anglia* (People and
                                        Places), Thames & Hudon 1960
                                        + H CLARKE, *East Anglia* (Regional
                                        Archaeologies), Heinemann 1971
Colchester: + booklets obtainable at the museum: *The
                                        Beginning of Roman Colchester* (1966) and
                                        The Story of Roman Colchester (1967)
                                        VCH *Essex* iii (1963), 90–122
                                        CA 26 (May 1971), 62–6
                                        Arch. J. cxxiii (1966), 27–61
                                        JRS lii (1962), 178
St Albans: + I ANTHONY, *The Roman City of Verulamium*,
                                        Official Guide 1970
                                        + K M KENYON and S S FRERE, *The Roman
                                        Theatre of Verulamium and adjacent
                                        buildings*, n.d. (guide booklet)

SS FRERE, *Verulamium Excavations* I, Soc. of
Antiq. 1972
Antiquity xxxviii (1964), 103–12
Bulletin of Inst. of Arch., London iv (1964),
61–82

Caistor St Edmund: *Arch. J.* cvi (1949), 62–5
    Britannia ii (1971), 1–26

Caister-on-Sea: *JRS* xlii (1952), 96–7; *ib.* xliii (1953), 121–2;
ib. xliv (1954), 97; *ib.* xlv (1955), 136
Norfolk Arch. xxxiii (1962), 94–107; *ib.*
xxxiv (1966), 45–73 (correct plan)

Burgh Castle: + DOE *Guide*, HMSO (pamphlet)
Proc. Suffolk Inst. of Arch. and N.H. xxiv
(1949), 100–20
Arch. J. cvi (1949), 66–9

Car Dyke: *Antiq. J.* xxix (1949), 145–63
Latimer: K BRANIGAN, *Latimer*, Chess Valley Arch.
and Hist. Soc., 1971
CA 20 (May 1970), 241–4

Welwyn   *CA* 27 (July 1971), 106–9
Harpenden: *St Albans Archit. and Arch. Soc.* v (1937),
108–14
JBAA xxii (1959), 22–3
JRS xxviii (1938), 186 (summary and plan)

Mersea: VCH *Essex* iii (1963), 159 61 (also information
sheet at site)

Thornborough: *Records of Bucks.* xvi (1953–60), 29–32
Stevenage: *Antiquity* x (1963), 39
Bartlow: VCH *Essex* iii (1963), 39–43

Chapter Five
Baginton: *Trans. Birmingham Arch. Soc.* lxxxiii
(1966–7), 65–129
CA 4 (Sept. 1967), 86–9; *ib.* 24 (Jan. 1971),
16–21; *ib.* 28 (Sept. 1971), 127–30

Lincoln: J B WHITWELL, *Roman Lincolnshire*, History
of Lincolnshire Committee 1970, ch. 3
CA 26 (May 1971), 67–71

Wroxeter: + DOE *Guide*, HMSO 1965 (booklet)
Antiq. J. xlvi (1966), 229–39
CA 1 (March 1967), 10; *ib.* 9 (July 1968), 231;

ib. 14 (May 1969), 82–6; *ib.* 25 (March 1971), 45–9

Leicester: K M KENYON, *Excavations at the Jewry Wall site, Leicester*, Soc. of Antiq. 1948 (much out of date)
Trans. Leics. Arch. and Hist. Soc. xliv (1968–9), 1–10
+ E BLANK, *A Guide to Leicestershire Archaeology*, Leicester Museums 1970 (booklet)

Wall: + DOE *Guide*, HMSO 1958 (booklet)
Trans. Lichfield and S. Staffordshire Arch. and Hist. Soc. v (1963–4), 1–47; *ib.* viii (1966–7), 1–38

Great Casterton: P CORDER (ed.), *The Roman Town and Villa at Great Casterton*, Univ. of Nottingham, 3 reports, 1951, 1954 and 1961
M TODD (ed.), *The Roman Fort at Great Casterton*, Univ. of Nottingham 1968
J B WHITWELL, *Roman Lincolnshire*, 1970, 61–4 (summary)

Ancaster: *ibid.*, 65–7

Caistor: *ibid.*, 69–72
Antiq. J. xl (1960), 175–87

Horncastle: J B WHITWELL, *op. cit.* 1970, 72–4

Chapter Six

General: V E NASH-WILLIAMS, *The Roman Frontier in Wales*, 2nd ed. revised by M G Jarrett, Univ. of Wales, Cardiff, 1969 (consult for *all* military sites)
I A RICHMOND, 'Roman Wales', ch. VI of *Prehistoric and Early Wales*, ed. by I W Foster and G Daniel, Routledge 1965
G SIMPSON, *Britons and the Roman Army*, Gregg 1964
+ K WATSON, *North Wales* (Regional Archaeologies), Heinemann 1965
+ C HOULDER and W H MANNING, *South Wales* (Regional Archaeologies), Heinemann 1966

R W DAVIES, 'Roman Wales and Roman military practice camps', *Arch. Camb.* cxvii (1968), 103–18

Caerleon: G C BOON, *Isca, the Roman Legionary Fortress at Caerleon*, National Museum of Wales, Cardiff 1972

+ G C BOON and C WILLIAMS, *Plan of Caerleon*, National Museum of Wales 1967

+ D MOORE, *Caerleon, Fortress of the Legion*, National Museum of Wales 1970 (booklet)

+ DOE *Guide*, HMSO 1970 (booklet)

Arch. Camb. cxix (1970), 10–63

Chester: F H THOMPSON, *Roman Cheshire*, Cheshire Council 1965

+ F H THOMPSON, *Deva, Roman Chester*, Grosvenor Museum, Chester, 1959

+ DOE *Guide*, HMSO 1972 (pamphlet on amphitheatre)

Brecon Gaer: + DOE *Guide*, HMSO (pamphlet)

Castell Collen: *Arch. Camb.* cxviii (1969), 124–34 (practice camps)

Y Pigwn: *BBCS* xxiii (1968–70), 100–3

Dolaucothi: *Antiq. J.* xlix (1969), 244–72

BBCS xix (1960), 71–84

Tomen-y-Mur: *JRS* lix (1969), 126–7 (Braich-ddu)

BBCS xviii (1958–60), 397–402 (Doldinnas)

Caernarvon: + DOE *Guide*, HMSO (booklet)

Caer Gybi: + DOE *Guide to the Ancient Monuments of Anglesey*, HMSO (booklet)

Carmarthen: *Carmarthen Antiq.* v (1964–9), 2–5; *ib.* vi (1970), 4–14; *ib.* vii (1971), 58–63

Caerwent: + DOE *Guide*, HMSO (booklet)

Tre'r Ceiri: *Arch. J.* cxvii (1960), 1–39

Holyhead Mountain, Caer Leb, Din Lligwy: + DOE *Guide to Ancient Monuments of Anglesey*, HMSO (booklet)

Chapter Seven

General: R M BUTLER (ed.), *Soldier and Civilian in Roman Yorkshire*, Leicester Univ. Press 1971

+ I LONGWORTH, *Yorkshire* (Regional Archaeologies), Heinemann 1965

+ T GARLICK, *Roman Sites in Yorkshire*, Dalesman 1971 (booklet)

+ T GARLICK, *Romans in the Lake Counties*, Dalesman 1971 (booklet)

B R HARTLEY, 'Some Problems of the Roman military occupation in the North of England', *Northern History* i (1966), 7–20

G B D JONES, 'Romans in the North-West', *Northern History* iii (1968), 1–26

York: RCHM, *Roman York: Eburacum*, HMSO 1962

R M BUTLER (ed.), *op. cit.* (see General), 16–17, 45–53, 97–106, 179–92

+ L P WENHAM, *Eboracum*, Yorkshire Arch. Soc. 1970 (booklet)

+ B HOPE-TAYLOR, *Under York Minster*, York Minster 1971 (booklet)

Britannia iii (1972), 265–6 (plaster)

CA 37 (March 1973), 49–50

Cawthorn: *Arch. J.* lxxxix (1932), 17–78

Wheeldale Moor: R H HAYES and J G RUTTER, *Wade's Causeway*, Scarborough & District Arch. Soc. 1964 (booklet)

Malton: P CORDER, *Defences of the Roman Fort at Malton*, Yorks. Arch. Soc. 1930

Ilkley: *Proc. Leeds Philosophical & Literary Soc.* xii (1966), 23–72

Blackstone Edge: + I D MARGARY, *Roman Roads in Britain*, Baker 1967, 404

Ribchester: + NT *Guide*

Britannia i (1970), 281; *ib.* ii (1971), 255

Piercebridge: *Trans. Arch. Soc. Durham and Northumberland* vii (1936), 235–77; *ib.* ix (1939–41), 43–68

Binchester: R E HOOPELL, *Vinovia, a buried Roman city*, Whiting and Co. 1891

Trans. Archit. and Arch. Soc. Durham and Northumberland xi (1958), 115–24; *ib.* (new series) ii (1970), 33–7

	Arch. J. cxi (1954), 195
Lanchester:	*ibid.*, 220–1
	Proc. Soc. Antiq. Newcastle, 4th series, iii (1927), 101–4
Ebchester:	*AA* xxxviii (1960), 193–229; *ib.* xlii (1964), 173–85
Bowes:	*JRS* lviii (1968), 179–81
	Britannia ii (1971), 251
	Yorks. Arch. J. xlv (1973), 181–4 (aqueduct); *ibid.* xxxvi (1946), 383–6; *ib.* xxxvii (1948), 107–16 (Scargill Moor)
Bowes Moor:	W F GRIMES (ed.), *Aspects of Archaeology in Britain and Beyond*, Edwards 1951, 293–302
Rey Cross:	*CW* xxxiv (1934), 50–61
Maiden Castle:	*CW* xxvii (1927), 170–7
Brough:	*CW* lviii (1958), 31–56
Brougham:	RCHM, *Westmorland*, HMSO 1936, 54
Temple Sowerby:	*ibid.*, 226
Whitley Castle:	*Proc. Soc. Antiq. Newcastle* i (1924), 249–55
	AA xxxvii (1959), 191–202
Maryport:	*CW* xv (1915), 135–72; *ib.* xxxvi (1936), 85–99; *ib.* xxxix (1939), 19–30; *ib.* lviii (1958), 63–7; *ib.* lxv (1965), 115–32
	CA 2 (May 1967), 36
	JRS lvii (1967), 177
Ravenglass:	*CW* xxviii (1928), 353–66; *ib.* lviii (1958), 14–30
Hardknott:	*CW* xxviii (1928), 314–52; *ib.* lxiii (1963), 148–52; *ib.* lxv (1965), 169–75
	+ DOE *Guide*, HMSO 1972 (pamphlet)
Ambleside:	RCHM, *Westmorland*, HMSO 1936, 1–3
Middleton:	R G COLLINGWOOD and R P WRIGHT, *Roman Inscriptions of Britain* I, Oxford Univ. Press 1965, no. 2283
Aldborough:	+ DOE *Guide*, HMSO (booklet)
	R M BUTLER (ed.), *op. cit.* (see General), 155–63
Hull:	+ I A RICHMOND, *The Roman Pavements from Rudston*, Hull Museum Publications 1963 (booklet)
Beadlam:	*Yorks. Arch. J.* xliii (1971), 178–86

Grassington:	*Antiquity* ii (1928), 168–72
Ewe Close:	*CW* xxxiii (1933), 201–26
Scarborough:	+ R G COLLINGWOOD, *The Roman Signal Station on Castle Hill*, Scarborough 1925 (booklet)
	+ DOE *Guide*, HMSO (pamphlet)

Chapter Eight

General: + OS *Map of Hadrian's Wall*, HMSO 1964
+ J COLLINGWOOD BRUCE, *Handbook to the Roman Wall*, 12th ed., rev. by I A Richmond, Andrew Reid, Newcastle, 1965
+ A R BIRLEY, *Hadrian's Wall*, HMSO 1963
+ R E BIRLEY, *Hadrian's Wall – the central sector*, Cameo Books 1972
E BIRLEY, *Research on Hadrian's Wall*, Titus Wilson, Kendal, 1961
J C MANN, *The Northern Frontier in Britain from Hadrian to Honorius*, Univ. of Durham 1969 (ancient texts)
+ B DOBSON and D J BREEZE, *The Building of Hadrian's Wall*, Univ. of Durham, 2nd ed. 1970 (booklet)
D J BREEZE and B DOBSON, 'Hadrian's Wall: some problems', *Britannia* iii (1972), 182–208
B R HARTLEY, 'Roman York and the northern military command', in *Soldier and Civilian in Roman Yorkshire*, ed. R M Butler, Univ. of Leicester Press 1971, 55–69
B R HARTLEY, 'The Roman Occupation of Scotland: the evidence of samian ware', *Britannia* iii (1972), 1–55
CA 15 (July 1969)

The first two works cited above give full details about how much of the Wall and its attendant structures are visible today, and should be consulted for all sites. Below are listed some articles dealing with work done since 1965, and also some guidebooks to individual sites.

South Shields: + I A RICHMOND, *The Roman Fort at South Shields, a guide*, n.d. (booklet)
CA 15 (July 1969), 110–12

JRS lvii (1967), 177

Corbridge: + DOE *Guide*, HMSO 1954 (booklet)
CA 15 (July 1969), 97–101
AA xlix (1971), 1–28

Chesters: + DOE *Guide*, HMSO 1959 (booklet)
Carrawburgh: *CA* 15 (July 1969), 106–7
+ C DANIELS, *Mithras and his Temples on the Wall*, Newcastle 1962 (booklet)

Housesteads: + DOE *Guide*, HMSO 1952 (booklet)
CA 15 (July 1969), 106–7
Britannia i (1970), 276; *ib*. ii (1971), 250

Chesterholm: *CA* 15 (July 1969), 109; *ib*. 23 (November 1970), 329–34
AA xlviii (1970), 97–155
+ R E BIRLEY, *Guide to Chesterholm*, new edition each year

Birdoswald: + P HOWARD, *Birdoswald Fort, a history and short guide*, Cameo Books 1969

Piper Sike: *Britannia* ii (1971), 250

Chapter Nine

§ 1, *Between the Walls*

General: S W MILLAR, *Roman Occupation of SW Scotland*, Maclehouse, Glasgow Arch. Soc. 1952
+ J G SCOTT, *South-West Scotland* (Regional Archaeologies), Heinemann 1966
+ J N G & A RITCHIE, *Edinburgh and S.E. Scotland* (Regional Archaeologies), Heinemann 1972
K A STEER, 'Roman and Native in S. Scotland', *Arch. J.* cxxi (1964), 164–7

Swine Hill to
Chew Green: I A RICHMOND, 'The Romans in Redesdale', *Northumberland County History*, xv (1940), 63–159

Pennymuir: RCHM (SCOTLAND), *Roxburgh II*, HMSO 1956, 375–7

Woden Law: *ib*., 169–72
Lyne: RCHM (SCOTLAND), *Peeblesshire I*, HMSO 1967, 172–5

Castle Greg: RCHM (SCOTLAND), *Midlothian and West Lothian*, HMSO 1929, 140

Birrens: *Trans. Dumfries and Galloway N.H. and Arch. Soc.* xli (1962–3), 135–55

Burnswark: *Arch. J.* cxv (1958), 234–6
CA 15 (July 1969), 114–6

§ 2, *The Antonine Wall*

G MACDONALD, *The Roman Wall in Scotland*, 2nd ed., Clarendon Press, 1934
+ A S ROBERTSON, *The Antonine Wall*, Glasgow Arch. Soc., rev. ed. 1970
+ OS *Map of the Antonine Wall*, HMSO 1969
B R HARTLEY, 'The Roman Occupation of Scotland: the evidence of samian ware', *Britannia* iii (1972), 1–55
CA 18 (January 1970), 197
PSAS ci (1968–9), 122–6

Cramond: *Univ. of Edinburgh J.* xx (1962), 305–8

§ 3, *Romans in the Far North*
General: O G S CRAWFORD, *Topography of Roman Scotland North of the Antonine Wall*, Cambridge Univ. Press 1949
R M OGILVIE and I A RICHMOND (ed.), *Tacitus' Agricola*, Oxford Univ. Press 1967, esp. 52–76
J K ST JOSEPH, 'Air Reconnaissance in Britain 1965–8', *JRS* lix (1969), 113–9
C DANIELS, 'Problems of the Roman Northern Frontier', *Scottish Arch. Forum*, Glasgow Arch. Soc. 1970, 91–101

Ardoch: *Arch. J.* cxxi (1964), 196
Britannia i (1970), 163–78

Kaims Castle: *Arch. J.* cxxi (1964), 196

Gask Ridge: *PSAS* xxxv (1900–1), 25–43
Arch. J. cxxi (1964), 196–8
Discovery and Excavation Scotland 1966, 37; *ibid.* 1968, 28–9

Inchtuthil: *PSAS* xxxvi (1901–2), 182–242

CRAWFORD, *op. cit.* (see General), 70–4
OGILVIE and RICHMOND, *op. cit.* (see General), 69–73

Cleaven Dyke: *PSAS* lxxiv (1939–40), 37–45
Kirkbuddo: CRAWFORD, *op. cit.* (see General), 97–100
Raedykes: *ib.*, 108–10
                       PSAS l (1916), 318–48
Normandykes: CRAWFORD, *op. cit.* (see General), 110–2
Glenmailen: *ib.*, 116–22
                       PSAS l (1916), 317–59
                       Britannia i (1970), 175–7

Chapter Ten

R MERRIFIELD, *The Roman City of London*, Benn 1965
+ R MERRIFIELD, *Roman London*, Cassell 1969
+ A SORRELL, *Roman London*, Batsford 1969 (reconstruction drawings)
+ *Londinium, a Practical Guide to the visible remains of Roman London*, Classical Association, London Branch 1971 (booklet)
W F GRIMES, *The Excavation of Roman and Medieval London*, Routledge 1968
+ H W YOUNG, *Roman London*, HMSO 1962 (London Museum booklet)
+ *Guide to the Antiquities of Roman Britain*, British Museum 1964

The early forum: *CA* 19 (March 1970), 219–20
                       The London Archaeologist (Spring 1969), 36–7
The palace: *CA* 8 (May 1968), 215–9
Lower Thames Street
   house: *The London Archaeologist* (Winter 1968), 3–5

Addenda

1   *York:* a new hotel to be built at the corner of Museum Street and Lendal will include a Roman bastion in the Forum Bar.
2   *Dorchester*, Dorset. A mosaic panel found in 1967 is on view *in situ* in Tilley's Show-rooms, 26 Trinity Street.
3   *Beauport Park*, near Hastings, Sussex. A small but very well-preserved bath-house attached to an iron-working area will be preserved. The site is at present covered and there is nothing to see: it is not expected to be open to the public before about 1978.
4   *Bearsden*, Scotland (NS 5472). The bath-house of the Antonine-Wall fort here has been excavated in advance of building-work and will be preserved as an A.M. It will be the only substantial Roman structure in stone visible in Scotland.
5   *Gatcombe*, Somerset (ST 5269). A short stretch of the late third-century defences of this small Roman town has been excavated and preserved.
6   *Exeter* (p. 69). Unfortunately not enough money was raised to ensure the preservation of the bath-house, and the site has been back-filled.
7   *Cirencester* (p. 105). This site has not been kept open on display, but the mosaics have been lifted and taken to the Corinium Museum.
8   *Caistor St Edmund* (p. 136). The interior of the Roman town is now permanently under grass, and crop-marks will not therefore be visible.
9   *London, British Museum* (p. 330). Reorganization has made some of the details of this paragraph out of date. *Two* plaster panels from St Albans are now displayed on the right of the door as one enters; the one here described is that mounted higher up on the wall. The Lullingstone busts now appear *after* the Mildenhall Treasure. Also, in the last paragraph of the book (p. 332), it should be noted that the statuette of Hercules is displayed in the third case, along with the Ribchester helmet.

Index 1—Sites

Only the main entry for each site is here given; passing references to these and other places with Roman remains, and all sites listed in Appendix One, are omitted.

Index 2—Types of Monument

This index is designed for those interested in following up some particular category of building: the entry gives the page number(s) on which *begins* the description of each visible example of the type. Sites listed in Appendix One are omitted.

County boundaries
England & W
before April 1

PEM